HIP-HOP
REVOLUTION

CULTUREAMERICA

Karal Ann Marling and Erika Doss, *Series Editors*

HIP-HOP
REVOLUTION

The Culture and
Politics of Rap

Jeffrey O. G. Ogbar

UNIVERSITY PRESS OF KANSAS

Photo credits: page 33, © John McCoy/Los Angeles Daily News/Corbis Sygma; 35, ©2007 by Dubelyoo of www.dubelyoo.net, from *Black Power . . . What It Is,* used courtesy of DJ Lord and by permission of the artist; 42, © Jesse Frohman/Corbis; 70 and 114, © Nancy Kaszerman/ZUMA/Corbis; 87, © Olivier Maire/epa/Corbis; 133, *Black Commentator* 17, 21 November 2002; 149 and 159, by permission of Universal Music Group.

Published by the University Press of Kansas (Lawrence, Kansas 66045), which was organized by the Kansas Board of Regents and is operated and funded by Emporia State University, Fort Hays State University, Kansas State University, Pittsburg State University, the University of Kansas, and Wichita State University

Library of Congress Cataloging-in-Publication Data

Ogbar, Jeffrey Ogbonna Green.

  Hip-hop revolution : the culture and politics of rap / Jeffrey O. G. Ogbar.

    p. cm. — (CultureAmerica)

  Includes bibliographical references (p.) and index.

  ISBN 978-0-7006-1547-6 (cloth : alk. paper)

  1. Rap (Music)—Social aspects. 2. Rap (Music)—Political aspects. 3. Hip-hop. I. Title.

  ML3918.R37O33 2007

  784.421649—dc22   2007038203

British Library Cataloguing-in-Publication Data is available.

CONTENTS

ACKNOWLEDGMENTS

This book has been a special endeavor, informed by the thousands of hip-hop songs, videos, movies, tags, articles, books, and conversations that I have experienced since 1979, when I was introduced to hip-hop. A number of people have helped shape my approach to this book by challenging me to think critically and creatively about culture, politics, young people, race, class, gender, and the like. Eric "Ease One" Anderson, Reggie "Kustafa" Roberts, Richard Walker, Mark Pope, Oscar Mendoza, Alan Wright, Zack "Omar" Flowers, and Chris "Hollywood" Fox provided my earliest grounding as my "Oaks Boys" crew back in Los Angeles. Few aspiring high school MCs were as memorable as Douglas "Tashiri" Burnside. Thanks to William "Cru1se" Tuggle for also helping me make my mark from Inglewood to the Valley. Major props to Ms. Jackie Thompson for making a little dude feel that he could really be big.

Among my college cohort, I cannot think of any group of MCs as "X-Clannish" as the Poetic Guerrilla Unit's own Fanon Che Wilkins and Maurice Raheem Mander. Adisa Iwa continues to encourage me to spit my "George Bush" rap many years after its introduction in 1991. (It is really that hot!) All those New York heads, Lee Clayton "Obe Shabaka" Jones, Aljuan Raiford, and Alton Allen were instrumental for introducing me to the styles, lexicon, and passion up close of your folk from the Big City of Dreams. Few cats have been my casual hip-hop conversation partners like Bill Benson and Dave Canton. You guys have been amazing. Shout-out to Jonathan Hanif Gayles, Charles Shakir McKinney, Darroll Andal Lawson, Anu B. Kemet, and all the brothers of KMT. I cannot ignore the debates and conversations with Abe De Leon, and Mark Beasley-Murray. Thanks for hooking me up with the latest and hottest joints from the streets. The hundreds of students over the last several years in my hip-hop classes have been very important to keeping me grounded and up on things.

While writing this project over several years, I have had ebbs and flows of energy. I owe tremendous thanks to John Akare Aden and Ira Dworkin for their encouragement, insight, thoughtful readings, and motivation to make this the best possible work. You mugs have no idea how much I owe you for your assistance and friendship during these last few years.

I have also enjoyed the surprise insight from plenty of folks who have tolerated my hip-hop-laced conversations, which have veered from politics to religion and sports. As always, the friendship with fellow traveling heads has been cool. Thanks to Kondo and Diane Bradley, Melanie Brown, Quinetta Roberson, Vincent Sutherland, Elyce Strong, the infamous Chunky Monkey, Amani, Emily Morse, Ryan Shanahan, Stephan Balkaran, Chris Tinson, Bill Armaline, Alex Torres, and, of course, Lecretia Cottonmouth for everything. You have been inspirational. Thanks also to Kevin Powell, Josette Jwa Harris, Temple Hemphill, Margot Early, Olu Oguibe, Christine Shaw, Kupenda Auset, Minkah Makalani, and Scot Brown. Many thanks to Algernon Austin for the graphs and information. I am so happy to know that I am not the only one using these data!

My fellowship at the Schomburg Center for Research in Black Culture of the New York City Public Library helped me in very important ways during the earliest years of this project. Fellowship director Colin Palmer, associate director Miriam Jimenez Roman, manager Diana Lachatanere, and Schomburg Center director Howard Dodson helped provide the physical and intellectual space and resources that have been essential to the project. Fellows Kim Butler, Chouki El-Hamel, Samuel Roberts, Rhonda Frederick, Jeffrey Sammons, Barbara Savage, Lisa Gail Collins, and Thomas Reinhardt provided incredibly thoughtful and helpful comments on my work. My fellowship at the University of Miami's (Florida) Africana Studies program was also a source of great discourse and encouragement while writing this project. Thanks to the Miami people: Terry-Ann Jones, Edmund Abaka, Donald Spivey, Monique Bedasse, Marten Brienen, and Gavin St. Louis.

I have been fortunate, perhaps guided by a higher power, to be at the right place at the right time to have chance encounters with a healthy number of hip-hop icons. Though we usually had nothing but a few passing words, I appreciate the thoughtful banter with (in order of appearance): Chuck D, Tupac, X-Clan, Boots (the Coup), Common, KRS-One, Scarface, Afrika Bambaataa, Bobbito DJ Cucumberslice, Crazy Legs, Russell Simmons, Chali 2Na (Jurassic 5), Rakaa Iriscience, DJ Babu (Dilated Peoples),

Apathy, J-Zone, Grandmaster Caz, Dre (Cool and Dre), Sheek Louch, and Styles P. Shout to Nas, Master P, and Talib Kweli for the "what's up." Thanks to Diddy for the "what's up," subsequent diss, and one of the funniest stories to retell.

My academic crew has also been very important to this project's development as well. Big shout to my partners in the Dynamic Duo + Three: Joseph G. Schloss, Jeff Chang, and Liz Mendez-Berry. W. Jelani Cobb provided incredibly helpful comments, making this a better manuscript. John L. Jackson, Brent Gibson, Fabienne Ducet, Richard Pierce, Peniel Joseph, Damion Thomas, Nikki Taylor, Amrita Chakrabarti Myers, Rose Lovelace, Ryan Dolan, Tinasha Amunugama, Ronald L. Taylor, Altina Waller, Willena Price, and my many colleagues at the University of Connecticut have been very helpful. Thanks also to my parents, aunts, uncles, cousins. Lorie McGee has been a bright light of joy, inspiration, fun, and partnership. Thanks for it all.

I owe considerable thanks to the University Press of Kansas for identifying me as a potential author of this contribution to the series. Thanks to former acquisitions editor Nancy Jackson for her initial patience while hearing me talk about my Black Power manuscript at the American Historical Association for a few minutes before I realized that she was interested in a different book altogether. The Press's patience, confidence, and encouragement throughout the years have been essential and appreciated.

Jeffrey O. G. Ogbar
Storrs, Connecticut

HIP-HOP
REVOLUTION

Introduction

Over the last several years, I have learned that no example of popular culture generates as much passion as does hip-hop. For people invested in the culture as MCs, writers (of magazines, of books, or of walls), deejays, b-boys and b-girls, producers, A&R (artists and repertoire) representatives, street team workers, video directors, or management, the passion is somewhat understandable. It is, after all, important to their livelihood and artistry. But how do we understand the emotion evoked in debates among average fans about the latest beef between hip-hop titans? What about the rivaling titans themselves? Why the anger? As the joke goes, you never heard of the Four Tops threatening to kill the Temptations. There were never shootouts between the camps of Gladys Knight and Aretha Franklin. Ask a fan about the merits of an artist's latest CD as opposed to his "classic" first release. Among the most reticent, there is always an opinion. Until recently, to witness a typical New Yorker discuss the aesthetic merits of the average southern rapper was to witness considerable emotional invective, with the provincial arrogance that is legendary among Gotham's own. Even hip-hop journalists are a passionate lot, with their own rivalries played out humorously on editorial pages, written on computers in comfortable Manhattan office buildings. Virtually every fan over thirty has had a spirited "has-hip-hop-gone-astray?" conversation, or at least an emotional "those-were-the-days" conversation about the "golden age" when the hip-hop nation was not divided into underground, commercial, gangsta, conscious, and other subgenres. Fundamentally, these discussions pivot on the notion of hip-hop's essential character—its authentic expression. Authenticity, however defined or imagined, has always been central to the culture.

Writing my tag "Speed" on walls and buses in Los Angeles with my partners in crime, including "Ease One" and "Cru1se," was invigorating and edgy for a fifteen year old. Though I never achieved major status, I viewed my activity as serious stuff. Getting up on a visible wall, and being so active that you'd stumble across your tag in places where you'd forgotten you'd hit, was part of the culture. Then there were those major figures. The dream of joining forces with big-time taggers "Soon" and "Legit" nearly came true for me with a chance meeting in 1985. They were so prolific that former Mid-City L.A. graf writer turned MC Rakaa Iriscience of Dilated Peoples similarly recalls their work: "Before [tagger] Chaka [of the early 1990s], Soon and Legit had the whole Venice Boulevard corridor on lock."[1] Legend held that these cats were straight from New York City. I can't recall if the accents were real or forced, but to me they represented the real thing. Their confidence, swagger, fat shoelaces, and windbreakers proved it. They even invited me to smoke a joint or two, and I could not admit to them that I no longer touched the stuff. I wanted to be down, closer to the standard of cool they represented. We never happened to cross paths again. But I remember the feeling of being close to the real McCoy, the brothers from New York who were, simply put, real.

Tagging was youthful rebellion. It was also fun. It was artistic, creative, destructive, and cool. It was hip-hop. Years later, after attending graduate school and becoming a history professor, I consulted with a prominent hip-hop journalist about my new course on hip-hop. He remarked that neither he nor I would have ever imagined our present conversation fifteen years earlier. As teenage "writers," or taggers, in New Jersey and Los Angeles, respectively, we never would have fathomed that we would actually earn a halfway decent living as "remixed" versions of hip-hop writers in our thirties. The nation's best-selling music magazines? Moguls in the Hamptons or Hollywood Hills? Congressional hearings? Outselling every other genre of music? Album of the year? A veritable "hip-hop studies" in the academy? Represented by native speakers of Arabic, Zulu, Polish, Korean, and Portuguese? In 1985 none of these were ever considered as hip-hop possibilities for me or many other heads. It was not that we did not think that it could happen; it would be more correct to say that it was not part of our immediate worldview, which was simply enjoying what we had. But even as we did not envisage the cultural juggernaut that hip-hop would become, it was clear to us that the cultural form was expanding its influence. Like the New York transplants in Los Angeles, Soon and Legit, hip-hop was going places on its own terms. It followed its own standards, codes, and symbols of cool. We followed suit. Hip-hop has transcended boundaries of class, race, region, and generation in fascinating ways, and seeing it mature has been fascinating.

The scholarship on hip-hop has grown considerably since the early 1990s, when a handful of academics engaged the new cultural phenomenon with considerable interest and sympathy. One of the first substantive and broad engagements on hip-hop written by an academic, Tricia Rose's *Black Noise: Rap Music and Black Culture in Contemporary America* (1994),[2] remains a powerful and insightful contribution to the field of cultural studies, youth culture, and ethnomusicology. Since the early 1990s, sociologists, literary critics, and scholars of American studies, African American studies, and cultural studies have added to the expanding corpus of hip-hop studies.

The history of hip-hop's origins among African American and Puerto Rican youth in the South Bronx is commonly recited.[3] In the early 1970s, as the Black Power movement and Puerto Rican nationalist activism began to wane, a convergence of factors gave rise to hip-hop in New York City. Deindustrialization had eviscerated the economic base for employment in some segments of the city. None was harder hit than the South Bronx, which was the poorest section of the poorest borough in the city. Gangs proliferated, even as some nationalist groups such as the Black Panther Party, Nation of Islam, Young Lords, and Revolutionary Action Movement attempted to politicize them. Simultaneously, court-ordered school busing was met with white resistance to integrated schools, as whites, including gang members, violently protested black and Latino students in white schools. White gangs such as the Golden Guineas and Fordham Baldies assaulted African American and Latino students at white schools like Christopher Columbus High School in the North Bronx. Victims of the attacks requested help from gangs like the largely Puerto Rican Ghetto Brothers and the mostly African American Black Spades. To some degree, these racial attacks politicized gangs, ultimately leading to a tenuous peace treaty. Initiated outside of police, school, or other efforts, gang members themselves, including Kevin Donovan of the Black Spades, emerged as leaders in this truce. Donovan, renaming himself Afrika Bambaataa, formed the Organization in November 1973. Renamed the Zulu Nation, after the formidable Zulu empire in precolonial Southern Africa, it systematically celebrated festive activities for local youth. An early recruit, DJ Macnificent, notes that the Zulu Nation was about peace treaties, "but if you resisted, sometimes peace came to you violently. We demanded peace; but a lot of gangs like the Ball Busters refused to join. One group, the Casanova Crew, joined . . . by force. In the end, there was peace, though."[4]

Also around this time, Clive Campbell, who had emigrated from Jamaica with his family at age twelve in 1967, attended parties at the Puzzle, a Bronx club frequented by graffiti artists and dancers of a new, nearly gymnastic style of dance. Eventually, Campbell, who moved away from graffiti, or "tagging," began hosting parties at 1520 Sedgwick Avenue on the west side of the Bronx in 1973. A fan of James Brown and Motown artists before he arrived in the United States, he was also influenced by the huge sound systems of outdoor parties in Jamaica. Known as Kool Herc, his parties were wildly popular. Soon other DJs emerged, including Afrika Bambaataa, who operated in Bronx River public housing in the southeast of the Bronx; Grandmaster Flash, on the south side; and DJ Breakout, on the north side. Crews of dancers competed against each other. Eventually known as "break dancers" or "b-boys" and "b-girls," these crews competed for dominance and popularity at the parties, supplanting gang violence significantly, though there remained occasional violent conflicts. Many who participated in the emerging culture also tagged their names on trains and walls. Names like Stay High 149 and Taki 183 marked trains throughout New York City. Graffiti artists began to heavily identify with the musical styles developing in the Bronx, although there were white graf artists who listened to rock music only and were virulently racist, having no contact with the emerging hip-hop scene in the Bronx.[5] Finally, DJs realized the need for lyrical assistants to help them as they focused on their records. DJs recruited other DJs to excite the crowd. Some of the most popular ones were Cowboy, Eddie Cheeba, Melle Mel, Kid Creole, and DJ Hollywood. Though one talented DJ, Grandmaster Caz, excelled at rapping and deejaying, these lyrical DJs began calling themselves "MCs," for master of ceremonies, to distinguish themselves from disc jockeys, who only manipulated the music. The four elements (deejaying, break dancing, graffiti art, and rapping) had come together by the mid-1970s. It was still a few years before the art broke from the subaltern into a commercially viable recorded style.

The first commercially successful rap song: "Rapper's Delight" (1979); first movie: *Wild Style* (1982); first platinum group: Run DMC (1985); first major hip-hop magazine: *The Source* (1988); first billion-dollar year: 1996;

first year in which hip-hop outsold every other genre of music: 1998; first Grammy for Album of the Year: 1999. Hip-hop has had its share of firsts, slowly penetrating the mainstream. Its impact is unquestionable.

This book explores the rise of hip-hop as a cultural juggernaut by focusing on the cultural and political landscape of the music and how it negotiates its own sense of identity. More specifically, I examine the lyrical world of hip-hop and how rappers and hip-hop-oriented writers engage the character of hip-hop authenticity. I focus on the nexus of race, class, generation, and gender to determine how America's latest cultural contribution to the world sees itself and hopes to be seen by others. I demonstrate that hip-hop is far from monolithic—admittedly so—even as its exponents demand "realness": a certain set of criteria that certify the nebulous notion of authenticity. Hip-hop, despite its inherent swagger, confidence, and boldness, appears quite insecure at times. Its agents often work very hard to prove how real they are to the "higher" (or "lower," depending on perspective) ideals of the art. There are scores of songs about how real an MC is. Herein lies my scholarly exploration of just what that "realness" means in an artistic form in which class, race, and gender are central to articulations of authenticity. And I examine how this realness is negotiated, interrogated, and articulated in a world where gendered and racialized stereotypes are pervasive. This book also reconsiders widely held beliefs about the threat that hip-hop poses to social norms. It challenges the notion that hip-hop is an anti-intellectual force that has led youth astray with lower standards of morality, industriousness, or civic duty. This book provides a social scientific interrogation of the hip-hop generation that goes beyond clichéd ideas of race, class, gender, and identity. In addition, I employ an element of historiography to provide context for our understanding of the art. I place the discussion of hip-hop authenticity and "realness" in a historical context that reflects the awareness and sensitivity to problematic black images such as the minstrel.

This is not a comprehensive study of the totality of hip-hop. There are already wonderful examinations of hip-hop graffiti, dance, and musical structure, as well as great works that incorporate examinations of lyrical style, structure, and poetic prose.[6] But this is a historian's take on musical verse in hip-hop, its political and social landscape, and its effect on the lives of its consumers. In some respects, this is as much a history book as it is an examination of contemporary cultural phenomena. It is not, however, a heavily theoretical cultural studies work. Though clearly an academic study in syntax, style, and content, it does not demand a working knowledge of postmodernist jargon and theory.

From the perspective of a historian, I explore the antecedents of popular music dating as far back as the mid-nineteenth century. It was in the troubled and dangerous world of 1840s America that the country found its earliest expressions of popular culture in the minstrel show. The minstrel show was also one of the most dominant expressions of America's terrible obsession with race in general and blackness in particular. But one cannot explore blackness without the "Other" that gives blackness meaning—whiteness.[7] Indeed, the two concepts are intimately bound together in powerful, painful, and complicated ways.

Though "authenticity" is used more frequently in this text, "credibility" and "realness" also reflect the same meaning of what it means to be authentic or real in hip-hop. While the definitions of "realness" or "authenticity" are slippery, I have determined some useful characteristics by considering the pervasive use of these terms. No song better represents hip-hop's obsession with "keeping it real" than Ice Cube's 1991 hit "True to the Game." Setting a standard for realness in hip-hop, Ice Cube raps about archetypal sellouts who "give our music away to the mainstream" by switching from "hardcore hip-hop" to being "white and corny." Cube also exclaims his commitment to the hood, living there, while some sellouts live in hostile white communities with "nigger go home" spray-painted on black homes. There are dozens of other songs that celebrate "real niggas," as an extension of the keeping-it-real ethos of hip-hop. Fundamentally, a "real nigga" refers to a tough urban black male who is intimately familiar with and willing to confront the many challenges of the "hood." But what exactly are these challenges, and how is the hood defined? The hood is generally understood as the urban space occupied by black working-class and poor people. It is not simply "urban" or "black." Few residential areas on earth are more urban than the Upper East Side of Manhattan. It is not, however, "hood" any more than the very exclusive and affluent black communities of Ladera Heights or Windsor Hills in Los Angeles. Neither is a rural community of abject white poverty "hood." So the convergence of urban economic despair and black or Latino space provides the criteria for what is popularly understood as hood, though people often lazily conflate race and class. For many, a black neighborhood is synonymous with a poor one. Data show, however, that about three-quarters of African Americans are not poor. The challenges of the hood, therefore, include underemployment, poverty, crime, and various other exigencies, such as the drug trade.

Any fruitful discussion of hip-hop's self-defined notions of authenticity must consider the diversity of opinions even within the hip-hop community of artists. An incredibly diverse collection of MCs from Common, to Juelz Santana, Lil Jon, and Fat Joe, have claimed to be "real niggas." That definition, however, is in flux. For example, Mos Def insists that hip-hop's obsession with "niggas fighting [and] gangster posturing . . . ain't no real nigga shit." But most songs referring to "real niggas" include references to graphic tales of violence and gangsta posturing, such as Notorious B.I.G.'s song "Real Niggas" (1995), "Real Niggaz" (1997) by Jay-Z and Too $hort, or "Real Niggaz" (2003) by the Diplomats. Finally, the conspicuous use of the term "nigga" must be considered as a particular affirmation of race, class, and gender identity. As discussed in greater detail in Chapter 3, the term has different meanings depending on context. It can be a term of racial contempt or endearment across racial lines. Still, its use here implies, in no uncertain terms, a masculinist black working-class identity that represents the core of hip-hop's character.

Evidence of these standards of location, class, race, and credibility in rap is also apparent when surveying battle raps, where MCs attack rivals for lack of credibility: B-Real attacks Ice Cube for going to school in the (mostly white) San Fernando Valley in "No Rest for the Wicked" (1996); Eminem attacks the Insane Clown Posse for living in white suburbs, while claiming Detroit (2001). He also attacks white rapper Everlast for being an "old" "redneck" white interloper to hip-hop who was not sincerely committed to the art in "Quitter" and "I Remember" (2001). Jadakiss has attacked 50 Cent for living in a Connecticut suburb in "Checkmate" (2005), while 50 Cent continues to shout out his childhood home of Southside Jamaica, Queens, as an obvious trope, which declares provincial credibility. Indeed, New York City's Marcy and Queensbridge public-housing projects, the Magnolia projects in New Orleans, Houston's 5th Ward, Miami-Dade's Carol City, and Compton near Los Angeles have become veritable markers of credibility by virtue of their reputations as poor urban spaces with high crime and tough streets. So realness, in this context, is inextricably tied to spatial notions that are represented by class and race assumptions as well as gender and generation.

Though emerging from African American and Puerto Rican communities in New York City in the early 1970s, hip-hop is anchored in an old American style of racialized cultural production. It owes much of its style to the African American badman narrative, the musical traditions of rock, R&B, and disco. It is a production of the Black Power era and is conscious of the cultural politics that have marginalized black artists who have had their art co-opted by white performers. Early hip-hoppers, as explored in Chapter 1, have been mindful of the racist ridicule experienced by their predecessors through much of the twentieth century. Still, as Chapter 2 shows, this does not stop rappers from pandering to some of the most pernicious stereotypes of black people, who celebrate being "real niggas." This assiduous attempt at realness has led to hyperbolic forms of misogyny in hip-hop, but as I discuss in Chapter 3, hip-hop has a feminist voice. Male and female rappers have addressed gender in very sophisticated ways, creating a fascinating dialogue as agents of organic intellectualism. Chapter 4 extends the discussion of social commentary and contest within hip-hop by examining the role of media and the insatiable desire for the rebel in hip-hop, public debates about hip-hop's place in society, and its utility as a source of influence. Then there is the visceral rejection seen by older generations (of various classes and races) who consider hip-hop crude, repugnant, and socially dangerous. Finally, Chapter 5 explores the prison industrial complex, its significance in the landscape of black and brown America, and the ways in which hip-hoppers of all political persuasions have engaged it.

Ultimately, this is an examination of the "cult of authenticity" that gives character to hip-hop. It dictates how performers walk, talk, and express themselves artistically. It also influences the larger consumer market. By studying the obsession with realness in hip-hop, I provide a necessary examination of the interplay between the market and the artists and the commercial structure of the music industry itself. What does it mean to keep it real? Who determines what is real? How are notions of realness contested or expressed? Are they static? If not, what forces change? What impact, if any, does hip-hop have in the lives of its consumers? These questions and others guide this exploration of hip-hop as the art itself continues its attempt to remain true to the game, while still being unpredictable and full of possibility.

1

The Minstrel Reprise:
Hip-Hop and the Evolution of the
Black Image in American Popular Culture

There has long been controversy within and without the Negro race as to just how the Negro should be treated in art—how he should be pictured by writers and portrayed by artists.

—W. E. B. Du Bois (1926)

Watching Bamboozled *in 2000, I thought, "OK, Spike, there's a little much. But life has become* Bamboozled. *I'm dancing with minstrels."*

—Ahmir "?uestlove" Thompson, of *The Roots* (2006)

In 2005 Little Brother, a North Carolina–based hip-hop group, released a critically acclaimed CD that garnered attention from even the most provincial northeastern underground fans who typically dismiss southern rap as primitive, simplistic, and wack ("except for Outkast," the cliché goes). Unlike the typical group from the Dirty South, Little Brother did not rely on tales of hypermaterialism, pimping, drug selling, violence, or gold or platinum teeth. The group, instead, grounded its style, creativity, and—in a sense— legitimacy on a peculiar historical icon: the minstrel. Their CD, *The Minstrel Show,* was not overtly political or heavy on commentary about hip-hop's loss of direction. It was, however, a bold display of lyrical creativity, humor, sophisticated production, and party songs that reminded folks of hip-hop's origins without sounding dated, bitter, or myopic. More important, the CD was a demonstration that hip-hop was more than a celebration of black pathology. Far from being the first in hip-hop to signify the minstrel, Little Brother, composed of Big Pooh, Phonte, and 9th Wonder, saw its own contribution to hip-hop as a satirical take on the state of hip-hop, which, according to many, has devolved into a mockery of itself—"the Biggest Colored Show on Earth." The CD was in many ways a direct reaction to the narrow notions of black authenticity expected in many hip-hop circles. Explaining the concept of the album title, Phonte states:

> When you turn on the TV and you watch these videos, you're not seeing real people, they're damn near like caricatures of what Hip Hop should be. So *The Minstrel Show* is us listening and examining Hip Hop and saying, "Ya know, if cats don't want to take responsibility for this s**t, if n*ggas want to keep making bulls**t records, if this is really what ya'll want to do with this music, than f*** it let's just go all out and make this s**t a minstrel show cause that's exactly what the f*** it's turning into."[1]

Little Brother expresses a strong sense of historical awareness, joining a discourse that transverses the whole of the twentieth century and extends into the twenty-first. More specifically, artists, intellectuals, and others have questioned the ways in which art effectively undergirds a system of oppression. Rooted in the antebellum era's crude and vicious notions of racial subjugation, the minstrel figure remains a touchtone for African American intellectuals, artists, and cultural critics alike. Since the Harlem Renaissance, African Americans have publicly interrogated the representations of black people in popular culture. The hip-hop generation is the latest to join this discourse. In this debate one finds a vibrant, intellectually engaging exchange over the merits of fictive characters given life, color, and dimension in the lyrics of rap's leading MCs. In many ways, the debate mirrors the debates of the Harlem Renaissance's leading intellectuals who similarly engaged in spirited discourse over the fate of a people and their cultural production.

The popular fixation of black people as criminal, lazy, witless miscreants in American popular culture has been well documented.[2] But the decades following the civil rights and Black Power movements have witnessed a full range of black images in popular culture. It is not uncommon to see black actors in roles as varied as medical doctors, judges, street thugs, or even president of the United States. But it is quite conspicuous that hip-hop—that unprecedented global cultural juggernaut—offers up only the most

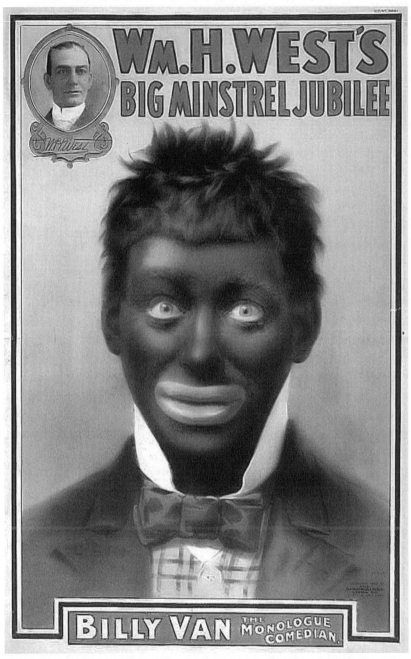

The minstrel figure, a stupid, lazy black caricature, is one of the most enduring images from the earliest era of American popular culture. It remained a central articulation of blackness in popular culture deep into the twentieth century despite black protest. This 1900 lithograph advertises a white performer, Billy Van, in blackface.

narrow and problematic representations of black imagery. Oversexed black men and women, nihilistic violence, impulsive, vulgar, and criminal behavior have marked all but a handful of platinum hip-hop albums since the early 1990s. For many, the "real niggas" of hip-hop are little more than a reprise of the minstrel. Debates within and without hip-hop have centered on these images and reflect a fascinating discourse on race, culture, and alarm. But among hip-hop artists and journalists, in particular, there is a pronounced sense of urgency over the direction of the art and the destiny of its core constituency—urban black and Latino young folk.

The Minstrel in American Popular Culture

Though the 1970s gave birth to hip-hop, its own cultural and political consciousness has deep roots in the expressive culture of African Americans, dating back to the era of minstrelsy. While the New York City–bred children of Caribbean people (primarily Puerto Ricans) were also creators of the art, hip-hop is firmly anchored into the performance of music, dance, and lyrical styles that descend from the earliest expressions of American popular culture, where blackness was at its center. As Imani Perry explains, "Hip hop music is black American music. Even with its hybridity: the consistent contributions from nonblack artists, and the borrowing from cultural forms of other communities."[3] To be sure, each culture is an example of a long and intimate exchange with other cultures. No culture is "pure." But claims that b-boying is derived from Brazilian capoeira or that MCing is derived from Jamaican toasting not only muddles the truth but ignores what the creators of the art say about their influences. Additionally, it tends to disconnect artistic continuities that provide context to the core character of hip-hop. The earliest b-boys explain that they were inspired by seeing James Brown's dance moves and by their own competitive spirit of dance innovation. Crazy Legs notes that break dancing, or b-boying, "originated with [some of the dance styles of] James Brown" in the late 1960s. In the early 1970s, these Bronx youths had never heard of or seen capoeira.[4] Jamaican-born, Bronx-raised hip-hop godfather DJ Kool Herc dismisses suggestions that rap found its origins in toasting. "Jamaican toasting? Naw, naw. No connection there. I couldn't play reggae in the Bronx. People couldn't accept it. The inspiration for rap is James Brown and the album *Hustlers Corner* by the

Last Poets."[5] The centrality of African American art to hip-hop helps contextualize the aesthetic symbols and creative expression found in the early hip-hop community and how they were inextricably tied to the era of the 1970s, which saw the minstrel as anathema.

From the emergence of American popular culture in the early nineteenth century, no term is as iconic of the obsession with blackness in popular culture than the minstrel figure. The minstrel was not only a central icon of early American entertainment; it functioned as well to articulate the terribly complicated racial landscape of the United States.

The development of what may be considered the earliest examples of American popular culture occurred in the early nineteenth century. It was during the Jacksonian era of the 1830s that suffrage was extended to all white men by eliminating property qualifications, which had barred poor white men from voting. This expansion of democracy had inflections throughout American society, including entertainment and its newest invention—the minstrel show. In early 1843 Dan Emmett's Virginia Minstrels performed at the Chatham Theatre in New York City. Though not the first minstrel performance, it marked a new age of commercial appeal and institutionalization of minstrelsy.[6] Characterized by buffoonish styles of singing, dancing and vernacular, minstrelsy depicted black people as infantile and pathological while underscoring the importance of race to the meaning of democracy in America. In an age that saw the expansion of voting to all white men, the ubiquitous image of the black minstrel, or "coon," affirmed the notion that black men were unfit for the responsibilities of democracy. It was beyond the pale that a childlike and indolent figure could make prudent decisions in any important arena of life.

White Americans were fascinated and entertained by minstrelsy and its celebration of what was passed off as authentic blackness. Whites from Abraham Lincoln and Mark Twain to poor Irish immigrants in the ghettoes of Boston and poor WASP dirt farmers in West Virginia were counted as fans of the minstrel show.[7] The effects of minstrelsy were profound. As Alexander Saxton writes, "Paced by the extraordinary popularity of blackface minstrelsy, theater expanded into an industry of mass entertainment." Moreover, the general popularity of black minstrels operated as a common racial reference for whites of various classes, helping to extend notions of white racial egalitarianism in both social and political contexts. The hostile images of black people in minstrelsy helped to promote alliance between northern white workers and southern planters by affirming a universal commitment to white supremacy and its corollary black subjugation. Southern fears that the North was dominated by rabid abolitionists with agendas of racial equality and emancipation were held at bay. The rise of minstrelsy also facilitated the spread of theater throughout the country while widening theater constituency beyond the upper class, giving rise to popular culture.[8] It was a class-open white space that at times allowed black artists to perform minstrel work; however, white performers handily dominated the field. Since over 90 percent of black people were enslaved in the United States and free blacks were generally barred from white theaters, the minstrel show remained an arena of near-total white consumption of "black" performance.

By the late nineteenth century, musicals, popular literature, plays, songs, dances, and children's stories relied on black caricatures for inspiration. These outlets pervaded the country, providing whites with no physical contact with blacks exposure to blackness in surrogate form. As proxies for black people, white men dressed in blackface and performed routines that ridiculed black humanity. The purpose of the minstrel was twofold. Minstrels provided easy and immediate entertainment to whites who simultaneously enjoyed the construction and dissemination of an ostensibly white American character by being the antithesis of the minstrel. The minstrel, or coon, was, in effect, an inversion of the white man. While white America prided itself on its scientific and technological achievements at world fairs, in government, in scholarship, and in other arenas, the carefree, happy, and irresponsible Negro offered a sharp contrast to articulations of whiteness and national identity. Additionally, the minstrel justified the sociopolitical and economic structure of the United States. The most important function of the minstrel was its role in rationalizing white supremacy. The enduring image of the happy, docile, cowardly, and shiftless coon insisted that black people were fundamentally ill equipped to compete with white people in any meaningful way. Blacks were barred from equal access to jobs, education, housing, military service, and democracy. The coon, therefore, assuaged the conscience of many whites who reasoned that things could not be too terrible if blacks were always happy.

Though African Americans have long fought against these images, it would be too simplistic to suggest that these caricatures were universal reflections of a capitulation to white supremacy. As W. T. Lhamon explains, blackface performance was not monolithic or static in its expression: "It seems most important to notice how blackface performance can work . . . against racial stereotyping."[9] For example, the nineteenth-century minstrel song "De New York Nigger" was sung by blackface performers, but it ridiculed white supremacy surreptitiously. Lhamon also argues that minstrels reflected a rejection of established codes of social respectability and convention. Their popularity was due, in part, he insists, to young white workers who identified with the hardscrabble Jim Crow figures: "The black figure appealed all across the Atlantic as an organizational emblem for workers and the unemployed. Hated everywhere, he could be championed everywhere alike."[10] Though Lhamon may be overstating the affinity that white workers shared with the coon characters of minstrel shows, this analysis raises important points of interest. The coon could be seen as an archetypal outsider who rejects the system that also rejects him. As appealing as this attempt to establish a new agency for the dispossessed is, this argument ignores the larger and more powerful currents of racism directed at black people from the very white workers who found "blackness" entertaining in its minstrel form. From deadly antiblack riots to exclusion from unions, neighborhoods, and public accommodations, African Americans were confronted with virulently racist action in the most obstreperous forms from white workers. In no uncertain terms, these stereotypes, or "controlling images," to paraphrase Patricia Hill Collins, affirmed the guiding principles of white supremacy by revealing the importance of white paternalism and domination.[11]

Despite the racist imagery and adoring (yet simultaneously hostile) audiences, some black people benefited from the offensive caricatures of their day. Scores of black entertainers enjoyed work as minstrels in the nineteenth century. Decades later, actor Lincoln Perry developed America's favorite coon, Stepin Fetchit, the self-described "laziest man alive," and became the wealthiest black entertainer of the 1920s and 1930s. Many other less-famous actors would express angst over their work while simultaneously enjoying the financial benefits accrued from it. Bert Williams, a talented black actor of the early twentieth century struggled with the limitations of his day, as would black performers in subsequent generations. Others like Willie Best offered little evidence of regret or frustration. Nevertheless, these images of the happy, careless, and emotionally primitive Negro were enduring.[12]

As entertainment media evolved from the nineteenth century, the nature of the minstrel image found new locations and mediums of expression.

From vaudeville to cartoons, silent movies, novels, advertisements, and music, minstrelsy thrived in the early twentieth century as a core expression of racial politics. In various ways, African Americans protested the overtly racist, crude, and vicious depictions. Though recalcitrance characterized the response to this black protest, the minstrel figure would eventually become insignificant in popular culture as the Civil Rights and Black Power movements made substantive changes to how race was publicly performed. Still, the imprint of minstrelsy has been indelible to the cultural expressions of African Americans. From the Harlem Renaissance to postwar jazz to the era of Black Power and beyond, black artists reacted by making copious expressions of resistive art that explicitly rejected the minstrel.[13] Hip-hop performers would be no different.

Hip-Hop and the (Anti)Minstrel

Hip-hop's earliest development was shaped by the thrust of the Black Power movement. In this era, African Americans initiated a vast corpus of cultural production that rejected minstrel-like figures. Borrowing from what Patricia Hill Collins calls "controlling images" of black women that function to reify dominant power relations of race, class, and gender, I argue that various controlling images can also function for black people in general. Black youth of hip-hop's founding cohort were reared in an age when controlling images of blackness were in flux. Many who were raised in the early 1970s had limited exposure to Mantan Moreland, Sleep 'n' Eat, or the many minstrel characters that most commonly represented black people in mainstream movies. By the late 1960s, television shows such as *I Spy, Julia, Hogan's Heroes,* and *Star Trek* featured black people in nonpathological and nondemeaning roles, even if they were rarely central to the cast. Black images on films such as those starring Sidney Poitier in *In the Heat of the Night* (1967), *Lilies of the Field* (1963), and *They Call Me Mister Tibbs!* (1970) reflected black characters as dignified, sophisticated, and intelligent in ways that were generally avoided in most pre-1960 white productions. As the Black Power movement matured and crested, however, the portrayals of blacks in films and television shifted toward more rebel-style antiheroes. Television shows of the 1970s such as *Starsky and Hutch, Good Times, Sanford and Son,* and even the *Jeffersons* offered black characters of some range, even though those roles were generally a departure from the more professional, straight-laced characters of the 1960s. In cinema, *Sweet Sweetback's Baadasssss Song* (1971), *Shaft* (1972), *Superfly* (1973), *Blacula* (1972), *Black Caesar* (1973), *The Mack* (1974), and a series of other movies valorized the badman trope that had been cultivated in black urban communities for decades. Indeed, these images were ubiquitous, even influencing comics and novels.[14] The transitory popular images of blackness during the late 1960s and early 1970s shaped the ways in which black youth of the era viewed the mutability of the black image in popular culture as no other generation had. Still, many of the urban blaxploitation films did fixate, however, on characters who were in many ways a new expression of a pathological other: sexually lascivious, criminally inclined, violent, and impulsive. Some critics, in fact, considered these images a postmodern minstrelsy.[15] But as Mark Anthony Neal explains, "Though these portrayals [in blaxploitation films] are rife with many problematic elements . . . [they] did usher in a cultural moment in which African-American male identity was presented in broadened ways."[16] Young black consumers of popular culture took notice of these cool, brave badasses of the cinematic urban landscape.

Hip-Hop and Blackness

Emerging out of the highly politicized era of Black Power, many of the hip-hop generation were keenly aware of the pernicious stereotypes of black people in American popular culture, even if the most naked minstrel figures were no longer popular. In no uncertain terms, the minstrel became the antithesis of hip-hop, significantly because of the historical moment of Black Power that precipitated a new racialized consciousness among black people.[17] In this historical moment, the unique provincial dynamics of New York City also significantly shaped hip-hop.[18] In the city, the quasi-nationalist group the Nation of Gods and Earths (NGE), better known as the Five Percenters, had a visible presence within New York's black and Latino youth. The first hip-hop organization, the Zulu Nation, philosophically borrowed from the NGE, as founder Afrika Bambaataa had known many "gods" and even attended temples of the Nation of Islam (from which the NGE was an offshoot) before he established the Zulu Nation.[19] Five Percenters also provided security for hip-hop's first DJ, Kool Herc, who called them "peace guards" for his very popular outdoor and indoor parties.[20] The philosophy of the NGE, that black men are gods and black women, "earths," created in the image of Allah, insisted that black people were innately wise. In fact, Five Percenters viewed knowledge, wisdom, and understanding as the foundation of their philosophy. A supreme alphabet, a system of numerology, complex codes, symbols and knowledge of "mathematics" were all part of being a privileged member of the NGE. Not to be taken lightly, Five Percenters were known to be street toughs who would beat members who failed to recite the daily wisdom properly. Many terms in hip-hop's lexicon find their origin in the NGE; for example, cipher (a circle, letter "O," or zero), "son," (originally "sun"—the black man), and "g" (originally short for "god"), among other words, reflect the influence of the gods and earths on hip-hop, not to mention their influence on many artists from Rakim to Wu Tang Clan. The fundamental thrust of a very important historical moment—Black Power—cannot be ignored in how hip-hop established its own identity in the earliest years. That a positive, racialized self-awareness was assumed among early hip-hoppers is essential to how we note hip-hop's own collective identity and its desire to appeal to those outside of its immediate community.

By the rise of the "Golden Age" of hip-hop in the late 1980s, there were clear messages from rappers that reflected a salient sense of historical continuity between the pernicious minstrel images and contemporary black cultural production. In fact, these comments mirror observations made by leading black intellectuals of the early twentieth century who engaged in spirited discussions about the importance of black images in entertainment. In 1988 KRS-One revisited the debates from the Harlem Renaissance of the 1920s when he decried the modern coon in "My Philosophy":

> But I don't walk this way to portray
> or reinforce stereotypes of today
> Like all my brothers eat chicken and watermelon,
> talk broken English and drug sellin'[21]

KRS-One represents a popular consciousness that rejects the controlling images of the minstrel while anchoring his discourse in the modern politics of the post–Black Power cultural landscape. "The Teacher" insists that he is "teaching real facts" about the insidious practices of the record industry,

which cultivates problematic images of blackness. Much like black intellectuals of the 1920s, he argues that white-controlled businesses would rather
promote tired black stereotypes. "Your record company," he raps, wants him
and others to "soften, dilute, or commercialize all our lyrics," instead of getting knowledge from "the intelligent brown man." KRS-One juxtaposes intelligence, racial pride, and militancy against the wack lyrics that celebrate
black pathos found among a growing number of rappers. Ultimately, he
also implies that the issue involves politics and power. It is, after all, a white
supremacist agenda that demands hostile stereotypes. White supremacy, of
course, is based on a system that demands political, economic, and social
marginalization of black people and other people of color.

"My Philosophy" echoes writings of earlier generations that explored
the same concern of myopic and offensive imagery. Many insisted, as does
KRS-One, that art and politics are inextricably connected. As a reaction to
the concerns of black artists and black cultural production in general, the
preeminent scholar W. E. B. Du Bois in 1926 organized a symposium,
"The Negro in Art: How Shall He Be Portrayed?" that engaged the questions of black representations in art created by both whites and blacks.
Commentators noted that black writers, as well as whites, must be beholden to better portrayals. Clearly, "better" was somewhat subjective, people noted. And some remarked that a range of black life experiences is the
nearly universal demand. There should not be an absolute erasure of the
black criminal or buffoon; however, these images should not dominate or
be the only ones available.

In the midst of these discussions and debates, some white benefactors
insisted that they were open to sympathetic black characters that included
dignified and varied figures. No work from a white benefactor or white author best represents this impulse than the controversial 1926 novel *Nigger
Heaven* by Carl Van Vechten. Called an "affront to the hospitality of black
folks" by Du Bois and others, the book was a best seller with a huge white
market. Its varied depiction of black life included rare glimpses of black
elites, intellectuals, and political radicals among the more common dregs.
Still, many black folk took offense, not only at the obvious sting of the title
but also at the characterization of black intellectuals and elites as snobbish
but politically inept, frustrated, and curtailed by racism. Even so, the book
was wildly popular, even among black readers. One estimate suggests that
Nigger Heaven sold more than all black-authored books combined during

the era.[22] Though Van Vechten had his public black defenders, in some ways his book represented the sheer powerlessness of black people in creating and protecting their images in literature and beyond. But the field of black-oriented literature remained open in the era, even if the market demanded narrow images.

Most black writers like Nella Larsen, Langston Hughes, and Walter White explored the complicated world of class and color diversity in black communities, refusing to fixate on poverty, criminality, or hopelessness. Jessie Fauset's 1929 novel *Plum Bun* provides an inside look at the world of elite African Americans, complete with snobbery and pretentiousness. It is such a contrast to how many whites—even liberal ones—were used to seeing blacks that the story seemed unbelievably outlandish to them. Mary White Ovington, a white cofounder of the National Association for the Advancement of Colored People, in disbelief at the story of black elites wondered if "such a colored world" really existed.[23] For many of the black intellectuals, Ovington's comments were an affirmation of the dilemmas faced by black people. The "disappointment" that Ovington expressed at reading about black elites reflected her ignorance of black life, despite working directly with black elites.

Du Bois, a patrician Harvard-educated scholar, understood the relationship between art and politics and noted that, while images of black pathos were dominant in art depicting black life, it was unrealistic to ignore the most downtrodden segments of the black community. Art, he noted, could not render invisible those who needed the most attention and assistance. "We have criminals and prostitutes and debased elements, just as [white people] have. When the artist paints us he has a right to paint us whole and not ignore everything which is not perfect as we would wish it to be."[24] In essence, Du Bois advocated for the a wider range of black humanity to be visible, as it was among whites, who laughed at white comedies, scorned white criminals, and admired the smart, industrious, and beautiful. Black people in most literature, plays, films, and songs, however, were simply servile figures or monstrous stereotypes of base living. There were several considerations to this dilemma, as there were many other black intellectuals who agreed with Du Bois's demand that black art be responsible to something larger than entertainment for its consumers.

In a somewhat similar vein to Du Bois, the Howard University professor and philosopher Alain Locke advocated for black art to be an invaluable tool of resistive politics against racial discrimination. Though he admired the organizational efforts of civil rights organizations, he stated that "more immediate hope rests in the revaluation by white and black alike of the Negro in terms of his artistic endowments and cultural contributions, past and prospective."[25] The intelligence, beauty, and complexity of Langston Hughes's poetic prose, Jean Toomer's fiction, or Augusta Savage's sculptures were inherently resistive to the prevailing stereotypes of the Negro. Some, like the National Urban League's Charles S. Johnson, even advocated that black art could supplant more overt agitation and protest. Du Bois and Locke, however, found this position absurd. Art was no panacea for racist policies that barred black people from jobs, housing, or education.[26] Politics requires militant protest in the forms of marches, petitions, and the like. Art alone was insufficient, they insisted.

Despite the divergence of perspectives of black artists and intellectuals in the 1920s, there were some fundamental truths that were undeniable: black people lived in a hostile and virulently antiblack country. The dominant expression of white cultural production reflected this racial pathos. Cultural critics understood the significance of black creative expression and the black freedom struggle. Most were critical of the emphasis on black pathology on the grounds that it did not represent the best of the race; however, many like Du Bois, Locke, and Wallace Thurman were not absolute about black cultural expression. It should, in fact, be diverse, they argued. The fundamental thrust of these debates recognized the intractable nature of white supremacy and its nexus to popular culture.[27]

This white artistic myopia pressed heavily on the black artist who understood the market demand for black characters that catered to the most offensive assumptions about black people. Most white readers were, in fact, uninterested in seeing black people in ways that were similar to their own lives. Though most whites were not middle class, the white reading public envisioned whiteness as closer to a middle-class ideal. Drawn to the exoticism of the Negro, the seedy tales of black urban dysfunction, or the buffoonish antics of the coon, white consumers anticipated—in fact, demanded—stories of black people that reminded them of attributed descriptions that made whites distinct from blacks: civilized versus barbarian, industrious versus indolent, responsible versus careless, and intelligent versus stupid. Not only did these images affirm blackness as an organic and absolute Other, they simultaneously gave added meaning to whiteness and

America's racial hierarchy. As clearly evident in these white reactions to black people is the notion that "primitivizing" the other was essential to demarcating the meaning and terms of relationships between the races. A binary discourse on savageness and civilization provided a simplification of the complexities of race and power not only on a national stage but in international relations as well. These artistic representations gave depth and purpose to the vast and daunting efforts to uphold white supremacy. In fact, blacks who lived lives that were stable, sober, middle class, educated, and healthy were "out of their place."[28] The visibility of black people, therefore, increased concomitantly with their distance from an ostensibly white middle-class cultural standard and aesthetic. The organic conscious of this dilemma became pronounced as hip-hop entered the era dominated by conscious artists who laced lyrics with a hard-edged black militancy. No group better represents this era than Public Enemy, who directly signified the minstrel in several songs.

No song by the late 1980s was as explicitly conscious of the ghost of minstrelsy as Public Enemy's "Burn Hollywood Burn" (1989). The song, which features lyrics from Big Daddy Kane and the consummate gangsta rapper Ice Cube, vilifies the film industry for its racist depictions of black people:

> But some things I'll never forget . . .
> So step and fetch this shit
> For all the years we looked like clowns
> The joke is over. Smell the smoke from all around.[29]

Chuck D's pun and reference to Stepin Fetchit reflects his rejection of the enduring coon image while offering a badman expression of militant retribution for years of racism. Similarly, Big Daddy Kane inveighs against the myopic roles of "butlers and maids, slaves and hoes." Cube, however, says nothing substantive about Hollywood and its representation of black people; however, he challenges racist authority with threats of violence.

A year later X-Clan, which represented the high-water mark of black nationalism in hip-hop, offered militant metaphors, witty references, and intertextual allusions to esoteric African philosophy in their seminal debut, *To the East Blackwards*. Wearing African clothing, medallions, and the black nationalist tricolor, lead rapper Brother J explores the meaning of blackness: "Now let me tell you about blackness: grits and cornbread, how can you act this?" You can't, he would say. Sensitive to the inaccurate representations of black people in film and television, X-Clan, in another song, addresses "actors and actresses who write a couple of lines on what black is." But in contrast to the fictionalized images depicted by these actors, Brother J is considered a "sin" because he "just speaks from within." His sin is his defiance and rejection of narrowly articulated and contrived blackness. For X-Clan, blackness is organic and not to be attained through symbolic cultural gestures like eating soul food, acting, or rapping. It is in this context that X-Clan criticizes the white rap group 3rd Bass, accusing the "cave boys" of "trying to play black." In essence, blackness cannot be performed.[30]

Other groups like KMD revisited the minstrel and coon in the early 1990s so-called golden age in incredibly creative ways. In 1991 KMD rapper Onyx declared that he was no "hoe-trickin' brother who likes to eat chicken," reflecting the thrust of rappers who considered the coon their antithesis. Perhaps the most dramatic example of the pervasive rejection of the minstrel was KMD's 1994 album *Black Bastards,* which was not released by its label (until 2001) because of the controversial cover depicting the hanging of a cartoon Sambo figure. In no uncertain terms, KMD saw the Sambo caricature of black people as loathsome and worthy of symbolic death. Their label Elektra Records, however, found the hanging of a black figure, even with its obvious political overtones, unacceptable.

Perhaps the most popular song to attack the coon figure was Ice Cube's hit "True to the Game" (1991), which best represents a gold standard in hip-hop's cult of authenticity. The song addresses three archetypes of black sell-outs: two figures earn large amounts of money and disassociate from black people, in fact, ingratiate themselves to whites, dating them, living with them, and tolerating racist offenses. Another figure, who is a rapper, actively seeks mainstream acceptance by tailoring his music for white consumption. The figure (who is parodied as an MC Hammer–type in the video) goes from "hardcore" to "white and corny" commercial success with "no more soul." Conjuring the spirit of the minstrel, the character gesticulates in comical ways, dancing and grinning. Ice Cube admonishes him to "wipe that stupid ass smile off your face. Niggas always gotta show their teeth."

Ice Cube celebrates an aesthetic that is not dependent on white acceptance, while simultaneously insisting on an image of blackness that is not the sophisticated image of earlier musicians like Duke Ellington, Miles Davis, or Marvin Gaye. Cube is clearly dismissive of white acceptance, lives in a black community, donates money to various community projects, and, unlike KRS-One, insists that he does not need anyone to correct his broken English. Cube, in fact, valorizes a ghettocentric sensibility that dominated hip-hop for the rest of the decade and beyond. It is a narrow articulation of black authenticity that, like Harlem Renaissance writer Wallace Thurman, finds the black middle class suspect and qualitatively "whiter" than the black working class and poor.[31]

Though members of the older generation of black intellectuals and artists during the Harlem Renaissance recoiled at the controlling images of blackness and sought alternatively propagandistic images, some younger artists rejected the notion that black art be beholden to political agendas to create "college types" to balance the tired bacchanalian images of the black community. Langston Hughes, for example, in his powerful essay, "The Negro Artist and the Racial Mountain" (1926), sums up the sentiment of some who felt that art must be beholden to the artists and their own aesthetic integrity, not white benefactors, a larger market share, or "self-hating" Negroes:

> We younger Negro artists who create now intend to express our individual dark-skinned selves without fear or shame. If white people are pleased we are glad. If they are not, it doesn't matter. We know we are beautiful. And ugly too. The tom-tom cries and the tom-tom laughs. If colored people are pleased we are glad. If they are not, their displeasure doesn't matter either. We build our temples for tomorrow, strong as we know how, and we stand on top of the mountain, free within ourselves.[32]

It is clear, however, that Hughes does not disavow political expression. His advocating of new artistic integrity is inherently political. But among the younger artists of the era, few critics were as vociferous as Wallace Thurman. A young writer from Salt Lake City, Thurman left the University of Southern California and moved to Harlem at the age of twenty-three. In 1926 he co-founded *Fire!!*, a quarterly fine-arts magazine that attempted to recalibrate the scope of black art. Viewing themselves as a systematic break from the older generation of critics, Thurman and his cohorts (which included such luminaries as Langston Hughes, Zora Neale Hurston, and Aaron Douglas) shunned appeals for commercial success and embraced a maverick style that did not anticipate propaganda. A costly venture with insufficient revenue, *Fire!!* failed after only one issue; however, its failure did not diminish Thurman's criticism of the old guard black art critics who were "spouting fire and venom or else weeping and moaning."[33]

It is not accurate to suggest that Thurman argued against politics in art. Indeed, he was sensitive to the racist work of Octavus Roy Cohen and other white writers of his day. Moreover, Thurman's writing was inherently political. He challenged, however, what he viewed as the tendency among black artists to offer "college types" of black folk, which amounted to myopic "honeyed manna on a silver spoon." These black artists should instead privilege the working poor over the middle class, "people who still retained some individual race qualities and who were not totally white American in every respect save color of skin."[34] What is problematic in Thurman's assessment of the black middle class is that they were qualitatively "whiter" than poor black folks. How this "whiteness" is quantified is unclear. Most white people did not graduate from high school in 1928, let alone see the inside of a college. That poverty is somehow more authentically black than being middle class echoes the perspectives of the larger white community that demanded the exoticized, ghettoized Other. One's political or cultural worldview or commitment to the uplift of the black community were simplistically reduced to class location, leaving college types like Du Bois, Locke, Hurston, Fauset, and Hughes suspect while valorizing the proletariat as more faithful to some nebulous concept of blackness. The implications of Thurman's vision reflect essentialist notions that conflate class into the conceptualization of race, thereby upholding dominant narratives of race. Echoes of Thurman's position are found in hip-hop today, where poverty and a "hood" life of crime are considered more authentically black than going to college.

Like Thurman, Ice Cube engages in this discussion with great zeal and sagacity, but he falls into essentialist and narrow notions of race. Both of these artists/cultural critics implicitly indict themselves, since they were both raised in middle-class households and attended college before dropping out to pursue their art. Ice Cube, too, joins Thurman in pandering to terribly problematic assumptions about one's commitment to uplifting the black community or one's political consciousness being determined by class.[35] Ultimately, the thug rebel articulated by Ice Cube serves itself as a sort of post–Black Power–era minstrel figure, complete with an impulsive, oversexed, violent, and generally pathological image, and Cube's hometown, South Central Los Angeles (which was officially renamed South Los

Angeles in 2003 to combat a negative image), represents a spatial icon of authentic blackness in which credibility is accrued by association with the crime, hustling, and urban turmoil that the area represents. It is, as Murray Forman explains, not simply a home base of local familiarity and social networks; it can be iconic for "more menacing elements that are also centrally implicated in establishing criteria of significance. . . . It may be threatening, alienating, and dangerous to its inhabitants."[36]

While credentials in hip-hop often come from shouting out one's hood background or friendships with infamous crime lords, rappers rarely acknowledge staples of a middle-class upbringing like college (Jadakiss, Redman, Ma$e, The Game). But this does not mean that celebrations of wealth do not appear. In fact, it is a dominant theme, but the cachet of being wealthy is indicated by implicit or explicit references that the wealth comes from illegitimate activities. From T.I., The Game, 50 Cent, Young Jeezy, and Clipse, tales of being a dope boy handily dominates hip-hop in the post-1990s. Rick Ross's 2006 hit "Hustlin'" best typifies a recent incarnation of a "drug boy" trope that extends back to the mid-1990s shift from a 40-oz. malt-liquor-drinking street gangsta standard (N.W.A, Geto Boys) to the champagne-drinking, organized sophisticate gangsta standard (Notorious B.I.G., Jay-Z). Ross's moniker alone builds on the reputation of the infamous drug kingpin Freeway Ricky Ross, who was the most significant drug supplier responsible for supplying thousands of dealers in Los Angeles. At his height of operations, the kingpin, with the help of drug dealers with ties to Central Intelligence Agency–funded Central American groups, made $1–2 million a day in untaxed revenue from his home base in South Central Los Angeles. Even though, by his own admission, Ricky Ross is responsible for the deaths, beatings, shootings, imprisonment, drug addictions, and suffering of scores of thousands of black and Latino people, many in hip-hop valorize him and others as hood heroes, regardless of the monstrous effects they have had on the lives of the very people in these communities. In many ways, the activities of people like Ricky Ross helped facilitate the passage of draconian laws that created the rapid expansion of the prison industrial complex in the United States, which incarcerates more people than any other nation on Earth. Black and Latino citizens are imprisoned at rates grossly disproportionate to their populations at large, as well as disproportionate to their use of illegal drugs.[37] These connections have not been lost on other rappers.

Hardcore rapper NYOil released a controversial video denouncing rappers who glorify drug dealing (and other themes) in hip-hop as modern minstrels. In "Y'all Should All Get Lynched" (2006) NYOil does not limit his attacks to just the buffoonish rappers; he goes after gangsta rappers like 50 Cent and Jim Jones with zeal, calling them "coon ass rappers" for their eagerness to attack black people but their willingness to be silent or even reluctant to criticize white racists. NYOil even praises Kanye West for being the only rapper brave enough to criticize President George W. Bush for vacationing extra days even as black people were drowning and suffering without drinking water or supplies during the August 2005 Hurricane Katrina disaster in the Gulf Coast. Though the video to "Y'all Should All Get Lynched" was banned from the popular website YouTube.com, he defends his song, which endorses the lynching of the "coons" of hip-hop by referencing Rick Ross and "crack music":

How are you going to call yourself [Rick Ross]? Do you know how many lives are ruined behind him? I've seen people on this drug. I've seen murders, death, theft, robbery, communities ravaged, beautiful families turned inside out behind money and this drug—and dude is biggin' this shit up! There is a section of rap called "crack music." Are you fucking kidding me, yo? And people have nerve to take issue with me saying, "Y'all should all get lynched?"[38]

He even points out—accurately so—that more black people have lost their lives to the drug trade than from all lynchings in U.S. history.[39]

Challenging the Neo-minstrel

Despite minor references to the minstrel (or its derivatives) made by some groups of the late 1990s, such as the Coup, the Roots, and Black Star, discussion and debate were muted until the post-1990s and the increase in "conscious" rap in both commercial and underground hip-hop. The more recent criticisms, however, have expanded on the role of the minstrel, or coon, while remaining aware of the staple features of the cultural icon. Paris, for example, calls gangsta rappers cowardly "wannabes" (2003) who operate in the interests of corporate "vultures."

Perhaps the most visible comment on the state of the black image in popular culture came from Spike Lee's movie *Bamboozled* in 2000. The movie follows the trials of a black television network executive who is pressured by racist higher-ups to develop a TV show that is racially "real." Played by Damon Wayans, the protagonist, Pierre Delacroix, is a stiff, nerdy Harvard graduate who represents a hyperbolic stereotype of black uncool. In fact, Delacroix's white boss Dunwitty, played by Michael Rapaport, tells his underling that, "brother man, I'm blacker than you." Dunwitty, who laces his speech with hip-hop slang, has a black wife, has black art in his office, and is a hip-hop aficionado. Out of frustration, Delacroix endorses an absurdly racist idea, "Mantan: The New Millennium Minstrel Show." To his surprise, the show is approved and becomes a national sensation, complete with "darkies" singing in the watermelon patch.

Hip-hop looms large in the movie. In fact, the real-life hip-hop antiminstrel group, the Roots, has a part on the Mantan show as the Alabama Porch Monkeys who perform music to adoring black and white audiences who celebrate the characters Sleep 'n' Eat, Mantan, Nigger Jim, Rastus, and Aunt Jemima. Another rap group, the fictionalized Mau Maus, led by Big Blak Afrika, played by Mos Def, represents black nationalist militancy, heavy with symbols and rhetoric but politically shallow. A sort of nationalist-inspired gangsta rap collective, the Mau Maus protest the minstrel show for fostering racist stereotypes, even as they gulp down 40-oz. malt liquor, play with guns, and represent an inarticulate, gangsta buffoon style that Lee calls "the minstrel of the 21st Century."[40] Lee's satire takes television, movies, and commercial hip-hop to task in the film. The message, given between expressions of over-the-top humor, is that the commodification of black culture continues to center on myopic representations of black pathos decades after Alain Locke, Wallace Thurman, and W. E. B. Du Bois debated the issue.

By the late 1990s many black intellectuals of the hip-hop generation were engaged in vigorous discussions about the merits of hip-hop's projected images of black people. *Vibe* magazine journalist Alicia Rice insists that the minstrel remains durable in the post-1990s as its derivative images thrive. "Its no joke," she notes, "that . . . playing a direct descendent of Step's jive-ass persona is still a bread-winning formula." In a similar vein, hip-hop journalist and activist Kevin Powell observes that following the success of *The Chronic* (1992), hip-hop had been "redirected, co-opted, commodified, and exploited to the point where it has become a modern-day minstrel show complete with . . . a self abhorrence of Black self."[41] Indeed, some argue that these images that are supposedly of "real nigga" tough guys are little more than cowardly Uncle Toms that "curtsy" to white supremacy. In fact, there is little debate over the importance the image of the violent black male is to gendered articulations of race by a white supremacist society at large. bell hooks notes that, "at the center of the way black male selfhood is constructed in white-supremacist capitalist patriarchy is the image of the brute—untamed, uncivilized, unthinking and unfeeling."[42] The appeal of commercial success is so great that few rappers are willing to depart from the winning formula of being the real nigga brute.

W. Jelani Cobb explains that the narrowing of black authenticity in hip-hop is, in part, due to the larger [white] consumer market, which will not tolerate offenses against whiteness while simultaneously enjoying the internecine orgy of hostility and violence among black folk. Cobb notes that "it is not coincidental that hip hop has made 'nigga' the most common noun in popular music. But you have almost never heard any certified thug utter the words cracker, ofay, honky, peckerwood, wop, dago, guinea, kike or any other white-oriented epithet. The reason for that is simple: Massa ain't havin' it. . . . And bitch is still allowed with the common understanding that the term is referring to black women. The point is this: debasement of black communities is entirely acceptable—required even—by hip hop's predominantly white consumer base."[43] This unthinking, uncivilized neominstrel has been given widespread promotion in various media. It has, in fact, handily dominated rap representations of black males to such an extreme that between Dr. Dre's gangsta standard *The Chronic* (1992) and 2006 only two adult solo black male rappers (Wyclef Jean [*Carnival*, 1997] and Will Smith [*Big Willie Style*, 1997]) have gone platinum without killing "niggas," referencing bitches, hos, and nihilistic violence on an album.[44]

In nearly every way these themes appear to correlate with the zip coon variant of the minstrel. The zip coon, an urban-set figure, is a criminally inclined, ignorant, and trifling character who revels in his deplorable conditions. So songs about teenage prostitutes, killings, drug dealing, and general pathos, such as Lil' Kim's 2005 hit "Lighters Up," are not only tales that give voice to the voiceless but veritable festive markers of credibility. They affirm one's authenticity and anchor the rapper as a real nigga or, in the case of Kim, the "hottest bitch." Rarely, however, do these hood narratives offer resistive messages or hope, inspiration, or defiance to white supremacy. Instead, they celebrate the ways in which a "nigga's" life can be taken almost casually.

While white consumers may be unwilling to embrace stories of killing "crackers" as much as tales of killing "niggas," there is a conspicuous pattern of consumption even among black folk. Many hip-hop consumers know of Mos Def, Common, and Talib Kweli, who have all gotten moderate exposure in hip-hop magazines, though none has gone platinum. Though not the darlings of Northeast-based hip-hop magazines, Chamillionaire, Trick Daddy, and Three 6 Mafia have all gone platinum with the help of droves of eager black consumers. What does it mean that the Ying Yang Twins are multiplatinum when the Roots have barely gone gold? More important, the oversexed, violent, and misogynist tales that are passed off as ghetto realness have become an established marker for credibility, as well as a racialized authenticity that conflates poverty, crime, misogyny, and all things "ghetto" with blackness. The ghetto itself becomes a spatial metaphor for black people, particularly ignorant and crude ones. It is such that calling someone "ghetto" represents a colloquial statement of one's crude behavior or otherwise unsophisticated and tactless style, which is implicitly black. Some whites have even begun referring to white women with large butts as having "ghetto butts"—butts that resemble those of black women. The association with blackness and the ghetto—and all that it represents—is clearly problematic.

While many from the hip-hop community have rejected the reprise of the minstrel show, there has also been an outcry from outside of the hip-hop nation. From Spike Lee to C. Delores Tucker, many African Americans have taken umbrage at many of the images in hip-hop. Few cultural critics have been as vituperative in describing the problematic images of black people in hip-hop as Stanley Crouch. Calling rap music videos "the new minstrelsy," Crouch inveighs against the "neo-Sambo [who] is sturdily placed in our contemporary popular iconography."[45] Crouch reflects no significant familiarity with hip-hop beyond these neominstrel types and offers what is typically a perspective of non-hip-hop critics. Unlike Powell, Bakari Kitwana, or other hip-hop journalists, Crouch simplifies hip-hop into an art that promotes disengagement from education and cultivates images that place black humanity under attack. The art appears monolithic in his observations, a departure from the jeremiad style of hip-hoppers who seek to redeem the art and realize its earliest ambitions to bring empowerment, peace, and pleasure to black and Latino communities.

Many hip-hop journalists see obvious parallels with the minstrel characters of the early twentieth century. Kevin Powell agrees with the work of hip-hop journalist Bakari Kitwana, who writes of the "minstrel-esque proven formula for success," when Powell charges that the art can do more for uplifting the black community and affirming black people. Instead, it has become a politically acceptable medium to ridicule black people, with echoes from the "buffoonish minstrelsy of yesteryear."[46] Though many have expressed decidedly opposing opinions on the modern hip-hop coon, some of the hip-hop generation have been more ambivalent.

Mark Anthony Neal refers to elements of hip-hop as "sonic blackface" that hail from a tradition known by many names: minstrelsy, coon-show, or "samboism." In fact, Neal humorously explains how his internal "'coon' meter" vibrates at the sight of King of Crunk rapper Lil Jon. With his brash lyrics of violence, hypersexuality, platinum-grilled smiles (what some black nationalists call "cooning for the camera"), and animated demeanor, Lil Jon and the Eastside Boys (or Trick Daddy or Flavor Flav, for that matter) appears as the quintessential postmodern super coon. The *Source*, on its November 2006 cover, questioned if hip-hop has become "a new minstrel show." The magazine takes to task several acts, including a popular 2006 YouTube.com video, "Fry That Chicken" by Ms. Peachez, an overweight female character, played by Dale Lynch, who raps about the joys of fried chicken to a bunch of rural, grinning black children. The article also examines VH1's hit show *Flavor of Love*, starring Public Enemy hype man Flavor Flav, who searches among a group of women for a mate. Flav, the article notes, is a "garishly dressed character whose appetite for fame is fed by a house full of women and buckets of fried chicken." The show has been called a "minstrel show" success by some for featuring the forty-seven-year-old as a comically surreal, carefree, outlandish figure. Some have argued that the formula for success is so evident that Flavor Flav has extended his antics for ratings.[47] In fact, it was not only the most popular show on VH1 but also was the most popular nonsports show on cable TV in 2006.[48]

The allegiance to the coon image is so strong that the two members of the Atlanta-based group the Eastside Boys have adopted names derived from the word *Sambo*: Big Sam and Lil Bo. For many observers, that grown black males would choose to call themselves "Sambos" reflects a pronounced stupidity and slavish adherence to white supremacy. Mos Def, exasperated, asks, "What's next, Kunte and Kinte? The South should know better. This is the same country that ran up in [Black Panther leader] Fred Hampton's crib and shot him in bed with his pregnant wife. You think the rules changed because niggas got No. 1 records? What are we supposed to tell our kids? After Malcolm, Martin and Du Bois we got Sam-Bo?"[49] Mos Def's outrage at the proliferation of "coonery" is mirrored by many of the hip-hop generation. In 2006 a group of educators and activists formed the "Stop Coonin Movement," which is aimed at "hustlin' consciousness to the hip hop community." Established by members of the hip-hop generation, the organization is committed to "challenging the misrepresentation of Black people prevalent in [popular culture]." Stop Coonin is one of the latest expressions of alarm over the direction of hip-hop.[50] The leading African American magazine, *Ebony*, even issued a special issue in July 2007 on the state of black images in hip-hop, insisting that the origins of hip-hop were never centered on such troubling depictions of black people. As editorial director Bryan Monroe writes, "We know better."[51] Within this discussion, there is a subtext that these minstrel inflections are part of an attempt to cater to a larger, hostile white audience of hip-hop consumers. Clearly, the divisions in the hip-hop nation around the representation of black people for a wider market have become increasingly salient.

Ultimately, however, Neal argues, this tradition of pandering to offensive and narrow definitions of black authenticity for a [white] consumer market is about white expectations as well as black self-preservation. "If such antics spared you the rod two centuries ago, it can surely earn you seven-figure salaries in this era of global digitized blackness."[52] Gangstas, thugs, masters of crunk, and many others have parlayed racist assumptions into a degree of financial success that has proved elusive to most black people (or white ones for that matter). They have created images that reify myopic ideas of black authenticity while achieving the material successes that have been largely unavailable to them. They have in fact, subverted the economic exigencies for their personal advancement. This does not mean, however, that they are above reproach, as the Boston-based group The Perceptionists argue. In their song "Black Dialogue" (2005), they dismiss the formulaic scheme to commercial success in rap:

> But does that mean we should be shucking and jiving
> Fucking and kniving just to keep our bank accounts thriving?
> See I walk the path my elders laid out
> Cause acting like a monkey for white folks is played out
> I get my own money, on my own terms.[53]

The Roots have remained part of a community of "underground" artists who have not enjoyed great commercial success but have enjoyed years of critical praise and moderate media attention. They have acted, according to member ?uestlove, contrary to the "minstrel" expectations of the market.

In a similar vein, the spokesman for The Roots, ?uestlove, explains that, despite the decade of critical praise the group has received, the media exposure, and work with giants of music like Jay-Z, Eve, and Erykah Badu, the group lacks commercial success largely because it does not conform to dominant expectations of hip-hop. "We're not minstrel. We're not cartoony. We're not gangsta. We're not ambiguously sexual. We're not overtly sexual. We're none of those things." Still, one cannot ignore the fact that the audiences at energetic and high-powered Roots concerts are typically overwhelmingly white. As Common notes, their typical concert is a sea full of "coffee shop chicks and white dudes." ?uestlove even jokes that one would see a typical Roots audience and "will think that [white rock band] Korn will be onstage any moment."[54] These observations demonstrate that consumption of black images is more than a concern over simple insatiable white appetites for the minstrel. The white hip-hop consumer market is not a monolith any more than the black or Latino ones. Most hip-hop consumers (regardless of race) have made their preference for "real niggas" clear. And it appears that the underground scene reflects the basic demographics of the commercial one: it is mostly white.

Conclusion

From the earliest caricatures of black people, African American artists, laypeople, and leaders have protested these deeply offensive images of lazy, infantile, and buffoonish figures. Still, some black people have always found space in minstrelsy for financial opportunity. Other black folk simply enjoyed the entertainment, despite its core racist thrust. Aware of this cultural heritage, hip-hop artists have demarcated their own contours of expression that engage the polemics of racial performance, making the minstrel an essential reference point. Indeed, the legacy of minstrelsy looms large in hip-hop as artists and others engage in a dynamic contest for the direction of its multibillion-dollar industry.

Though the arch of the black experience since the mid-nineteenth century has continued to bend toward freedom and an expansion of democracy, it is not without its challenges. The expansion of democracy and freedom in the United States has always been met with stiff resistance from defenders of white supremacy, patriarchy, and intolerance. Without question, the status quo has sought to maintain itself through multiple levels of influence. William Stanley Braithwaite's comments about black folk in 1920s popular culture oddly sounds identical to contemporary comments about hip-hop when he explained that black people were reduced to being "a shuttlecock between two extremes of humor and pathos."[55] Braithwaite, Du Bois, and others vilified the Negro found in white-produced art: one who was "sordid, foolish and criminal."[56] It was in this context that the proponents of the New Negro sought to deconstruct the hegemonic depictions of blackness, offering a vituperative challenge by way of their own artistic creativity. The insistence that the powerful maintain their domination with much greater efficacy by utilizing the will of the oppressed bears weight in understanding the dynamic at play with hip-hop's own self-image. The marginalized, therefore, embrace dominant ideas and narratives, even if doing so engenders their own oppression.[57] Many black people, therefore,

This image represents a cross-section of hip-hop's history, influences, and artistic icons, from its origins in the waning years of the Black Power movement (the clenched fist, the woman with the afro) to hip-hop's classic lyrical homage to materialism. James Brown, who influenced the audio style of hip-hop in prolific sampling as well as the earliest b-boys and b-girls, is also prominent. Malcolm X's iconic pose peering out the window with an assault rifle is redone by DJ Lord, who harnesses a turntable as his weapon of choice.

endorse narrow definitions of black authenticity. One is not "real" by doing well in school, being raised middle class, or even speaking proper grammar. The articulation of a "real nigga" among many MCs reads nearly exactly as a "zip coon" character of the early twentieth century.

In the final analysis, the idea of the "controlling images" of black people reflects the role that black artists, from nineteenth-century minstrels to twenty-first-century thugs, assume in articulating dominant ideas about black people, reducing them to tired stereotypes that help apologize for prevailing structures of oppression and racism. These images are not always simplified into Manichean roles. They are often convoluted and dynamic figures that follow no set boundaries of expression. They do, however, foment considerable discussion and debate, suggesting that the durability of racism reveals its uncanny ability to mutate and adapt to changing social and cultural currents. Moreover, black artists and intellectuals are incessantly adapting to and resisting dominant narratives that tend to circumscribe their humanity.

2

"Real Niggas": Race, Ethnicity, and the Construction of Authenticity in Hip-Hop

Hip-hop was Black music. It's becoming harder to tell these days. Is this music defined by the culture that inspires it or the white palms that purchase the CDs and sign the checks?

— *Source* (March 2001)

In October 2001 Bubba Sparxxx, then a new rapper on the national scene, explained during an interview with MTV News that "hip-hop has always been about authenticity." As a white southerner, Bubba celebrates his "authenticity" in a music video for his hit song "Ugly," which features overweight, rustic southerners—black and white—engaging in raucous fun chasing pigs in mud, tumbling in hay, eating boiled peanuts, and racing tractors. Like the video, Sparxxx in his CD proudly gives homage to his poor roots. Proud of his heritage, he remains cognizant of the inevitable questions about his right to represent hip-hop. In several tracks Sparxxx conspicuously affirms his marginalization in society as a poor white southerner. A rural, southern white landscape as an expression of hip-hop authenticity is nearly anathema to hip-hop's origins in 1970s New York City. But as ironic as this appears, he finds no incongruence with extolling his southern white roots in order to affirm his legitimacy in and love for a black art form.[1]

Bubba Sparxxx represents the fluidity and dynamic manner in which credibility and authenticity are understood in hip-hop. Race and ethnicity have long loomed large for hip-hop artists since the earliest block parties in the South Bronx. It was in the poorest sections of New York's rough-and-tumble ghettoes that African American and Caribbean youth developed the four pillars of America's newest artistic gift to the world. That era of the art's birth bears great responsibility to the oppositional culture that remains the cornerstone of hip-hop, which was largely an extension of the Black Power movement that waned as hip-hop crystallized among urban youth.

By 1998 hip-hop records outsold every other genre of music in the United States. From cinema, clothing lines, magazines, and American vernacular, hip-hop's influence has made an indelible mark in popular culture. Some view this as a portentous sign of hip-hop's decline and corruption. Others welcome it as an example of young black talent and business expertise and even as a salve for America's old wounds of racism. Regardless of the opinions surrounding hip-hop's success, an examination of the art reveals fascinating examples of how America's popular culture has conformed to and deviated from conventional notions of race.

This chapter explores the dynamic notions of "authenticity" in hip-hop and explores the role that race figures into the definitions of "realness." I pay particular attention to rap music (instead of deejaying, break dancing, or graffiti art), exploring the lyrics of rappers of European, Caribbean (Spanish- and English-speaking), Asian, and Mexican descent to show that, although figurative passing occurs, cultural appropriation and cultural melding also take place in rap, further extending the precept that race is socially constructed. These rappers at once affirm their ethnicity as non–African Americans while simultaneously appropriating significant cultural markers and semiotic styles from African American rappers in order to declare their legitimacy in rap music.

From its beginning, hip-hop has been as obsessed with artistic authenticity as the United States has been with race. As an art spawned from the black and Latino ghettoes of the race-obsessed United States, hip-hop has long predicated its popular understanding of authenticity in highly racialized terms. An examination of how hip-hop engages "realness" in the American context of race reveals fascinating social and cultural examples of the malleability of both race and authenticity, which remain inexact and dynamic in hip-hop. Hip-hop's mostly white audience and the growing visibility of non–African American rappers have forced observers and participants to reexamine the notions of realness and artistic function in hip-hop since the early 1990s as race and identity formation remain salient components in an art form in constant contest with itself.

Keepin' It Real: Definitions in Flux

Despite the multiethnic nature of the founding community of hip-hop, young African American working-class, urban males emerged as the art's central representatives. From this vantage, the art pulled qualities from the pervasive sensibilities of black "oppositional culture" that had become increasingly popular in the 1960s and hegemonic in black America in the early 1970s. In essence, oppositional culture is the system of beliefs and practices that operates counter to the dominant culture and ideologies.[2] Oppositional culture was woven into the tapestry of hip-hop from its inception. In over twenty-five years of hip-hop's existence, the art has been mostly regarded as exceptional and peculiar within the realm of the American musical and artistic mainstream. But to narrowly define hip-hop as an oppositional art or an art that inherently resists racism or oppression is an oversimplification. The art not only resists the overarching themes of racial discrimination inherent in American popular culture, it also affirms the racial status quo while simultaneously offering alternative perspectives. Fundamentally, hip-hop is a varied, complex art form with plenty of room for expression along various ideological lines. But as revealed here, all artists position themselves as authentic and "true to the game." The criteria for that authenticity, however, are in constant flux, reflecting larger social and political currents in society at large.

At its most fundamental level, "realness" in hip-hop implies an intimate familiarity with the urban, working-class landscapes that gave rise to hip-hop in the 1970s. Additionally, it recognizes that the conditions in the South Bronx around 1974 are not unfamiliar to poor urban communities elsewhere. Implicit in this spatial notion is a class consciousness that is inextricably connected to race. It implies (somewhat narrowly) that black communities are synonymous with poor communities. A brash intimacy with crime has also been assumed within the dominant definition of hip-hop authenticity during the last decade. Conversely, middle-class status, suburban living, and whiteness have been further removed from hip-hop authenticity psychically, spatially, and culturally.

Although this definition has been the dominant articulation of hip-hop authenticity since the mid-1990s, competing expressions remain. There is the black-conscious rebel authenticity that had been largely relegated to the margins of commercial hip-hop until war and worsening urban conditions emerged under the administration of the second president Bush. Commercial rappers like Jadakiss, Ludacris, Jay-Z, and The Game have been political in ways that were virtually absent in commercial hip-hop between 1994 and 2002. They have all expressed a black consciousness that was pervasive a decade earlier, during hip-hop's "Golden Age." Additionally, other more explicit political commentaries are made by commercial rappers that address war, poverty, and police brutality in very sophisticated and highly racialized discourses.

Despite the centrality of African Americans in articulations of authenticity, hip-hop has roots that are, in fact, more diasporic than popularly perceived. Hip-hop not only owes its origins to lyrical and instrumental musical styles from North America, such as the urban folkloric badman narratives, R&B, blues, jazz, and disco; it also is influenced by the early sound-system techniques of Jamaican music, as well as by *plena* and *bomba* music from Puerto Rico.[3]

This idea is not novel. Dozens of scholars have taken note of the various influences on hip-hop. As Robin D. G. Kelley notes, "Hip-hop's hybridity reflected, in part, the increasingly international character of America's inner cities resulting from immigration, demographic change, and new forms of information, as well as the inventive employment of technology in creating rap music."[4] All the same, other observers often marginalize or entirely ignore the non–African American contributions to hip-hop. Aïda Croal argues that "no one questions the origins of rap—that it came out of the Bronx and out of black urban culture."[5] In a similar vein, Marvin J. Gladney argues that hip-hop is "the most recent 'seed' in the continuum, of Afrikan-American culture."[6] For Gladney, hip-hop is inextricably tied to the Black Arts Movement of the late 1960s and early 1970s, and by extension, hip-hop is bound to the musical, folkloric, and stylistic traditions of African Americans. While his argument has significant merit, he fails to mention the influence or participation of non–African Americans in the formation of the art. The centrality of Puerto Ricans is ignored for sake of the "black aesthetic," and while some overlook the contributions of non–African Americans, others simply argue that only black men are authentic representatives of hip-hop. In 1999 the *New York Times* hosted a two-sided debate entitled, "The Hip-Hop Nation: Whose Is It?" in which the writer Toure argued that, despite the multiracial origins of the hip-hop nation, its "leadership is and will remain black. As it should."[7]

Even the hip-hop media have maintained the hegemonic hold that African Americans have on the art. Despite being cofounders of hip-hop, Latinos generally were marginalized in the hip-hop media until the post-1990s, when they were slightly more visible. For example, a survey of the *Source,* and the other leading hip-hop magazines, from the 1988 to 2002 found only one Latino soloist on a magazine cover, Big Pun, and one Latino group, Cypress Hill, out of over one hundred covers of magazines.[8]

Several other academic and popular press writers have likewise erased non–African American contributions. Some simply locate all contributions under the rubric of "blackness." While it is easy to situate Caribbean people (English, Spanish, or French speaking) within the framework of "blackness," the popular understanding of what it means to be "Latino" exists outside the parameters of the popular understanding of being black.[9] But, as revealed here, identity formation among Puerto Rican youth in the United States is a complicated one and further textured by hip-hop. Thus, the discussion of "authenticity" and race in hip-hop is complex.

Black people have been most visible in the deejaying and MC facets of hip-hop. Though still central, African Americans have been less dominant in graffiti art and b-boying, in which Latinos have had a long and visible presence since the earliest years.[10] Though Latinos were involved early in rapping, like Charlie Chase, they have been less involved in MCing. This has led to a general ignorance about the involvement of Puerto Ricans to the origins of hip-hop. The cause of this historical myopia stems chiefly from the marketing of hip-hop. Corporate America has generally been unable to market break dancing and graffiti art, both of which fell outside the confines of an easily commodified art. The music, which has been the center-piece of the culture, was easily marketed throughout the 1980s and 1990s. African Americans had long held dominance in those two elements—dee-jaying and rapping. Though turntablism traces its roots to Jamaican-born, NYC-raised DJ Kool Herc, African American DJs like Grand Wizard Theodore and Afrika Bambaataa dominated the scene.[11] Rapping, rooted in urban African American "badman" narratives, gave hip-hop its force and character.[12]

The question of authenticity and how race and ethnicity intersect with it is addressed most easily by isolating the music from hip-hop, particularly from the lyrics of rap. It is in this lyrical realm that the intellectual process of affirming one's place in hip-hop can be addressed most effectively. The

Grandmaster Flash and Nas represent an arc of hip-hop, from its earliest years on the streets of the Bronx to a multibillion-dollar art with broad global influence.

rhymes and styles of rap reveal fascinating examples of how race is perceived in a genre obsessed with "keepin' it real" and in a society at large where race is an obsession. In rap, the realest is often the blackest, though the meaning of blackness is in constant flux. For some, "authentic blackness" is clearly expressed in the black militant expressions of nationalism among groups like dead prez. For others, a ghettocentric expression is the iconic expression of blackness with an artist like 50 Cent.   ·

The desire to affirm authenticity and skill is a ubiquitous artistic quality in the "rap game." The criteria for authenticity, however, are dynamic. Since the early 1990s the thug ethos has handily dominated hip-hop, after a short period of black nationalist dominance. Thus rappers celebrate thug behavior as an expression of their authenticity, and while being a thug is not solely the domain of African Americans, thugs in rap clearly conform to a standard established by young, working class, urban African American males. Out of this thug appeal the celebration of being a "real nigga" has become common. In fact, "thug" has become synonymous with being a "real nigga." The list of rappers who claim to be "real niggas" runs like a list of who's who in hip-hop: T.I., Yung Joc, The Game, Jay-Z, Fat Joe.

Dozens of songs laud realness. Whether gangsta or conscious, being a real nigga has currency in rap. N.W.A took realness to new heights with *Efi14zaggin* (1991). Subsequent rappers like Tupac and Jay-Z have celebrated the thug life while underscoring their real nigga status. Within this framework, rappers who extol ghettoized pathology (drug selling, gang banging, violence, pimping, etc.) affirm their realness. All other groups become peripheral and must conform to the standard established by this group. So lyrically and stylistically all artists place themselves within this contextual framework and to varying degrees appropriate young African American male styles and cultural markers. In order to secure greater points in the realm of realness, pathology must also be added to the mix. Not to overlook the black nationalists, Jeru the Damaja in "One Day" (1995) refers to himself as a "real nigga" who rescues hip-hop from the corrupt, greedy and materialistic forces of the industry. So-called conscious rappers like Common and Talib Kweli have also referred to themselves as "real niggas," further obfuscating the meaning of the term as a signifier of gangsta sensibility. It must be noted, however, that the last two rappers first used the term in reference to themselves in songs that were done with self-described thugs Fat Joe, Big Pun, and DJ Quik. Perhaps each rapper sought to affirm his versatility and lyrical agility by ascribing to the typical tropes of gangsta rap while sharing the mic with thug rappers. To be sure, one does not want to appear "soft" by comparison.

Realer than Real

In "Real Niggas" (2000), the rappers Nas and Ruc provide homage to their friends and fallen comrades from Queensbridge public housing in New York. After each line of names the chorus, "real niggas," reminds the listener of the respect due to their associates. Ostensibly victims of and players in the crime and dysfunction pervasive in the housing project, the people named are so numerous that Nas states that "the list is gettin' too long for this track." Not only does the song valorize their friends, it manages to lionize the rappers by association. Raised in the same projects, the rappers exclaim, "Real niggas come out the projects." Several other rappers proudly wear their previous residence in public housing on their sleeves. The Marcy projects in Brooklyn and Magnolia projects in New Orleans have been to Jay-Z and Juvenile what Queensbridge is to Nas: instant credibility.

While celebrating location has always been an essential trope in hip-hop, it was not until Boogie Down Productions' "South Bronx" (1986) that hometown homage ventured into gangsta themes. Still, most songs, such as Run DMC's "Hollis Crew" (1984) or LL Cool J's "Hollis"(1990), simply provided recognition of location, a figurative declaration of affinity with public space. N.W.A's "Straight Outta Compton" (1988), however, introduced new styles into the urban tales in hip-hop. The song features a new level of violent lyricism about murder, mayhem, and misogyny. Implicit in the song is that the working-class Los Angeles suburb was a tough place not to be taken lightly, where they will "shoot a motherfucker in a minute." The seminal first album from N.W.A represents the most unadulterated form of gangsta rap, replete with songs featuring fiercely romantic tales of shootings, drive-bys, and nihilism. The album introduced a fundamental shift in the way in which authenticity was judged.

While machismo posturing had predated *Straight Outta Compton,* no group relied so heavily on the crude and obstreperous tales of ghetto myth as did N.W.A. Moreover, N.W.A significantly based its credibility on its gangsta narrative. The gangsta tales raised the bar of oppositional culture, inherent in the art. In many ways, the group conformed to the standards of hip-hop while pushing its boundaries. Hip-hop has always been about one-upmanship. Competition has always driven the art to new levels of creative expression. As Noam Chomsky writes, "Creativity is predicated on a system of rules and forms, in part determined by intrinsic human capacities. Without such constraints, we have arbitrary and random behavior."[13] In relation to hip-hop culture, N.W.A adhered to its norms of expression: developing hyperbolic tales, graphic first-personal stories, and the surrounding world. N.W.A, while aware of the fanciful nature of the tales found in its songs, also knew that the tales were a loose reality for friends or cohorts. That no member of the group was ever in a gang or served time in prison did not produce cries of figurative plagiarism. Instead, the group was praised for its raw and bold depiction of ghetto life in postindustrial Los Angeles.[14] Ultimately, N.W.A's gangsta tales reflected an intimidation factor never before seen in hip-hop. The group refocused intimidation from lyrical ability and self-aggrandizing tales of wealth and women to base, street-level conflict. It was an extension of the hip-hop style of fictive displays of self-promotion in rhyme. For example, early MCs generally rapped about having huge amounts of cash, women, and fame. Few complained that these early rappers more often than not lived with their parents, owned no cars, and lived in areas with a median poverty-level income. Hyperbole is intrinsic to rapping. N.W.A's hyperbolic style fixated on violent tropes that were outlandishly surreal and not to be taken literally. They were, however, more firmly associated with the "bad nigger" trope that has been reconfigured as the "real nigga."[15] By the mid-1990s the gangsta genre had established hegemony in rap, causing commercial rappers to eagerly declare their "real nigga" status. Thus, non–African Americans who aspire to represent the real do so by celebrating the same activities that performers like N.W.A, Geto Boys, Ice-T, and other gangsta rappers had established as standards of ghetto authenticity in the late 1980s.[16]

From Puerto Rocks to *"Eses"*

The group Cypress Hill, composed of two Los Angeles–based Cuban rappers and an Italian-American DJ, released its first album in 1991. Though not African American, the two rappers did not hesitate to promote the prevailing gangsta-inspired themes that dominated rap. Though not relying as heavily on the misogynist styles of their peers, Cypress Hill continues to valorize gang life with songs about drinking malt liquor, smoking marijuana, and killing "niggas." In "How I Could Just Kill a Man," they rap: "Sawed off shotgun, hand on the pump, sippin' on a forty / puffin' on a blunt / pumped my shotgun / the niggas didn't jump . . . look at all those funeral cars." Emerging from the tumultuous world of gangs and drive-bys, the rappers fused the styles of the L.A.-area's Chicano and African American gang systems in their brand of gangsta rap. Mixing Chicano and African American slang, the group situated itself between two distinct gang systems in which violence has historically been intraethnic. Black gangs concentrate on attacking rival black gangsters in a system known as the Crip-Blood binary. Similarly, Latino gangs prey mostly on Latinos in a separate and distinct system known as the *Norte-Sur* binary. With a relatively small Cuban community, Cypress Hill affirmed its street credibility with gangsta styles that borrowed from both *cholos* and mostly black Bloods and Crips.[17] Unlike Chicano rappers such as Kid Frost, group members unabashedly call themselves "niggas," and Cypress Hill became the first Latino group to go platinum and appear on the cover of major hip-hop magazines.

Though Cypress Hill effectively adopts African American semiotics, the group produced a brilliant song in a curious bilingual style, "Latin Lingo" on its first CD. The song employs Chicano street slang mixed with African American street slang against a musical backdrop of Cuban congas and rhythms. *Calo* words like *"vato," "hynas," "simon,"* and *"ese"* are peculiar to California Chicano slang. Moreover, the group gives a shout-out to *"la raza,"* the Latino people; however, the term coined among Chicanos and Mexicans is typically used as a reference to Mexican-descended people. Here, Cypress Hill demonstrates an interesting process of group-identity formation. Sen Dog, a dark-skinned Cuban with kinky hair, is typically considered black by American observers. B-Real, with lighter skin and an Afro (ca. 1993), looks markedly different from the typical Chicano phenotype common in Los Angeles. The visible African ancestry may have prompted the Cuban rappers to adopt African American cultural markers while granting them access to the coveted acceptance from hardcore rappers. What may at once appear to be semiotic ambiguities are a testimony to the malleability of race and ethnicity. Cypress Hill rappers are of African and Latino descent in a city with little history and cultural precedent for African Latinos.[18]

The group incorporates elements from the disparate gang cultures of blacks and Latinos in the city, giving a new and unique provincial expression to hip-hop, which tends to absorb regional styles and expressions, while conforming to generally universal tropes. In addition, Cypress Hill helped establish an important tone for Latino expression in an art that had a limited Latino presence in rap.[19] The group not only brought visibility to Latino rappers; it also affirmed gangsta styles and themes that had begun to dominate hip-hop in the early 1990s. It did this while adhering to an image of Chicano/African American street realness that was peculiar to the Los Angeles area. That the members were neither Chicano nor African American did not evoke criticisms that they made infractions against hip-hop's sacrosanct code of authenticity.[20] Instead, Cypress Hill's success reflects the group's ability to transcend conventional notions of race and ethnicity while simultaneously celebrating, and bringing attention to, those very cultural markers that give race and ethnicity meaning. Simply put, Sen Dog and B-Real are "black" and Latino.[21] That they are not African Americans did not prevent them from employing African American Vernacular English (AAVE) or using in-group terms such as "nigga" with impunity. That they are not Chicano did not prevent them from adopting Chicano cultural markers as their own. In fact, the group went so far as to release an LP, *Los grandes éxitos en Español* ("Greatest Hits in Spanish"; 1999), with cover art featuring Aztec motifs. The Aztec symbolism ostensibly represents a nod to their Latino "roots," although Aztecs did not occupy pre-Columbian Cuba. At once, Cypress Hill cultivates both an African diasporic and trans-Latino perspective in their expression of hip-hop. It may be argued that conventional notions of race and identity formation are ineffective for fully interpreting the cultural interloping in which the group participates. But to suggest that Cypress Hill passes for Chicano circumscribes the boundaries of Chicano street youth culture and evokes an essentialist perspective that resists non-Chicano participation in Chicano semiotics. This Cuban adoption and celebration of distinctly Chicano semiotics does not undermine the "Cuban-ness" of the group, nor does it suggest a particular longing to be Chicano. For example, few would suggest that white youth are making efforts to actually pass as black by listening to hip-hop, wearing hip-hop clothing, and employing vernacular terms born of black youth, such as "bling," "wack," "phat," or the several other terms in the mainstream American lexicon. Cultural cross-fertilization does not mean a conscious effort to abandon whiteness or become black, any more than a black fan of NASCAR, monster truck races, and Trace Adkins is trying to pass as white. Cypress Hill's adoption of disparate cultural markers represents the groups' attempt to affirm authenticity by conforming to popular notions of gangsta culture and "representing" their hood while adhering to the larger hegemonic forces in society that demand pan-Latinoism. In some ways, their identification with Chicanos was not their choice. The very term "Latino" makes a certainty of group identity that they can either embrace or reject. Whether or not they were advocates of trans-Latinoism, many non-Cuban Latinos would identify with them for their artistic achievements. In fact, Cypress Hill is highly regarded in the Latino rap community for being trailblazers.

Los Angeles rap group Funkdoobiest has not only praised Cypress Hill but exclaimed that it was due time for Latinos to get recognition for their contribution to hip-hop. Said one member of the group: "I'm up on that Latin supremacy shit. I mean, we was there from the giddy up and nobody gave us fuckin' no props."[22] Throughout the 1990s, Cypress Hill sold millions, becoming one of the most successful rap groups ever. In 1999 Nuyorican Big Punisher (aka Big Pun) became the first Latino soloist to go platinum. His incredible skills on the mic, thugged-out lyrics about violence, misogyny, and materialistic references earned him an unquestionable status as "real." He even promotes himself as a "real nigga" on several songs. Much of the same can be said of Fat Joe or lesser-known Latino acts like the Beatnuts and Cuban Link.

Caribbean Latinos have not hesitated to call themselves real niggas, nearly universally: Big Pun, Fat Joe, Juju and Psycho Les of the Beatnuts, Cuban Link, and several others. What is stark, however, is the way in which Chicano rappers affirm their realness without use of the n-word. Kid Frost, the Mexakinz, MC Man, and others conspicuously avoid calling themselves or others nigga while simultaneously glorifying street credibility with rhymes about general gangsta tropes. Houston-based South Park Mexican, however, does call himself and others "niggas," demonstrating that, though it is rare, it is not unprecedented for Chicano rappers to use the contested word.[23]

This bifurcation in the Latino rap community reflects (1) the historical, cultural, and social relationships between different Latino nationalities and African Americans and (2) African diasporic connections between people in the Caribbean and North America. Since the early twentieth century, Puerto Ricans and African Americans in New York City have had relatively close social relations in various cultural and political institutions from sports teams (professional and recreational), to residential areas, to musical groups, and to politics. Quasi-black nationalist Harlemite and bibliophile Arturo A. Schomburg provides the most celebrated example of the relationship between the two groups. In the early 1970s, the Puerto Rican Young Lords emerged as the most visible expression of Puerto Rican nationalism of their time. They explicitly modeled themselves after the Black Panther Party and worked as close allies with the Panthers in New York and elsewhere. Roberto P. Rodriguez-Morazzani even suggests that, to the uninitiated observer, similarities between the two groups could lead to the assumption that they could be viewed as one, "a hyphenated signifier, i.e., African American–Puerto Rican." But the relationship between African Americans and Puerto Ricans has never been simple or entirely affable.[24] Nevertheless, the close proximity of housing and shared public space in New York City and the cultural continuities shared by the two groups gave rise to their creation of hip-hop.

Caribbean-descendent rappers, whether Dominican, Puerto Rican, Cuban, or Haitian, generally emerge from islands and a cultural background with palpable traces of African heritage. The influence of Africa is manifested in song, dance, and religion, as well as in the physiognomy of the people. While there were scores of thousands of Africans brought to Mexico up to the nineteenth century, most have been absorbed into the larger mestizo framework and, according to some, systematically erased from the collective memory of Mexico. Chicano rappers, therefore, have considerably less cultural and historical affinity with African diasporic communities than their Caribbean counterparts. But as Caribbean rappers conform to dominant African American standards, they are not reticent about their own ethnicity. In fact, most produce songs that conform to AAVE as well as in their own Creole or Spanish. Wyclef Jean, a producer, rapper, and member of the most successful rap group ever, the Fugees, has on many occasions celebrated his Haitian heritage in songs in Creole.

In "Yele," Wyclef raps about an immigrant kid who, driven by poverty, sells cocaine and is arrested. The tragic story of a poor immigrant in a wealthy country is a cautionary tale that ends with Wyclef imploring listeners to find God, be disciplined, and be responsible. On "Jaspora," Wyclef vilifies "Jaspora," or ex-patriot Haitians who return to the island nation to exploit young girls and the poor after making money abroad. He castigates them and instructs listeners to disrespect them wherever they are found. On "Original Kopa," Wyclef devotes an entire song to Haitian women. He celebrates their beauty and proudly exclaims his special adoration of them.[25]

What is particularly salient about Wyclef's songs is not so much his celebration of Haitian culture but that it is done exclusively for Haitian people. Performing in Creole, Wyclef excludes the overwhelming majority of listeners from appreciating his messages.[26] In a sense, the songs are inside-group creative expressions that are not necessarily dependent on the aesthetic standards or understanding of outsiders.

While Caribbean-descended rappers universally conform to the general tropes of hip-hop, there is a clear difference in the degree to which anglophone Caribbean rappers acknowledge their island heritage vis-à-vis their Latino counterparts. In fact, anglophone Caribbean-descended rappers like Notorious B.I.G., Busta Rhymes, Heavy D, and Ja Rule make virtually no mention of their Caribbean heritage, perhaps reflecting the degree to which they have been absorbed within the larger social framework of race, as understood in the traditional black-white binary. The conspicuous absence of (im)migrant narratives, however, can not be simply attributed to who is "black." Wyclef Jean has consistently heralded both his blackness and his Haitian heritage since the Fugees' first CD, *Blunted on Reality* (1994). In contrast, Juju of the Beatnuts simultaneously calls himself a "real nigga" while informing listeners that he is Latino and "not black." Reminding his listeners of his Dominican background, Juju explains that "we're never gonna deny where we come from. A lotta people think I'm black . . . I make it clear that I'm not."[27]

Though many Latino rappers like Juju bring attention to their ethnic identity, some want to be better known as good MCs than good Latin MCs. Miami-based Pit Bull emerged as one of the hottest rappers from Florida with his Reggaeton hit "Culo" in 2004. With national attention, he was typically referred to as a "Cuban" rapper. Conscious of his ethnicity, even using the Cuban flag in his promotional efforts, Pit Bull sees race and ethnicity as complicated parts to his persona. Reflecting the general sense of camaraderie typical among African Americans and Puerto Ricans in the Northeast, Pit Bull notes that hip-hop resonates with Latinos as well, despite some resistance. Fat Joe, Pit Bull explains, had to prove himself to skeptics: "Hey this is a Black [man's] game, but shit we grew up the same way; we live the same culture." Not only does hip-hop resonate powerfully with Latinos, but Pit Bull sees music in general and hip-hop specifically as a force to bridge racial and ethnic chasms in important ways: "It's a revolution. Everybody's strong together. They running and we just putting out good music that everybody's vibing to." In the final analysis, he is proud to be Cuban, but "I rap and I just happen to be [Latino]." Ja Rule, he notes, is of Bahamian descent: "So what, he's a Bahamian rapper? He's just a rapper, doing it like the rest of us."[28] Implicit here is that he would like to also be recognized as a good rapper, without any ethnic qualification. But one cannot avoid the obvious Cuban flag, Spanish lyrics, or cultural references that bring attention to Pit Bull as a rapper who is culturally, politically, and expressively Cuban American. Perhaps the essence of his remarks suggests that, inasmuch as Jay-Z, Common, or Mos Def can make references to their blackness but be recognized as a "great rappers," Latinos—and presumably other non–African Americans—should be afforded the same luxury.

Latino rappers have created scores of songs in Spanish while simultaneously adhering to particular African American cultural markers in other songs. Building upon the credibility he has developed, Big Pun offers a well crafted and richly layered rhyme scheme that presents the talent for which he is known, using AAVE, while recognizing his own ethnicity. Big Pun raps, "I'm the first Latin rapper to baffle your skull / master the flow, niggas be swearin' I'm blacker than coal / like Nat King, I be rappin' and tongues packin'."[29] The verse utilizes metaphor, pun, wordplay, tropes, and similes while placing the rapper as the quintessence of the art. His use of the AAVE conjugation of the verb "to be" is consistent with AAVE style and syntax. Note that Pun brings attention to the confusion over his ethnicity resulting from his lyrical mastery. Pun adroitly employs AAVE and switches to Spanish on several songs. On "100 percent," Big Pun explains "*Puerto Puro,* not Menudo no I'm not the one / I'm studying judo, judo don't know if I got a gun." He proudly states that he is "like G. Rap, 'Pac, Master P all balled up with a twist of Marc Anthony." Here Pun compares himself to prominent African American rappers and offers a nod to a popular Puerto Rican singer.

Similarly, Juju of the Beatnuts raps that he is a "thug nigga, only fuck wit *muchacha mala.*" In the virtually all Spanish "Se Acabo," the Beatnuts take pride in being bilingual: "Nigga, I'm like a Jay-Z duet: two voices, one talent." Not to conflate all Latinos, Magic Juan raps: "*No soy Boriqua,* so don't call me *papi.*" But to further affirm their commitment to hardcore rap, they explain that theirs is no Caribbean sound, but urban and tough: "Don't get it twisted, this ain't salsa."

The historical relationship between Caribbean people and African Americans has facilitated the former's affirmation of realness in hip-hop. From the barrios of Spanish Harlem to the projects of South Bronx, Puerto Ricans, Dominicans, and Haitians have successfully celebrated their Caribbean heritage in rap while absorbing African American cultural markers. The same cannot be said of anglophone Caribbean rappers. The conspicuous absence of immigrant narratives reflects the degree of assimilation vis-à-vis their Latino counterparts. Clearly, the role that language plays cannot be minimized, nor can the general notions of race of the larger U.S. society, which has tended to subsume English-speaking immigrants of African descent into the larger African American community.

While Latinos have been with hip-hop since its beginning and have played central roles to the development of break dancing and graffiti art, Asian American and white rappers have had a more arduous time acquiring the valued authenticity enjoyed by the "realest" in the game.

Yellow Brotherhood

In 1991 Ice Cube's song "Black Korea," a 45-second lyrical attack on Asian shop owners in black communities, was vilified for its anti-Asian lyrics. Under protest, Cube eventually issued an apology to Korean and Japanese American communities and sponsored dialogue between local black and Asian communities following the 1992 Los Angeles Rebellion in the wake of the Rodney King verdicts. Cube's hostility to Asian Americans is an extension of the contentious relations that many blacks and Asians have experienced in communities across the country. While scholars have explored the friction, Asian American hip-hop artists to varying degrees have transcended the more pronounced animosity of the early 1990s. Groups like Fists of Fury, Asiatic Apostles, Yellow Peril, and Seoul Brothers emerged with rhymes that challenged white supremacy and aligned themselves with the politically conscious impulse of the era. Although all these groups conform to the cultural standards of hip-hop, none embraced pronounced thug styles in an attempt to affirm their legitimacy. Instead, groups like Yellow Peril and Fists of Fury wrote politicized rhymes that were inspired by Public Enemy. Seoul Brothers even performed at a black festival and opened for Attallah Shabazz, daughter of Malcolm X. A product of the problack lyrics of the late 1980s and early 1990s, lyrics by many Asian American groups affirmed their credibility in the rap game through progressive antiracist political rhymes. Though few Asian American rappers have achieved commercial success, the underground scene of the late 1990s included respected rappers like the Mountain Brothers, Jin, Jamez, and Tabu of Black Eyed Peas. Chinaman, of the 1980s and early 1990s raunchy group 2 Live Crew, is also of Asian descent, as is Foxy Brown (although she does not make it a reference point, other than in her LP title, *Chyna Doll*). The all-Asian American Invisible Skratch Piklz are widely considered one of the best collectives of turntablists in the world, winning several major DJ contests and producing several popular CDs, videos, and tapes for the underground scene.[30]

In terms of the continued negotiation of credibility, many Asian American rappers have used hip-hop as an expressive gesture of defiance and racial and ethnic pride against a dominant mainstream social narrative of white normalcy. Similar to other non–African American MCs, Asian American rappers have chosen to use their racial and ethnic identity as a touchtone for their own articulations of authenticity. Inasmuch as blackness itself has been historically marginalized in the United States, all other people of color have employed the trope of racialized marginality to represent on the mic. In bold rejection of white cultural hegemonic assumptions, Asian American rappers have been less willing to embrace an assimilationist model of expression or to assume the role of the quiet, timid "model minority" who is rarely seen or heard.

Jamez, a New York-based rapper, released his first full-length album *Z-Bonics* in 1998. Building upon hip-hop's ability to absorb any musical style or instrumentation, his album offered typical hip-hop beats with a fusion of Korean music like Poongmul drumming. Part of what he called an "Azian/Pacific Renaissance," Jamez views his art as connected to political, social, and cultural currents in society at large. With this in mind, his music is shaped by social commentary. His songs "FOB," "Day in the Life," and "7-Train" address immigration, race, class, and the urban landscape in a myriad of ways. Echoing the conscious artists who view their art as a tool of education and entertainment, Jamez notes that he aspires to educate Korean American young people about their history and culture. He explains that "so many of us are influenced by Western standards of beauty, speech and music. I want to expose Asian Americans to their rich legacy of music, our beat of life."[31] Indeed, he has heralded his identity politics in the hip-hop underground in the late 1990s and post-1990s in creative ways that provide further examples of hip-hop's uncanny ability to absorb disparate styles while adhering to a definable and palpable hip-hop aesthetic. Hip-hop is about "being real"; however, this realness is never static, thus allowing for continued shifts of expression in politics and race.

Though no Asian soloist MC has been a commercial success, the career of Jin, a New York–based Chinese American rapper from Miami is a fascinating tale of the intersectionality of race, class, and authenticity in hip-hop. In 2002 Jin, who had been raised on hip-hop, entered BET's "Freestyle Fridays" MC battles. As a battle MC, Jin was well aware that his being Chinese would be used as fodder on the show with a largely African American audience. Preempting his opponents, Jin created masterful rhymes that catered to the urban, tough-guy sensibilities of hip-hop and simultaneously brought attention to his ethnicity: "Yeah I'm Chinese / Now you'll understand it / I'm the reason your little sis's eyes are slanted / If you make one more joke about Chinese food or karate / The NYPD will be searching Chinatown for your body."[32] The formula worked. Racial references by his opponents appeared tired or desperate attempts to gain points for something other than MC skills. The mostly black audience and judges gave Jin successive victories that ultimately led to a record deal with Ruff Ryders later that year.

In the fall of 2003 Jin released his first single, "Learn Chinese," with a video that made references to Chinese archetypes, including the industrious and humble Chinese food worker and the Chinatown crime boss. Both characters were played by Jin, who necessarily affirms street credibility as the latter character. As a well-dressed mobster, Jin evoked the braggadocio typical of hip-hop while declaring at the start of the song that he is Chinese, but no longer the happy Chinese food deliverer: "The days of the pork fried rice and the chicken wings coming to your house by me is over." As is typical with Wyclef Jean or many Latino rappers, Jin demonstrates his bilingualism on the track, giving further salience to his racialized expression. In line with dominant hip-hop tropes, Jin affirms his sexual prowess, popularity with women, and ability to vanquish rivals with intimations of violence. To anchor himself within a historical context of racialized marginalization, the child of immigrants references the exploitation of Chinese laborers to build U.S. railroads: "We should ride the train for free, we built the railroads." At about 100,000 units, his debut did not go gold; however, Jin has received more commercial attention than any Asian American solo singer or rapper—ever.[33] Part of the invisibility of Asian Americans in U.S. popular culture can be attributed to the dominant expression of "permanent foreigner" status ascribed to the larger Asian American community. Jin, Jamez, and others reject these narratives while fundamentally adhering to hip-hop's oppositional styles that provide space for counterhegemonic discursive expression. In fact, hip-hop nearly demands a counterpoint to the mainstream in some way, even as it endorses many staple assumptions from the mainstream. To rap in hip-hop without expressing some sort of a rebel style is to call into question one's own legitimacy as a rapper. In other words, to laud the political establishment, police, or conventional racial values (or silence on all of the above) evokes suspicion and detracts from the appeal of a genre in which being real is being rebellious. Although Asian American rappers have remained largely marginal, they have expressed hip-hop's dominant discourse by carving out their own space in hip-hop.

White like Me

The relationship between whites and hip-hop authenticity has been a complicated one, which is specifically a result of the historical relationship between black art and white people and, more generally, the result of ubiquitous white supremacy. Since the minstrelsy of the late nineteenth century, whites have been fascinated by commodifiable black cultural production, despite the brutality and open acceptance of white supremacy among whites for most of the country's history. Many scholars and cultural critics have explored white relationships with African American art.[34] Some argue that white Americans have long enjoyed co-opting black creative expressions in what appears to be a form of cultural banditry. There is no debate about white adoption of black musical styles and semiotic gestures throughout the twentieth century and beyond. Greg Tate notes that a long line of black "impersonators" from Paul Whiteman, Elvis Presley, and the Rolling Stones to Britney Spears, Pink, and Eminem have reaped the financial benefits of cultural mimicry.[35] Even Vanilla Ice's debut CD, *To the Extreme* (1990), the iconic representation of white intrusion and cultural banditry, outsold all but a handful of hip-hop LPs for a decade. But can current white performers and consumers be fairly compared to naked racists of the 1930s? Moreover, are the current social and political circumstances similar enough to find current white adoption identical to that of the 1950s?

In Bakari Kitwana's thoughtful consideration of whites and hip-hop, he explains that the centrality of blackness to hip-hop is far too established and salient for the same kind of white co-optation that happened with rock and roll: "It would take an army of Eminems to divorce hip-hop from young black men, who after thirty years still dominate the art form."[36] The centrality of black people to hip-hop notwithstanding, the question of authenticity and white rappers has been a perennial dilemma for white MCs since Vanilla Ice's contentious rise and decline in the early 1990s.[37] Though not the first white rapper on wax, his emergence on the rap scene occurred in the middle of an era characterized by black nationalist affirmations of black authenticity as well as competing street-level gangsta tales. On one end of the pendulum was the intensely popular Public Enemy, and on the other was N.W.A. Both groups rebelled against the cultural and political status quo while simultaneously offering themselves as models for a new, urban youthful representation of blackness. The fun-loving Beastie Boys, who released their first rap album in 1986 on Def Jam, predated the popularity of both gangsta and black nationalist expressions of realness. Enjoying the status that came with associating with Run DMC and being label mates with Public Enemy, the white Beasties were viewed by many more as tolerated zany friends than as cultural bandit interlopers. Vanilla Ice enjoyed none of this tolerance or black peer validation.

Vanilla Ice's lift of the Alpha Phi Alpha fraternity chant "Ice Ice Baby," his appropriation of black vernacular, dance, and general style evoked curiosity about his roots. In various press releases and interviews, he embellished his past to affirm his place in hip-hop. His claim that he was raised in a tough black neighborhood in Miami and involved with criminal activities proved false. Vilified by various segments of media, Ice represented to many (of various ethnic groups) the latest in a long line of white cultural bandits. Even other white rappers mocked him, like 3rd Bass, with his chant of "Elvis, Elvis, baby, no soul, no soul." This mockery of the hook for Vanilla Ice's hit song reflected the historical consciousness of white cultural banditry and the legendary Elvis Presley, widely believed to have publicly expressed racist comments as he appropriated black art.[38] The legacy of Vanilla Ice would be a shadow over eager white MCs for years. In fact, Vanilla Ice's own attempt to re-create himself as "real" proved a pitiful mockery of himself in 1993 with his sophomore release. In the video for his first single, Ice roamed alleys and, with dark, bass-heavy beats, rapped about being a thug. His blonde dreads, sagging pants, and tattoos were a further attempt to accrue props for realness, as were his lyrics about shooting people in the head and smoking marijuana. The second most successful rapper ever, he was unable to muster a gold CD with his sophomore effort.[39]

After the decline of Vanilla Ice, other white rappers struggled for acceptance in various ways. White rappers Marky Mark, 3rd Bass, and Young

Black Teenagers inveighed against racism in their songs and took shots at Vanilla Ice in a process that helped to affirm their credibility and mitigate allegations of cultural theft. Additionally, they all cultivated images that were intimately familiar with the inner city in their videos and songs. From expressions of violence or malt liquor consumption, all three groups pandered to the widespread currents of credibility pervasive in hip-hop at that time.

In 1992 House of Pain entered the scene with a catchy song and style that achieved a generally favorable reception in hip-hop circles. It was no surprise that the Irish-American rappers of House of Pain affirmed their street credibility both in lyrics and in a video that featured an urban, cool toughness with a simultaneous affirmation of white ethnic pride and appropriation of dominant gangsta styles from the West Coast.[40] Though House of Pain achieved a level of respect, white rappers did not gain serious admiration until the meteoric rise of Eminem, a talented underground lyricist from Detroit who was discovered by former N.W.A member Dr. Dre in 1998.

Eminem proved to be a conundrum for many hip-hop fans, particularly older aficionados who sometimes warn of a potential "takeover" that whites can realize with rap, similar to what has been done with jazz and rock. The concern over white appropriation has made many cautious about white participation in hip-hop, even of those white artists with black endorsement. Eminem has lived through this antipathy throughout his professional career.

Though booed and ridiculed on stage before he could ever spit a rhyme, Eminem adopted an old African American adage while on the underground battle circuit: to be recognized, you have to be twice as good. Honing his skills and developing richly creative uses of similes and punch lines, he struggled on the battle circuit earning respect from skeptical white and black hip-hoppers alike. He released his first full-length LP *Infinite* in 1995 and the *Slim Shady EP* in 1997. In 1998 Eminem became the first white rapper to appear in the *Source*'s prestigious "Unsigned Hype" column, which features a promising unsigned artist. Famous alumni include the Notorious B.I.G., Common, and Mobb Deep. After being discovered by superproducer Dr. Dre, Eminem ascended into stardom with his first big-label commercial release LP, *The Slim Shady LP* in 1999. Released on Dr. Dre's Aftermath label, it sold four million copies, catapulting him into rare multiplatinum success.

Eminem sold seven million with his second, *The Marshall Mathers LP* in 2001. He was the most successful music artist of 2002, selling seven and a half million copies of *The Eminem Show*. In October 2004 he released *Encore,* selling over four million copies in the first five months, making him the second most successful rapper ever, only following Tupac. The greatest example of Eminem's acceptance in the hardcore thugged-out crowd of "real niggas" is probably the 2000 Up in Smoke tour, which featured the pioneers of gangsta rap: Ice Cube, Dr. Dre, MC Ren, as well as Snoop Dogg and Xzibit. Amid all the gangstas from South Central L.A. and its surrounding environs was the white rapper from the Midwest, holding his own. His presence in the Up in Smoke Tour was significant in that it represented a profound endorsement that had currency for the larger hip-hop consumer market, black, white, and other.

Following Vanilla Ice, no white rappers had enjoyed high-profile endorsement from black artists, and the largely white hip-hop consumer market did not automatically rush to the scores of white underground artists around the country, artists like Cage, RA the Rugged Man, the High and Mighty, Necro, or White Dawg. Eminem's acceptance among hip-hop heavyweights, however, validated him as his skills could not alone. Poverty, a white rapper from Portland, Maine, explains that "white people are scared of liking what they do when it comes to rap. They wait for blacks to like it first."[41] Eminem similarly recognizes that Dr. Dre's endorsement gave him commercial validation as a white rapper in his song "White America," further confirming the opinion that black people remain the epitome of hip-hop and are deferred to for trend setting in the art. Despite Eminem's acceptance and commercial success, there were almost immediate allegations of fraud. Interviews focused on what high school he graduated from. "None," was the answer; though he attended Detroit's Lincoln High School before he dropped out after flunking the ninth grade in 1989. Eminem has addressed the question of authenticity on numerous occasions. He has carefully noted that he lived in tough black neighborhoods in Detroit, rapped for years, hung out with black folks, and grew up in a poor, dysfunctional household.[42] Despite affirmations of his credibility from such pillars of hip-hop as Jay-Z, Nas, Dr. Dre, Snoop Dogg, and others, Eminem was harshly attacked from many corners of the white hip-hop community. Whether jealousy is to blame for the white-on-white attacks is unclear.

The several early battles with white MCs such as Everlast, Cage, Evidence of Dilated Peoples, and Michigan-based Insane Clown Posse created exciting exchanges centered on traditional accusations of artistic fraud and contrived imagery. Conforming to the general tropes in hip-hop battles, these exchanges reveal fascinating articulations of race and authenticity within white-on-white rapper beefs.

Eminem made early verbal attacks at boy bands and teen singers with his second major release in 2000. In 2001 the opportunity emerged for him to take his battling skills to a worthy opponent with a reply to a diss made by Everlast who attacked him as an insecure neophyte attempting to represent "real peckerwood status" in rap. In a fierce rebuttal, Eminem attacked Everlast for his artistic shift to acoustic fusion with rap music and the departure from a strictly hip-hop style. Eminem called the former lead of House of Pain a white poseur who had "no respect in the hood / fled to his neck of the woods / Got in touch with his roots, found the redneck in his blood / and said, 'heck, country western rap records are good!!'" The musical shift was, according to Eminem, indicative of Everlast's spatial and cultural distance from the locus of real hip-hop. He identifies Everlast as an inauthentic white performer who enjoyed an ephemeral commitment to the (black) art of hip-hop.[43]

Eminem eagerly embraced the race card to expose his rival Everlast, much as others attacked him in the years he spent in the battle circuit prior to 1999. He ridiculed Everlast as a "redneck" who abandoned rap and "crossed over to country." Fundamentally, Eminem affirmed his own place and legitimacy in hip-hop by adopting crude tropes of black criticism at white participation, even calling Everlast a "white devil," "honkey," and "cracker."[44] Moreover, he relegated Everlast's adoption of bluesy riffs and acoustic style as gravitation to an ostensibly white aesthetic. The irony, of course, is that blues originated with black people. Eminem inadvertently obfuscated the history of black cultural production by implying that his white rival abandoned black style and retreated to his "redneck" roots of blues and country. This implication unintentionally validates the efforts of white interlopers who dominate black art forms, claiming them as their own. Eminem, however, makes no mistake about hip-hop's origins. "I do black music," he explains. His battle with Everlast, therefore, centers on accusations of artistic fraud and race while simultaneously reinforcing popular ignorance about the histories of various musical genres.

Similarly, Eminem attacks fellow Michigan rappers Insane Clown Posse for claiming "Detroit" when they are really from the suburb of Warren County, north of the famous 8 Mile road that divides mostly white communities from mostly black ones. For Eminem, his own inner-city roots bestow currency. In interviews he has recounted his life of poverty, low-wage employment, urban blight, and crime. His hometown was closer to the urban landscape of the South Bronx, Compton, Houston's 5th Ward, Brooklyn's Marcy Projects, or the many other famous landmarks that signify a racialized class location in hip-hop. What appears as class marginalization in the larger society is not necessarily so in hip-hop. Indeed, Carol City, Miami, or New Orleans's Magnolia Projects become references points of credibility and intimate familiarity with the hardscrabble life of (black) urban poverty that gives hip-hop much of its expression. Some have even called Eminem a "nigga" for his familiarity with these conditions and hip-hop itself.

One of Eminem's longtime friends once insisted that Eminem was a "nigga" who "ain't white" but "might have some white in him."[45] Cultural critic and writer Farai Chideya notes that "today, race is performative" in ways unlike years prior. "To a great degree," she explains, "Eminem does come from a place where this kind of black performance identity was not unnatural to him. . . . What Eminem demonstrates clearly is that race now is not just about the color of your skin, it's also about your psychology. It's about your positioning yourself. It is a mix of conscious and unconscious factors that situate you in a demographic which your skin color might even deny."[46] From a slightly different position, Bakari Kitwana notes that Eminem's impoverished background makes him an "outcast outsider" who is also oppressed. But one cannot ignore the tables of data that confirm that white supremacy continues to shape America in how people are hired, educated, housed, or paid or how they receive justice.[47]

Although some may say that Eminem has become a veritable "nigga" by virtue of his class location and hard-knock life, such a figurative identity simplifies the intractability of race and its nexus with the landscape of class in America (not to mention the distasteful moniker attached to black people). In fact, the majority of the poor in the United States are white, and most African Americans are middle class or working class.[48] Though poverty rates are twice as high among blacks than among whites, it is problematic to conflate class and race into simplistic assumptions of black poverty and white affluence. In fact, to allow Eminem to remain fully "white" is to

acknowledge the complicated role that class has long played in racial politics in America. For most of the country's history, elites have conveniently
used race to divide black and white (and Asian and Latino) workers across
the country: in Chicago's stockyards, New York's garment industry,
California's railroads, and Pittsburgh's steel mills. Desperately poor white
southerners of the nineteenth century who lived near starvation were
loathe to consider that they had more in common with most black farmers
than the minority of wealthy whites who oppressed them all. Poor white
workers, unwilling to recognize their own terrible class position, historically embraced dominant notions of race privilege (as limited as the privilege was at times) rather than accept that they shared more in common
with similarly oppressed black workers. Taking their cue from the pervasive
racism among white workers, many black militants and nationalists have
historically refused to consider working with even the most dedicated white
radicals, viewing them all with a jaundiced eye.[49]

One of the most sophisticated examples of this class consciousness
comes from Bubba Sparxxx's debut album's title track, "Bright Days, Dark
Nights":

I probably won't even fault you if you dismiss me as the demon
It is true, I am not you, my skin's the tone of piss and semen
But if we fight this evening, I assure you, we'll both bleed red
And it'll take your whole slum and all your guns to leave me dead
Plus all that blood we shed will do nothin' but serve their purpose
So let's unite these bright nights and dark days, then see who nervous.

In this song, "bright days" and "dark nights" operate as a metaphor for
white and black people, respectively. Bubba explores his own poor roots
and the painful history of white supremacy in the South and admits that he
has no animus toward black people and, in fact, understands any racial hostility toward him. But he insists in typical hip-hop confidence that he is no
coward and will fight any rival to the death. Ultimately, however, the power
of transcending racial conflict is significantly greater than valorizing it. He
even intimates a class-consciousness that mirrors nineteenth-century
southern populism when he states that after their unifying we can see "who
[is really] nervous" that poor blacks and whites are no longer fighting each
other. On the symbolic significance of this interracial interrogation of class

and oppression, S. Craig Watkins notes that performers like Bubba Sparxxx and Eminem represent a profoundly subversive message: "When [racial] boundaries are violated, if only symbolically, so too are the powerful myths and power relations that sustain the status quo."[50] Indeed, the exaggeration of white affluence, which has been an important component of the larger super structure of white supremacy, is undermined by the visibility and voice of poor whites.

In Eminem's many narratives of economic despair, there is a salient recognition of class, race, and shared experience with the black poor that (1) helps legitimate him and (2) reflects the power and utility of interrogating the meaning of race and offering a more sophisticated discussion of class in America. In "White America" and "Mosh," Eminem refers to uniting races through his music, even as he addresses modern expressions of white supremacy that have benefited him as a rapper: "If I was black I would have sold half / I did have to graduate from Lincoln High to know that." Dressing up as Elvis in his video for "Without Me," he references the black accusations and charges of white co-optation. In self-mockery, he raps, "No I'm not the first king of controversy / I am the worst thing since Elvis Presley / to do black music so selfishly / and used it to get myself wealthy."

Despite his remarkable acceptance in the hip-hop community and sharp social commentary, Eminem experienced a different type of maelstrom when ten-year-old audiotapes surfaced in the fall of 2003. Released by the very anti-Eminem *Source* magazine in its February 2004 issue, the snippet features a homemade rap made by a teenage Eminem who declares that "black girls are dumb and white girls are good chicks." The magazine also alleged that he called black girls "bitches" and black people "niggers," as it denounced Eminem with vitriol. Rapper Styles P said that "his fucking teeth should have been knocked out. But all the Black people who are sucking his cock should be ashamed of themselves." Killer Mike explained that "this is a black and Latino culture and art form. If you're not sensitive to that, then your card is gonna be pulled." Though Killer Mike had not yet heard the song, he indicated that he was "not in favor of white men bashing black women." Similar comments came from many others in hip-hop.[51]

In a press release Eminem reported that he was "stupid and angry" when he created the tape following the breakup with his black girlfriend. Though he admitted to degrading black girls, Eminem denied that he called black people niggers. On his autobiographical "Yellow Brick Road" (2004), he offered further context and an unorthodox apology for singling out an entire race: "'Cause no matter what color a girl is she's still a [ho]." His statement reflects the fundamental hypocrisy of the *Source*'s outcry at his comments about black women. Nearly every commercial rapper—including those praised by the *Source*—calls black women "bitches" and "hos" in their songs, including Styles P and Killer Mike. Assuming that only black men can denigrate and dehumanize black women, or that misogyny must be confined to intraracial performance does nothing to resist sexism or assist black and Latina women. Chuck D similarly sees the outcry as suspect, considering widespread acceptance of anti–black woman remarks from black male rappers:

[Russell] Simmons, the *Source* and others have endorsed this attitude like a house slave watches the field yet eats from the kitchen. Blackfaces of these Negroes endorsing "nigga-ism" are responsible for having the world look at us black people in America [as] inferior to everyone else here. Negroes like this have used culture to, in essence, sell us back into slavery. Now after drinking from the same jug of "selling the integrity out" they wanna point their crooked ass fingers at a white boy they've tried to sell this attitude to in the first place.[52]

Ultimately, the responses to Eminem's lyrics about black women reflect the limitations on race and white acceptance in hip-hop. Despite his widely praised lyrical skills, battle MC pedigree, and urban, impoverished background, he is, at the end of the day, still a white "cultural bandit" to some. His performance and familiarity with widely considered essential tropes of authenticity in hip-hop fail to grant him the level of acceptance enjoyed by black rappers. Ice Cube, for example, with his two-parent, middle-class background, crime-free record, and dozens of songs referring to killing black people and referring to black women as bitches and hos was never put under "credibility tests." Instead, he was awarded a "Lifetime Achievement" award by the *Source* in 2000. Such treatment is elusive to Eminem. Perhaps no better example of the limitations of acceptance imposed upon white rappers is the use of the word "nigger"/"nigga."

While gaining credibility is important to all MCs, few white ones have been able to achieve the ultimate "ghetto pass": free usage of the n-word. Eminem has achieved more acceptance than any white rapper in hip-hop, but he has not uttered the troublesome word in any song (at least not since his commercial career began.) In 2002, he noted that "it's not my place to say it. There's some things that I just don't do."[53] To be sure, few words in English evoke as much emotion, and many have considered it so vile that a euphemism—"the n-word"—has taken its place in the public domain. The word can, in one sentence, connote warmth and companionship as well as hostility and hate. It often means diametrically opposed things to its black users. In *Goodfellas* the 504 Boys use the word nearly forty times, shifting from affection: "[I] put it down for my niggas, plus I love the South" to violent hatred: "[I'll] murder your muthafuckin' ass, nigga."[54]

Detractors of the word argue that it is so vile, born of intense oppression and violence, that no one of any race should use it. Some who use the word, however, insist that by not pronouncing the "-er" that it has become a different word with a different meaning. We must keep in mind, however, that for centuries white southerners, by virtue of their regional accent, did not typically pronounce the "er," either. "We'll lynch that nigga" was just as vile an expression. Another defense of using the word in hip-hop typically argues that it is a "term of endearment," appropriated from racists and rendered powerless as a racist epithet. But despite this justification, the hip-hop community that uses it does, in fact, recognize the word as a deeply offensive term of white supremacy.

In 2000, Dr. Dre expressed his hostility over the use of the word in an acoustic cover of an N.W.A song, "Boyz-N-The-Hood," by a white band, Dynamite Hack.[55] Many attacked Eminem for allegedly uttering it as a teenager on a private basement mix tape. In November 2006 a huge outcry emerged when "Seinfeld" star Michael Richards called a black patron a "nigger" multiple times during Richard's comedy routine in Los Angeles. After a video of the racist rant was released and televised nationally, Richards publicly apologized, claiming that he was no racist. Many in hip-hop were enraged and did not accept his apology, insisting that it was illegitimate.[56] Despite the near universal use among black rappers, it is conspicuously absent among white ones. In fact, the only rappers to go gold or platinum since 1997 who have not used "nigga" on a song have been white: Eminem, Bubba Sparxxx, and Paul Wall. Each rapper, however, has recorded a song where a fellow MC, who is black, is calling someone a nigga. A telling truth of the word's accepted use is demonstrated in the brilliant satirical film *Fear of a Black Hat* (1994). When an eager white rapper, "Vanilla Sherbet," attempts to gain acceptance with N.W.H. (Niggaz With Hats) by using the n-word, the good-natured conversation abruptly shifts into a vicious beating. Even the context of Sherbet's friendly exchange with N.W.H. was not enough to deflect their intolerance for his use of the word. The word still maintains profound potential for racist hurt and anger, despite incessant claims that black people's usage has rendered it sterile for racist offense. In fact, many black people have been calling each other niggas since slavery; however, the word remains just as much a racist offense in the twenty-first century as it was in the nineteenth whether rappers use it or not.[57] With such emotion enveloped in this word for African Americans, it is somewhat conspicuous that Puerto Ricans use it with impunity.

Nearly universally, Puerto Rican rappers use the word with great agility and zeal. As "family," there has been no notable protest over their use of the word.[58] The New York rapper, Fat Joe, who is of Puerto Rican and Cuban descent, had his career's biggest hit single with 2004's "Lean Back" with a chorus that insisted that "my niggas don't dance; they just pull up their pants." And when Fat Joe got into a beef with 50 Cent in 2005 he called his rival a "bitch nigga" and was called a "fat nigga" in return. No eyebrows were raised as Puerto Ricans, as seen above, have long enjoyed a level of acceptance in an African American–dominated art that Puerto Ricans cocreated. Not only did hip-hop come primarily from African Americans and Puerto Ricans, the two groups have shared cultural, political, and residential intimacy in northeastern cities like New York, Newark, Bridgeport, and Hartford, among many others. They share common African roots as well. The racialized term, therefore, appears less caustic when used, even in anger, between Puerto Rican and African American rappers. The same cannot be said of white hardcore rappers like RA the Rugged Man, Haystack, or Bubba Sparxxx, who appropriate all other staples of gangsta rap: beatdowns, shootings, misogyny, and the routing of various adversaries in and outside the rap game. They all affirm their place in the realm of realness by recognizing their impoverished backgrounds. Growing up in poor black neighborhoods, in particular, further confirms their narratives as authentic. Tennessee native Haystak raps, "I grew up in the projects / that's why I speak in Ebonics." Similarly RA the Rugged Man presents a self-effacing "poor white trash, stinkin'" description of himself. The rapper Poverty, conspicuously named, has used his troubled upbringing, which included homelessness, as reference points in his rhymes over references to his race. "I talk about my life situation, not my race," Poverty explains. For many, however, being poor is racialized as an extension of being black or brown; therefore poverty has currency in the pursuit of authenticity in rap. Still, these white rappers avoid use of the word "nigga," even calling themselves "crackers," "honkies," and "white trash." Though the word evokes vitriolic responses from many black folks when whites use it, a few white rappers have proudly and unabashedly used "nigga" in their rhymes.

White Dawg, a South Florida–based thugged-out rapper, not only employs "Bama" vernacular,[59] he calls for "niggas" throughout the South to get "crunk" on his song "Skraten Up." Cage, a white underground rapper from Buffalo, similarly uses the word and has justified his use by exclaiming that he was raised in a black community and was called a nigga his entire life. Most of his friends are black, and he could care less what people think of what he says. Necro, a Brooklyn-based white rapper, uses nigga as well. Despite the marginal use of the word among a handful of underground white rappers, controversy has not yet arisen. Instead, the mostly white underground fans of White Dawg, Cage, Necro, and others have generally embraced the word as a word with multiple meanings. There is little question that when Cage attacks Eminem as a "bitch ass nigga," Cage adopts the widely held African American and Puerto Rican meaning of the word and affirms his place as an authentic and real member of the rap game—without restrictions.[60] Though a handful of white underground rappers have employed the word, no white rapper of note has declared himself to be a "real nigga." Interestingly enough, however, many white rappers are called "niggas" by their black peers. Yung Redd affectionately calls Paul Wall "my nigga" in "Chick Magnet" (2004), and ironically Benzino calls Eminem a "nigga" in his anti-Eminem song "Pull your Skirt Up" (2003). Both songs demonstrate the malleability of the term, used for both affection and contempt, depending on context. But as evidenced in the reaction to Eminem's "lost tapes," his calling black people "niggas" in a hostile context is an intolerable infraction, even among those black folk who employ the term. Despite the mutability of the word, it still maintains certain limitations in the realm of widely accepted expression.

These debates about the n-word and the direction of hip-hop reached a new level of fervor following the April 2007 on-air remarks by radio shock jock Don Imus, who referred to the mostly black women's basketball team of Rutgers University as "nappy-headed hos." Employing disparaging remarks to express how ugly he found these women, he selected a term that stressed a racial physical characteristic of these players as an aesthetic marker in his insistence that they were physically repulsive. Of course, he simultaneously used sexist language as well. Following the outcry, Imus and his defenders indicated that rappers who had used similar terms had somehow escaped criticism from black folks. This is, of course, untrue. As Bakari Kitwana notes, people must "let the record show that media justice advocates such as Davey D Cook (of the organization daveyd.com), Rosa Clementes (of R.E.A.C.H. Hip-Hop) and Lisa Fagers (of industryears.com) have for years been very loudly challenging the music industry and rappers to raise the bar."[61] The community activist Rev. Al Sharpton also weighed in when he explained that "we have for a while said to the hip-hop community that we believe in free speech, but at the same time, we also have the right to say this whole sexist, racist overuse of the word 'n—a' and 'ho' we need to deal with in our community."[62] But others of the hip-hop community offered new opinions on these invective words. Following the Imus incident, Russell Simmons, hip-hop mogul and co-founder of Def Jam and the Hip Hop Summit Action Network, urged that record labels "voluntarily remove, bleep, delete the words 'bitch,' 'hoe' and the racially offensive word 'nigga.'"[63] Even hip-hop generation youth in the NAACP offered to symbolically bury the n-word at the organization's 2007 national convention. And Houston-based rapper Camillionaire, who went platinum with his first CD, noted that his 2007 sophomore major release will not have him calling women bitches or hos or using the n-word. It appears that hip-hop was significantly affected by the Imus comments. But the discourse post-Imus is really an extension of debates that have been going on for years over the n-word and the word "ho."[64]

The black intolerance for white use of the n-word clearly reflects the sensitivity of the word to black people and the resilience of its power. But it also highlights a degree of resistive black agency, in that black people have moved the offensive word from black private discourses to the public and from white public discourses to the private (if they choose to use it). Moreover, black people have refused whites opportunity to partake in the term, whether they hope to use it affectionately or not. Even as whites are the major consumers of hip-hop and all of its raunchy, badass style, there is some question about the degree to which whites can *really* participate. This is evident in the ways in which Jay-Z requests his white fans to avoid repeating the word as they recite his lyrics aloud at his concerts. Chris Rock notes how white friends who knew the lyrics to rap songs skipped reciting the word, even as they all rapped along to a song. Embracing hip-hop fashion, lexicon, semiotics, even being affectionately called "my nigga" by black folks can be markers of acceptance for white hip-hop heads. But, in the final analysis, the n-word remains (publicly at least) a word used on black people's terms, even if the black community is not in agreement with its use. Many black people, of different classes and generations, remain opposed to the word, as a term of affection or scorn—by black or white folk. Whites who use it with each other are generally cautious about using it among any random black person—out of respect or fear. But ultimately, it is black offense, anger, and rage at the very core racist meaning of this word that has determined its public unacceptability among whites.

Conclusion

"Keeping it real" has long been central to hip-hop. In a highly racialized society, "realness" in an African American-dominated art has special meaning. Rappers who attempt to secure and affirm their place in the rap game have often contrived, repackaged, and embellished their images to locate themselves at the center of what it means to be legitimate in hip-hop. Fashion, style, language, and personal history all play crucial roles in the construct of realness, though it is often in flux. The decline of black-conscious rap has meant the decline of a pro-black standard of authenticity that both challenges white supremacy and lauds black people. Since the early 1990s, authenticity has been less measured by any quasi-black nationalist politics than by ghetto authenticity, shaped by romanticized notions of pathology and dysfunction.

The fundamental thrust of the notion of authenticity rests on an essentialist premise that presupposes that there are particular traits or characteristics innate to black people. African American young males are typically viewed as naturally criminal and violent. Deviations from this ideal evoke allegations of being "bitch made" or being an "herb nigga." Conversely, a prison sentence ("Everyone on Death Row got a case!"—Tupac, valorizing his record label, 1996), drug use ("You don't even smoke buddah"—a Cypress Hill diss of Ice Cube for not smoking marijuana, 1996), or general violence

("These words I say are what I do"—Shyne, a rapper who rapped about shooting people and was convicted of a 1999 shooting in a New York City night club) affirm credibility. In 2001 rapper Jay-Z excoriated fellow gangsta rapper Prodigy in a public battle after it became known that the latter took ballet lessons as a child. Around the same time Nas attacked Jay-Z in a song for never having a criminal case before rapping. In 2005 Jadakiss attacked 50 Cent for claiming Queens when he lived in suburban Connecticut. Similarly, Fat Joe attacked 50 Cent for hiring police as security and for not shooting the man who assaulted his boss Dr. Dre at the 2004 Vibe Awards. In 2006 Spider Loc and The Game exchanged battle rhymes that questioned each other's gangsta pedigree. Each insisted that the other was not really shooting, robbing, drug selling, or otherwise engaged in criminal acts. Realness (and its corollary, blackness) is thus relegated to poverty, dysfunction, and pathology. Indeed, the pathological becomes normative. This problematic position circumscribes blackness into a narrow expression. The limited expressions of "realness" in rap reflect the pernicious stereotypes promoted by society at large about black and Latino youth.

It is too simplistic to argue that the insatiable white appetite for self-destructive black violence and exoticism explains the gangsta themes in rap. Though the art is inextricably tied to the consumer market, artists also determine their own perspectives, along with larger institutional forces, such as labels, radio stations, and television stations. Black creative and consumer culpability must be recognized as important to the direction of hip-hop. Without doubt (and as explored in Chapter 3) much of the lyrical pathology is simply artful fantasy and badman style that reflects the intense competitive spirit of hip-hop's cultural unorthodoxy: I am badder than you. But in terms of consumption, white audiences not only purchase the majority of gangsta rap; they also purchase the majority of its conscious rap, reflecting the general demographics of young people, who are hip-hop consumers: they are mostly white. Groups like the Roots, Jurassic 5, and Common have remarked that their concerts are almost totally white. But most hip-hop consumers—black, white, and Latino—simply prefer gangsta themes over others.

Throughout the reign of ghettocentric rap, the hip-hop community has had its own conflicts over how authenticity is determined. Gangsta rappers have not gone unchallenged by their peers who have accused them of being "Uncle Toms," "house niggas," "studio gangstas," and cowards. They have

Though stylistically different, Kanye West and Jay-Z have parlayed their musical talents into hugely successful careers as label executives, with a combined net worth of over half a billion dollars. Both have made bold political statements on issues ranging from blood diamonds to clean water in Africa.

been parodied in songs and videos. Even hip-hop journalists have attacked them.[65] The emergence of hip-hop "purists" from the underground in the late 1990s also led to a shift in the way authenticity is judged. Underground artists like the Roots, Little Brother, Apathy, the Perceptionists, the Last Emperor, and the High and Mighty rely less on gangsta tropes and more on a fierce allegiance to lyrical development and a celebration of the full range of hip-hop culture, while embracing a braggadocious style. To quote Jurassic 5, "Without the [four] elements, it's all irrelevant."[66] They have also voiced intense criticism of their commercial peers as inauthentic interlopers. This new movement has moved to the awareness of the national scene as commercial-underground collaborations become more common, as witnessed by Kanye West's commercially successful work with Common, Dilated Peoples, and Talib Kweli. Similarly, Jay-Z's work with the Roots reflects this trend. This all suggests that as the core thrust of rap styles are in flux, there is no doubt that the core thrust of what it means to keep it real will likewise remain dynamic.

3

Between God and Earth: Feminism, Machismo, and Gender in Hip-Hop Music

I am America. I am the part you won't recognize. But get used to me. Black, confident, cocky; my name, not yours; my religion, not yours; my goals, my own; get used to me.

Muhammad Ali, *The Greatest* (1975)

The professional career of Muhammad Ali operates as a metaphor for hip-hop. From his humble origins in Louisville, Kentucky, a poor black boy found space for opportunity, leisure, and pleasure in boxing. Slowly climbing the ranks of the boxing world, he eventually experienced huge crossover popularity after defeating heavyweight champ Sonny Liston in 1964. No longer going by his birth name, his new identity included a new name, style, consciousness, confidence, and defiance. His political sensibilities, influenced by black nationalism, and—quite importantly—his perceived arrogance infuriated many whites and old-school Negroes alike. But despite the legal disputes, journalistic attacks, public criticism, and anti-Ali campaigns, he became a beloved icon of American sport—on his very racialized and gendered terms.

Ali represents, according to Imani Perry, "part of the foundation for the explosion of hip hop, an artistic variation of traditional black cultural forms, into the American popular cultural framework."[1] Like Ali, jazz, and rock and roll, hip-hop moved from the margins to the center of American popular culture, despite considerable hostility. But unlike its musical predecessors, much of hip-hop's core expressions have been boldly centered on a black masculinist identity that has unapologetically insisted on both racial and gender markers. Though not inherently antifemale, the dominant male-centered discourse eventually endorsed strong misogynist themes among commercially successful artists by the early 1990s. They would dominate hip-hop through that decade and beyond.

Misogyny has been a central focus of cultural critics who denounce the "degenerate lyrics" of many rappers. Additionally, hip-hop's hypermasculine style has been blamed for much of the contemptuous expression directed at women.[2] While some have reduced hip-hop to its cruder, antisocial forms, prominent and respected artists have long expressed strong positions of resistance to the subjugation of women by realizing a feminist voice in hip-hop, even male artists. In examining the development of gendered language in hip-hop music, I consider in this chapter a feminist voice, its contextual framework, and the dynamic contestation of female agency in general, while simultaneously discussing the hypermale trope in hip-hop. It also examines the ways by which artists have conformed to or deviated from conventional definitions of feminism. In hip-hop, there are often contrasting messages in the artistic work of any given artist. I explore this incongruence, broadening our understanding of the contours and complexities of hip-hop's gendered landscape. Finally, I contextualize the social and cultural expression of hip-hop and how women must contend with the overarching themes of masculinity that underpin this art form.[3]

Feminism

The historian Nancy Cott asserts that a working definition of feminism has three core components. The first is an opposition to sexual hierarchy, an opposition that demands sexual equality in terms of access to resources and opportunity. The second maintains that the condition of women is socially constructed, "historically shaped by human usage rather than simply predestined by God or nature." The third component of feminism, tied to the second, "posits that women perceive themselves not only as a biological sex but as a social grouping." Cott also points out that men, too, can be feminists.[4] But as Judith Grant points out, feminist theory is not a monolith: "Feminist theory is multicentered and undefinable. It is divided according to its attachment to one or another of several male theories whose terms it has attempted to appropriate and whose male-biased assumptions it has tended to mitigate."[5] While this may be particularly obvious in discussing "liberal feminism," "Marxist feminism," or "existentialist feminism," it is not so apparent when discussing black feminism, which does not wholly rely on a male theory for its own theoretical basis.

There are more specific definitions of feminism as they relate to black women who have had different historical experiences with discrimination than the white women who have been the chief focus of mainstream (white) feminist scholarship.[6] Patricia Hill Collins explains that

> black feminism's fundamental goal of creating a humanistic vision of community is more comprehensive than that of other social action movements. For example, unlike the women's movement in the United States, black feminism has not striven solely to secure equal rights for women and men, because gaining rights equal to those of black men would not necessarily lead to liberation for African American women. Instead, black feminism encompasses a comprehensive, antisexist, antiracist, and anti-elitist perspective on social change. Black feminism is a means for human empowerment rather than an end in and of itself.[7]

Perhaps more central to my focus is what Collins considers the second core thrust of black feminism: the search for voice, or the refusal of black women to remain silenced. She explains that, "in order to exploit black women, dominant groups have developed controlling images or stereotypes claiming that black women are inferior. Because they justify black women's oppression, four interrelated controlling images of black women—the mammy, the matriarch, the welfare mother, and the jezebel—reflect the dominant group's interest in maintaining black women's subordination. Challenging these stereotypes has been an essential part of the search for voice." To be sure, the agency of women in general is essential to feminism. Women cannot be expected to assume the position of passive forces in society who are acted upon and without the agency to define themselves, their ambitions, and their lives. To this end, they must reject narrow definitions of femininity that circumscribe them and the fullness of their humanity.

The last core theme in black feminism, described by Collins, is empowerment in the context of everyday life: "Black feminism cannot challenge race, gender, and class oppression without empowering black women to take action in everyday life."[8] Here, Collins implies that feminism must be anathema to oppression and its many shades. It cannot, in fact, reaffirm the dominant ideologies that marginalize, exploit, and dehumanize people with war, poverty, little education, no health care, or no shelter. Feminism must inspire to free humanity from the perils of intolerance, ignorance, and hate, she insists.[9]

The Badman

In the context of hip-hop, feminist articulations run up against dominant narratives of the ubermasculine trope of the badman. In the expression of this masculine discourse, manhood is typically reduced to three very common core points of reference to (male) authenticity: (1) willful ability to inflict violent harm on adversaries, (2) willful ability to have sex with many women, (3) access to material resources that are largely inaccessible to others. These images are grounded in the tales of Stagolee (whose name has been adopted by a white New York rapper) and blaxploitation movie figures like Shaft and Dolomite (who have been referenced in hip-hop songs). Perhaps one of the most colorful and charismatic figures to emerge from this tradition is Muhammad Ali, whose self-promotional style and boastful displays in and out of the boxing ring are legendary. As Perry explains, Ali is "one of the forerunners of hip hop" by his very public usage of African American vernacular badman style.[10] Indeed, his bold, audacious flaunting of skills, braggadocious demeanor, and defiance to established authority runs identical to descriptions of hip-hop. Too, his unapologetic and conspicuous blackness (including, among other things, being a member of the largest black nationalist organization in the country, the Nation of Islam) marked a departure from public displays of race among black athletes. He was grounded in the black community and made no requests for white acceptance. The mainstream must accept or reject him on *his* terms. In many respects, Ali was the physical incarnation of the spirit of the Black Power era, which gave birth to hip-hop. Moreover, Ali's style would influence professional sports as black star athletes from Charles Barkley, to Allen Iverson, to Terrell Owens have emerged as major figures: characteristically cocky, boastful, defiant, and damned good at what they do.[11]

Like other forms of cultural expression, black men have created a palpable celebration of their masculinity in the form of hip-hop discourse and style. This style is rooted in the historical, social, cultural, and economic experiences of black men. In a patriarchal society in which most black men of any age were called "boys" and denied the right to vote, the right to obtain adequate employment, or even basic human rights, many black men by the mid-twentieth century compensated for their powerlessness by creating the hypermale. This was manifested in a coolness that typified black manhood, particularly young urban working-class black men.[12]

An essential part of this hypermachismo is the conspicuous value placed on power and status in urban folkloric tales and sayings. Many of these songs celebrate the sexual prowess of the male storyteller while simultaneously reducing women to mere props to men's sexual and material exploits. As early as 1979, in the first hit rap song "Rapper's Delight," all of the staples were present: a braggadocious hypermaterialism and female subjugation. Rapper Big Bank Hank brags about being the "ladies' pimp" while his partner extols the joy of his bodyguards, a pool, a Lincoln Continental, and a sunroof Cadillac. While these rappers create a fictitious world of conspicuous consumption, status, and prestige, their style is anchored in an oral tradition that has existed for decades, as detailed by Robin D. G. Kelley. In explaining the rise of this hypermale or "baaadman" trope, Kelley writes:

> Both the baaadman and trickster embody a challenge to virtually *all* authority (which makes sense to people for whom justice is a rare thing), creates an imaginary upside down world where the oppressed are powerful, and it reveals to listeners the pleasures and price of reckless abandon. And in a world where male public powerlessness is often turned inward on women and children, misogyny and stories of sexual conflict are very old examples of the "price" of being baaad.[13]

A generation of rappers has continued the tradition of fictive first-personal tales of grandeur, or toasting, which had its origins in the badman narratives that developed in African American communities in the early twentieth century. Though the lyrics from "Rapper's Delight" are largely considered indigenous to New York and originated with the Sugar Hill Gang and Grandmaster Caz, aka Casanova,[14] evidence suggests that the rhyme is anchored in classic urban badman styles found throughout urban centers in the United States. In fact, a rhyme found among Chicago

street gangs in the 1960s is identical to part of the first commercially successful rap song:

> I'm nemp the hemp, the women's pimp
> Women fight for my delight
> I'm the ass kicker, the city slicker
> The world shaker, the baby maker.[15]

Compare these lyrics to "Rapper's Delight":

> I'm imp the dimp the ladies' pimp
> the women fight for my delight
> but I'm the grandmaster with the three mcs
> that shock the house for the young ladies.[16]

These similarities do not detract from the creativity of the commercial rap
song. They do, however, reflect a style that was not unique to New York or
hip-hop's early years; it was, in fact, part of a tradition and festive ritual that
young black men developed as a creative outlet. With fanciful rhymes and
witty references to materialism, sexuality, and cool, these male-centered
modes of expression gave hip-hop its core sensibilities and thrust. Moreover, these raps are inextricably connected to precise social and political
conditions. As Angela Y. Davis notes, "Great art never achieves its greatness
through an act of absolute transcendence of socio-historical reality. On the
contrary, even as it transcends specific circumstances, it is deeply rooted in
social realities. Its function precisely is to fashion new perspectives on the
human condition—in its specificity and in its generality."[17] In the case of
the hypermasculine trope in hip-hop, the social realties were generally not
as rappers insisted. The great majority of rappers have not been the wealthy,
globetrotting players that they portray in the music studio. These MCs have
carefully formulated a fanciful world of self-absorbed conspicuous consumption, profound sexual prowess, fearlessness, pugilistic skills, and an
uncanny willingness to kill anyone who attempts to get in their way.[18] The
hyperbole is clear. But as hip-hop established itself as an extension of the
supermacho narrative, it assumed a misogynist character. As hip-hop continued to develop, however, it proved much too dynamic and innovative to
become limited in content or scope.

Early Female MCs

Within its first few years, hip-hop had visible female rappers who carved spaces for themselves and contested the contradictions within this new musical art. Sha Rock was the only female rapper in the group Funky Four +1 More, which emerged in the late 1970s in New York. Later Sha Rock teamed up with Lisa Lee, a native of the South Bronx—hip-hop's birthplace—who had begun rapping in 1976. With Debbie Dee, the three formed Us Girls, the first all-female rap group to get any radio play. The name reflected a gender consciousness in a realm that was not only male dominated but in which the discourse was also decidedly male centered. On the *Beat Street* movie soundtrack, they affirmed the ability of female rappers in the theme song "Us Girls Can Boogie Too."[19]

Us Girls found that although they received some accolades from other rappers, they were limited in scope to their artistic expression, unlike their male peers. For male rappers, boasting and bragging necessarily included aggressive verbal challenges to "wack MCs" as well as tales of sexual prowess in their rhymes. For women, raps about sexual exploits—regardless how fictive—were potentially destructive to their image and career. As Lisa Lee explained, if women gyrated, grabbed their crotches, or took off their clothes on stage as men did, the responses would be very different. "If a male does that, the audience will say 'Man they're crazy. I like that.' If a girl does it, they'll say 'Oh my God! They were disgusting and nasty.' That's how they judge it."[20]

Clearly, the hypersexualized stereotype of the black woman—the jezebel image—was what many black artists resisted. Still, the assumption that women in general must adhere to "acceptable" expressions of limited sexuality reflects patriarchal impulses. Indeed, the terrain of women's sexuality reflects the ultimate effort to control women as extensions of male provenance. For most of American history women were considered by the larger patriarchal structure to be extensions of male social, familial, and economic interest. In this custom female sexuality had to be controlled, otherwise patriarchy itself would be threatened.[21]

Like the sexuality of women in general, the image of the sexually lascivious black woman was derived from deeply rooted notions. Slavery demanded personality types that operated as a justification for the awful and inhuman conditions under which enslaved people languished. Sexual relations between white male enslavers and the women whom they enslaved demanded the jezebel, or hypersexual woman. The sexuality of enslaved women was, in many ways, contested territory, and, though many women resisted, they became extensions of the domain of white men in general and the enslaver in particular.[22] Though these images grow out of the barbarity of nineteenth-century slavery, their utility has not been totally erased. Inasmuch as racism and patriarchy continue to function, the need for useful rationalizations helps perpetuate these images. Like the male minstrel figure, the jezebel figure survives in American popular culture and in hip-hop in particular. As Patricia Hill Collins explains, these injurious "controlling images of Black women are not simply grafted onto existing social institutions but are so pervasive that even though the images themselves change in the popular imagination, Black women's portrayal of the Other persists."[23] The rejection of such images is, on one level, essential to black feminism. Black women rappers, however, found themselves circumscribed by what they considered a double standard in artistic expression. This limits the agency of women in hip-hop and even conforms to other patriarchal rationalizations, such as the madonna/whore dyad. The difficulty of determining the nature of feminist agency is not as clear-cut as one may hope when examining the early years of hip-hop.

Many early female rappers like those in Us Girls wore miniskirts and high-heeled shoes "to guarantee a favorable response" and otherwise conform to a feminine style.[24] While female MCs assumed the bravado and boasting style of their male counterparts, they were also limited to the degree in which women could express their passion. As Nancy Guevara notes in her 1987 study of women in rap, their feminine image "appears to constrain their ability to develop styles in the direction of political assertiveness as well."[25] This contestation for artistic expression took a very different turn in 1984 with the release of the first female battle song against male rappers.

UTFO's 1984 hit "Roxanne Roxanne" describes the frustration experienced when a girl named Roxanne disses the protagonists in the song. She is criticized as "stuck-up" because she would not give the rappers any attention. Later that year, a fourteen year old from Queens, calling herself Roxanne Shante, released "Roxanne's Revenge," which was a frontal attack on UTFO and a defense of women who are vilified by men for not favorably responding to their amorous advances. Disrespecting girls, she says, is "played out." Shante explains, "Talking about girls is good as long as you've got something good to say. Why do you always gotta say girls are stuck up?" Her response launched one of the most popular battles in hip-hop history, producing at least seven "diss" songs, all centered on the mythical Roxanne character. Shante even performed with UTFO at concerts, challenging the male rappers in front of thousands. Responses like hers, she stated, are needed to "put guys, or anyone else with a crazy ego, in their place."[26] Not limited to the verbal challenge, Shante also rejected the miniskirt and high-heels for jeans and sneakers. The image of female MC was forever changed.

Three years later, in 1987, Salt-n-Pepa released *Hot, Cool, and Vicious*. The album was a commercial success and featured three women who demonstrated brash confidence, challenging womanizers while also boasting about their ability to take another woman's man. In their hit "Push It" (1987), the rapping duo of Salt-n-Pepa made sexual innuendos with catchy hooks and danceable beats. The song's festive style is typical of the era, while it also celebrates the implied sexual freedom of the MCs. The second hit song, "Tramp," builds upon a song originally recorded by Lowell Fulsom in 1965–1966. Otis Redding and Carla Thomas later covered it in 1967 as a dozens-type of dialogue between a would-be player and a woman who is skeptical of his claims of grandeur. Twenty years later, Salt-n-Pepa extended the discussion to call out womanizers who similarly make grandiose claims to lure women. As Russell Potter notes, "The male voice, dominant in Fulsom and comically punctuated in Thomas/Redding, is completely marginalized here, appearing only as a one-dimensional comic foil."[27] In their version, Salt-n-Pepa ridicule the ambitious player and do so by rendering his voice nearly mute as his monologue is barely audible behind the beats and the rappers' own verses.

Salt-n-Pepa continued a winning formula of sexy lyrical and visual performance and subtle (and not so subtle) political messages. The group's DJ, Spinderella, joined the two rappers in videos for "Whatta Man" (1993) and "Shoop" (1993), as the three women wore less clothing, revealed chiseled bodies, and made a more conspicuous display of their own sexuality. In "Whatta Man" they offered their praise of their men who are not reduced to simple beefcake objects but who instead represent smart, caring, strong, sexually satisfying, and handsome total packages:

My man is smooth like Barry, and his voice got bass
A body like Arnold with a Denzel face
He's smart like a doctor with a real good rep
And when he comes home he's relaxed with Pep.

Not to confuse his love and sensitivity with anything less than a truly masculine specimen, Pepa's man's deep voice, muscular physique, and intelligence depart from the popular constrictions of manhood that are popularized in hip-hop. "He's not a fake wannabe tryin' to be a pimp," doesn't cheat on his woman and is "never disrespectful." This song reflects a somewhat anomalous style in hip-hop music. Few songs from male or female rappers offer visions of an ideal, healthy amorous relationship. Black Star's "Brown Skinned Lady" (1998) and Strange Fruit Project's "Honey" (2006) also extol intelligent, sexual, and loving partners. Typically, however, songs referencing male-female relations are reduced to exploitative unions that generally weave fictive ego-driven tales. From Snoop Dogg's "Ain't No Fun" (1993), to DMX's "Shorty Was the Bomb" (2001), through Lil' Kim's "Suck My Dick" (2001) and beyond, rappers generally offer cautionary tales of deceit or crude expressions of sexual domination.[28]

Advocating sexual responsibility in "Let's Talk about Sex" (1992) and women's liberation in "Ain't Nothing but a She Thing" (1995), the group reflected a profound expansion of female expression in hip-hop. Salt-n-Pepa demonstrated their ability to reject the feminine image expected of them with a sexuality that was not as bold or raunchy as some male rappers, but it was no longer suppressed. Additionally, they reflected a profound sensitivity to social issues like AIDS, sexism, and racism. Though not as political or caustic as artists like Public Enemy or Ice Cube, the group broadened the range of gendered expressions in hip-hop in significant ways.

MC Lyte, the first solo female rapper to earn a gold single ("Ruffneck"; 1993), developed a style that was largely in tune with the general currents of the time, much like her female contemporaries. She eschewed the skirts of earlier female rappers and embraced typical braggadocious styles that spoke to her womanhood as well as her agility on the mic on songs like "I Am Woman" from her 1988 debut Lyte as a Rock. On her 1989 hit "Cha Cha Cha," she is a self-described "Uptown brainiac" who will "blind you with the science that the others have yet to find." Her self-referential comment about her smarts reflects the popular sense of intellectualism that pervaded hip-hop in the late 1980s and early 1990s. Rappers, particularly New York–based ones, celebrated their intelligence in scores of songs while simultaneously remaining hardcore and authentic.[29] In contrast to the madonna/whore dyad, MC Lyte insisted in "I Am Woman" that certain labels don't apply to her. Being referred to as "Queen" was "too corny," while "Sexy" made guys "too horny."[30] Settling simply on "the Best," Lyte implies that her classification transcends gendered limitations. She is not the "Queen Mother" prototype that author Cheryl Keyes identifies.[31] Nor is she the sexualized vixen or "jezebel" character, whose roots extend to the era of slavery. She is simply the best, not just the best among women, either. In no uncertain terms, MC Lyte affirms herself by adopting the dominant styles while simultaneously subverting traditional notions of female place and agency.

The expansion of feminist expression is best represented in the traditional definition with the release of Queen Latifah's *All Hail the Queen* in 1989. Latifah, a native of New Jersey, joined the burgeoning black nationalist trend of hip-hop as a freedom fighter for the black world. She celebrated the contribution of women to liberation struggles in Africa and the United States. On "Ladies First," she invited other female MCs to praise a progressive sisterhood:

> Use your imagination, picture this
> Any male or female rapper trying to diss
> Here for excitement and enticement
> With my competitors killed I go build with my enlightenment
> Teach the youth, feed the needy
> Confident descendent of Queen Nefertiti
> The mother of civilization will rise . . .
> Acknowledge the fact that I'm black and I don't lack
> Queen Latifah is giving you a piece of my mind
> A rhyme spoken by a feminine teacher.[32]

The video for "Ladies First" depicts film clips of women engaged in activism around the world, including iconic figures like Angela Davis, Sojourner Truth, and Winnie Mandela. Queen Latifah, who controls a massive chess board in the video, represents authority and control in the world (at large and within hip-hop, in particular), where women are largely politically marginalized in a patriarchal system that transcends national boundaries.

Latifah engaged in similar celebrations of female agency and power in songs like "The Evil That Men Do" and "U.N.I.T.Y."[33]

In "U.N.I.T.Y.," Latifah inveighs against the type of misogynistic expressions that were growing dominant in hip-hop in the early 1990s, while she also extols black male and black female love and affection. The chorus, "Love a black woman from infinity to infinity," and "Love a black man from infinity to infinity," was a challenge to the cynical chants from gangstas that argued that "life ain't nothing but bitches and money."[34] Other gangstas were simultaneously claiming that life is "M.O.B.: money over bitches."[35] In the song, she hits a man in the eye who grabs her booty as he calls her a bitch. Latifah not only condemned the men who insisted on calling women "bitches" and "hos" but also offered healing options to black male and female relations, while not appearing too corny or conciliatory to infractions against women. Her willingness to punch the offensive man in the face reflected the sort of brash and confrontational style that had become prominent in hip-hop in the early 1990s. To offer an olive branch to the man who grabbed her butt and called her a bitch would have most certainly appeared very uncool and inordinately passive to fans. But taken in its larger context, the song was more affirming in male and female relations than not.

High Fashion Gangstas

By 1991 female MCs were continuing to expand their artistic horizons. They were no longer confined to only certain types of artistic expression, and some even demonstrated the same hypersexuality and vulgar displays of violence that some of their male peers had. As hip-hop's criteria for authenticity and rebel coolness shifted, so did female expressions in the genre, which had always been coterminous with the dominant male notions of authenticity. Though the gangsta tropes are dependent on hypermasculine sensibilities, female MCs quickly adopted them, simultaneously suffusing these styles with uniquely feminine inflections. In 1991, two groups emerged on both coasts with identical gimmicks as hypersexualized vixens. Perhaps taking a cue from the immensely popular N.W.A (Niggas With Attitude), BWP (Bytches With Problems) and HWA (Hoez With Attitudes) hit the rap scenes in New York and Los Angeles, respectively. They made songs about men with little sexual stamina and small penises, as they rapped in scantly clad outfits.

As many anticipated, they were ridiculed and criticized for their representation of female sexuality. Some thought that record companies, who
expected a promising monetary return in the exploitation of female sexuality, were manipulating the groups. Others argued that the artists themselves
were chiefly to blame for their images and lyrics with song titles like "Fuck a
Man" and "Hoe I am." In response to their critics, members of BWP stated
that their images were the product of their "anger at woman's roles and a
desire to poke fun at double standards."[36] The groups marked the first artistic attempt in popular music made by female artists to claim the term
"bitch," traditionally used as a term of contempt for women. Deconstructing the term and modifying its spelling, a member of BWP insisted that the
term "bytch" means "a strong, positive aggressive woman who goes after
what she wants. We take that on today and use it in a positive way."[37] The
term was also an acronym which represented an alternate meaning: Beautiful Young Thing College Honeys en' Shit. Using feminist slogans such as
"No Means No" and rapping about revenge fantasies against misogynists,
the group offered a militant style that was fundamentally unique in hip-
hop. In many respects they employed what bell hooks identifies as a defiant
language that inherently challenges the patriarchal and racist system, its
codes, and expectations of deference. In some respects, these expressions
reflected what became known as "Third Wave Feminism," a poststructural-
ist reading of gender and sexuality that engages the dynamic nature of gender itself. Third Wave feminists have been known to position themselves as
less explicitly political than earlier feminists, rejecting conventional notions
of what is, or is not, good for females.[38] Moreover, the style mirrored the
brash styles that had emerged among those rappers who had fused the uplifting styles of East Coast "conscious" rap with the violent and often vulgar
expressions of the West Coast gangsta rap. Like gangsta and black nationalist fusions, the gangsta and feminist fusions resulted in an expansion of violently resistive narratives. BWP affirmed its place as authentic, as the decidedly gangsta styles of hip-hop had begun to establish hegemony in the
music, while adhering to a peculiar feminist perspective.

These groups became what Perry calls "badwomen," and by their presence in male space they inherently challenge hip-hop gender norms. Badwomen "use their presence to call into question the masculine designation
of those spaces, and to at times even offer a feminist critique by using the
power vested in these spaces."[39] Despite the raised eyebrows, neither group

of early badwomen developed much market appeal and simply disappeared into the backdrop of rap gimmick groups like the Afros or Young Black Teenagers.

It would not be until 1996 that a new genre of hypersexualized female MCs would not only take sexuality to extremes but also become some of the most successful and visible rappers ever. Lil' Kim and Foxy Brown emerged out of New York as the reigning queens of female hypersexuality and uber-materialism in the rap game. When they first appeared on the music scene, both women belonged to larger cliques that included successful artists like Jay-Z, Nas, the Notorious B.I.G., and Puff Daddy. They exhibited a sexuality that simultaneously rejected the double standards of sexual expression expected in hip-hop and embraced the oversexed vixen image that many feminists oppose. Still, some argue that the rappers are short on talent and long on gimmick and shock value. Men, such as Jay-Z, wrote lyrics for Foxy Brown, and reports have surfaced that attribute some of Lil' Kim's lyrics to the Notorious B.I.G.

Blending an image of the gold digger, sexually lascivious vixen, and the violent mob girl, both Lil' Kim and Foxy Brown, who knew each other since childhood, took the hip-hop world by storm, each selling millions of albums. With strong production, name recognition, and visibility, Foxy Brown (the "Ill Na Na") and Lil' Kim ("The Queen Bee") appropriated the common tropes of braggadocious sexuality and materialism once reserved for male rappers—to the consternation of many feminists. In her rhymes, Kim compares herself to famous porn stars Heather Hunter and Janet Jackme and in several songs extolled the joys of all sorts of sexual pleasure, including anal sex, cunnilingus, and fellatio. Referring to herself as the "Queen Bitch," Kim also raps that she is a "kill a nigga for my nigga by any means bitch—[a] murder scene bitch."[40] Foxy Brown, like Kim, revels in her sexuality, but puts more emphasis on naming expensive brands in her rhymes. Enamored of high-end designer labels, Foxy raps about her Mercedes, Dolce & Gabbana, and Movado. "Never settle for less, I'm in excess."[41] And like Kim, she has a moniker that suggests her violent side, the "murderess mami."

The commercial success of the hypersexual and violent female MC opened doors for other women rappers who employed this style. Eve, Trina, Gangsta Boo, Remy Ma, Jackie-O, and others would employ the formula of Kim and Foxy in the late 1990s and beyond. In fact, no commercial female MC since 2000 has gone gold, let alone platinum, without the typical tropes of violence and hypersexuality. Even Missy Elliot, who is not typically seen as the gangsta sexual vixen, manages to engage the common tropes of violence in her style, referring to her ability to kill adversaries and to herself as a "ho" and a "bitch."[42] This is, of course, a significant departure from the styles of Salt-n-Pepa, MC Lyte, Queen Latifah, Lauryn Hill, and other female MCs from the decade before.

Some feminists have argued that the hypermaterialistic and violent female MCs, like their predecessors, BWP and HWA, simply complement the sexist/racist/classist interests of the music industry in particular and corporate America generally. This point is particularly salient, considering that the lyrics of some women MCs have been widely known to have been written by men.[43] Clearly, many of these women depart from the strict definitions of feminism used here. Patricia Collins, as explained earlier, sets the rejection of stereotypes such as the oversexed jezebel as central to black feminism, along with a commitment to eradicate class elitism. But what is also important to this discussion is the way in which an ostensibly working-class girl evolves into a nouveau-riche vixen whose sexuality is essential to her expression of authenticity. To be affluent and living in the suburbs inherently detracts from the credibility factor in hip-hop, unless such affluence comes from "doing dirt," such as "moving weight" (drug selling).[44] Additionally, for men and women rappers, hypersexuality becomes an expression of authenticity. Collins writes that, "to be real, [Lil' Kim] must sell sexuality as part of working-class Black female authenticity."[45] In many respects this dovetails with the most pernicious stereotypes of black sexuality in general and that of poor people as well. The association of hypersexuality among the black working class reflects hegemonic notions of culture, class, race, and personal responsibility. Indeed, it has a recurring role in the Welfare Queen stereotype discussed by Ronald Reagan's administration, as well as the jezebel character from slavery.[46]

Neither Kim nor Foxy seems interested in rejecting the more pernicious controlling images that Collins discusses. Both rappers revel in ostentatious displays of wealth while deriding those who are too poor to afford such luxuries. In fact, their self-representation appears dependent on the most destructive stereotypes of black people in general and black women in particular. Akissi Britton, who defines herself as a young black feminist, takes umbrage at Lil' Kim being called a "feminist." As Britton explains, "To carry that label means that you are engaged in the battle to fight political,

In 1998–1999 Lauryn Hill's talent as a singer, rapper, producer, and writer resulted in significant media exposure, commercial sales, and unprecedented Grammy wins for a woman and hip-hop artist without pandering to controlling images of black women.

economic and social sexism." Embracing the dominant definitions of the term, Britton insists that feminism is inherently resistive to oppression. Moreover, it is about undermining the narrow assumptions about the power of women. Women's power is broad enough to extend beyond patriarchal assumptions about "pussy power" and sex as a tool for meaningful agency. Rejecting the notion that the contemptuous term "bitch" has been reclaimed and imbued with feminist power, she tells the rapper in an open letter that, "no matter how you define it, Kim, a bitch is a bitch. And sex equals money equals power is not a feminist principle." Ultimately, "because a voice is feminine doesn't mean its feminist."[47] But when historically contextualized, the agency of both women appears to suggest that in some ways they are reflections of a peculiar type of resistive female politics. Some even insist that their lyrics are "manifestos of a new age of womanhood."[48] Iterations of Third Wave Feminism, as mentioned above, are also found here. While Kim's work can be viewed as a expression of hegemonic patriarchal controlling images of black women, her politics are not beholden to any strict, static definition of "proper" feminist expression.

She seeks opportunity for herself as a black woman, which can be viewed as a rejection of (black) women's subordination and passivity.

Kim and Foxy entered into a male-dominated art form that clearly had limitations for female participants. Whereas women like Queen Latifah, The Boss, Yo, MC Lyte, and others expanded the boundaries of the female MC, none received the level of popularity that Lil' Kim and Foxy Brown had by 1997, each appearing on the cover of dozens of mainstream magazines from *Interview* to *Essence* and *Rolling Stone*. They simultaneously rejected the limitations of female sexuality, demonstrating that a female rapper could be as sexually explicit as any male rapper, while garnering respect from male peers and music consumers. One cannot deny that they have rejected limitations imposed upon female MCs. Yet they also reflect profound self-doubt and limited agency even as they laud their self-determination.

In February 1999, Foxy Brown became only the second female rapper (the other was Lauryn Hill) to debut at number 1 on the Billboard 200 with her sophomore release *Chyna Doll*. In a revealing article in *Essence*, Foxy Brown explained her hardcore image as grounded in hip-hop style: "[My] right home is hip-hop. I'm never going to stray from that. I'm always going to be gritty, grimy hip-hop, 'cause that's what I do." Despite her insistence on her comfort with her "grimy" image, she equivocated on her sexual image. In fact, she hoped to "gradually" contain fewer obscenities. Moreover, she expressed dismay at her controversial cover for the 1999 December/January issue of *Vibe*, where she appears so scantily clad that some stores refused to use the posters of the cover, considering them too lewd. Her mother and fiancé, rapper Kurupt, were similarly upset with the cover. Ultimately, she insisted that she had profound insecurity about her beauty as a girl: "If you take any beautiful dark-skinned sister nowadays, guys are like, 'oh she's beautiful.' But back in the day, it was not a cool thing. That was something I had to get over, because for a while I couldn't stand myself." Brown's mother suggests that this childhood experience partially explains her daughter's need for attention and affirmation.[49] Still, the marketing forces of her label and management played an active role in shaping Foxy Brown.

Violator (a subsidiary of Def Jam) helped make Inga Marchand into Foxy Brown, a "ghetto glam-girl." She admits that "that was my gimmick. I thought being a sex symbol was what I had to do to make it work."[50] The question of her own feminist expression and resistive politics are further scrutinized when considering that Jay-Z wrote her verses for her first album and that her image was contrived by men. The power of female sexual liberation in this case appears to be little more than a male-constructed vision of female sexuality, complete with stock jezebel references. But, of course, the dialogic quality of this image is complicated. Can the "ghetto glam-girl" be an extension of resistive cultural production if males contrive it? If men can be resistive to patriarchy, then the consideration must be made.

In several instances, Lil' Kim, the archetype of this style, displays bravado, confidence, and arrogance that are typical, even obligatory, for any rapper. In doing so, her identity as a woman and as a black person is inherently resistive to dominant ideas of gender, race, place, and power. Unfettered by the forces of racism, classism, or sexism, Lil' Kim infiltrates any social world. She enjoys the finest hotels, jewelry, clothes, and automobiles available. She lives an affluent life that is elusive to the overwhelming majority of white males, yet she can still party in some of the grimiest hoods of Brooklyn. In a society with a long history of circumscribing the power of women and people of color, she admires Oprah Winfrey, whom she calls a "gangsta bitch" for her unparalleled success in corporate America.[51] In "Single Black Female," Lil' Kim affirms her own self-determination when she raps that she writes her own rhymes and that her image is her own doing. Implicitly, this image has afforded her the power to improve the quality of life for many others. She even gives her friends "businesses for Christmas":

If I talk freaky—then that's my business
If I dress freaky—then that's my business
Got folks praticin' how to spit like this
Sexy C-E-O makin' hits like this
HUH?! I know you pissed, but take some advice from me
In five years, you'll be as nice as me
But right now, nah, ya'll ain't ready
I'm a single black female and this goes out to Heddy.[52]

Though decidedly bold and brash, Lil' Kim's confidence, ability to earn large sums of money, and ability to employ others does not offer any radical critique of society. It does not vilify the social, political, and economic conditions in which she lived until her music career. It instead uses her past as a marker for authenticity—hood girl makes good—but it fails to even mention the inherent limitations that make her success (or Oprah's) so exceptional. Instead, her lyrics, like the lyrics of most commercial rappers, offer a loud gloating, as if she is telling listeners, "I came up. Now watch me roll through the 'hood on my 22's. Better yet, tune in to see my ostentatious, self-indulgent lifestyle on MTV's 'Cribs.'" As the humanistic thrust of feminism—as defined by Collins—asserts, Kim is no feminist.

Joan Morgan, a self-defined hip-hop feminist, addresses the complexity of Foxy and Kim. But, as Morgan explains, "There will be those who choose to empower themselves by making less than womanist choices—and they are free to do so."[53] What Foxy, Kim, and their stylistic peers—Da Brat, Trina, and Eve—create is a style that challenges traditional assumptions and demands on womanhood. Jason D. Haugen calls these styles "alternative femininities" that provide a space for an expression of power for these MCs.[54] The sexuality of some of these female rappers operates as a counter-hegemonic text that will not pander to traditional or acceptable boundaries of female sexual expression. Relative to Nancy Cott's definition of feminism, Foxy, Kim, and other badwomen have been able to oppose sexual hierarchy with a salient identity as women. Some may argue even that sexualized lyrics force consideration of Audre Lorde's idea of the erotic as power:

> I believe in the erotic and I believe in it as an enlightening force within our lives as women. I have become clearer about the distinctions between the erotic and other apparently similar forces. We tend to think of the erotic as an easy, tantalizing sexual arousal. I speak of the erotic as the deepest life force, a force which moves us toward living in a fundamental way. And when I say living I mean it as that force which moves us toward what will accomplish real positive change.[55]

And though several songs such as Foxy Brown's "Ill Na Na" and "Ride (Down South)" and Lil' Kim's "We Don't Need It" explore erotic themes, they fail to explore intimacy beyond selfish and cynical types that render trust, affection, and love corny notions for the ignorant and gullible. In essence, they adopt the dominant misogynist sexual tropes that pervade hip-hop. Men become sexual objects to be exploited and used.

In "Queen Bitch" (1996), the Queen Bee demands that male figures satisfy her with cunnilingus, while she watches cartoons. Similarly in "Suck My Dick" (2000), Lil' Kim offers a subversive take on the misogynist catch-all phrase. Here, she raps that many men "ain't shit" and constructs a tale of objectification of male bodies:

He asked me did I love him
I said what came to mind, like niggas be doing:
"Yeah baby, I love you long time"
Look I ain't tryin' to suck ya
I might not even fuck ya
Just lay me on this bed and give me some head
Got the camcord layin' in the drawer where he can't see
Can't wait to show my girls; he sucked the piss out my pussy.[56]

This verse relegates men to being only extensions of female pleasure and need. Male agency rests primarily in affirming the women in sexual relationships that are neither healthy nor trusting. And though this exemplifies what hip-hop journalists Bakari Kitwana and Kevin Powell note as the crisis in black male and female relationships, the song, for some, proves to be a cathartic counter to the hundreds of sexist songs that pervade hip-hop, as well as the general sexist pulse of society at large. Ever since N.W.A's "Gangsta Gangsta" (1988) line that "life ain't nuthin but bitches and money" these songs have become standard tropes in commercial hip-hop. Jay-Z's 1999 hit "Big Pimpin'" best represents the general thrust of these dominant commercial songs:

You know I—thug em, fuck em, love em, leave em
Cause I don't fuckin need em
Take em out the hood, keep em lookin good
But I don't fuckin feed em . . .
I'm a pimp in every sense of the word, bitch

Miami's Rick Ross in "Hustlin'" (2006) reminds listeners that, eighteen years after the release of *Straight Outta Compton,* life is still "bitches and business." For most commercial rappers, women are always a necessary adornment to male sexual needs and egos, but rarely in a respectful way. As Kim explains in an interview over her lyrics that objectify men, many women appreciate the attacks: "A lot of them [were] supportive because they were, like, 'oh, my gosh. I couldn't wait for a female to come back and go after men.'"[57]

    Lil' Kim and Foxy Brown's ultrasexual image appealed to an important segment of the market. Young male consumers enjoyed the X-rated lyrics, which were backed by catchy beats and glitzy videos. But Kim and Foxy, despite their professional success, are mere advocates of dangerous stereotypes, many insist. It's important to acknowledge that women can also be agents of female subjugation while personally experiencing privilege and acceptance typically reserved for men. As scholar Joan Smith notes, "We are all exposed to the prevailing ideology of our culture, and some women learn early on that they can prosper by aping the misogyny of men; these are the women who win provisional favor by denigrating other women, by playing on male prejudices, and by acting the 'man's woman.'"[58]

While debates emerged around how to interpret the meteoric rise of the Queen Bee and the Ill Na Na, the lone female member of one of the most successful rap groups released her solo CD in 1998. In its first week *The Miseducation of Lauryn Hill* sold more units that any female artist of any genre of music in a similar length of time. Lauryn Hill, a member of the Fugees, wrote and produced her solo effort, which received near universal praise, considered an instant classic by some critics. The album was nominated for ten Grammy Awards, of which Hill collected five (a record for a woman). Her award for album of the year was the first given to a hip-hop album. Hill was the most visible winner for an awards show with so many female winners that it was called by one magazine "the year of the woman."[59] Hill's image as a mother, rapper, singer, actor, producer, writer, and socially conscious artist proved that the limitations of women in hip-hop had been single-handedly broken as never before. Moreover, her touted beauty was even more significant in that her dark skin, modest-sized posterior, and dreadlocks were anomalous to the dominant representations of beauty in hip-hop videos or society at large. At once, Hill transcended the jezebel trope that some argued was essential for a woman rapper to go platinum. She also rejected the gangsta and hypermaterialist style that pervades hip-hop while embracing a sophistication that is not dependent on name brands and conspicuous consumption. But despite her powerful impact in the industry, her lyrics are not decidedly feminist. Like most rappers, she offers a boasting style that involves some social commentary, including exhortations to women to demand respect from men and for men to assume responsibility and maturity in their relations with both women and men. Hill is not alone in achieving success while constructing new representations of female MCs in hip-hop.

Philadelphia-based rapper Bahamadia released her first CD *Kollage* in 1997 to very warm receptions in the nascent underground community of hip-hop. Her complex lyrical ability, well-developed styles that utilized intelligent wordplay and rhyme schemes, demonstrated that she shared company with the best of hip-hop MCs:

> completed like seven
> to overshadow the triple six
> complimenting zig-a-zicks
> with wisdom like the 5 percenters when doing mathematics
> flips scripts like acrobatics
> intrinsic in rapping like insulin to diabetics
> text is didactic with nutrients like Muslix.[60]

Stylistically similar to Mos Def, Talib Kweli, Common, and The Roots with her internal rhymes, similes, puns, and metaphors, Bahamadia demonstrated that women, too, can hold on to the creativity that characterizes communities of MCs that do not rely on the commercial tropes of violence and pathology in their music. Other female rappers as well have expanded artistic boundaries since the mid-1990s.

Missy Misdemeanor Elliot emerged in 1996 as a writer for recording artists as diverse as Janet Jackson and Lil' Kim. With impressive self-produced tracks as well as coproduced work with Timbaland, she went platinum with her debut CD in 1997. Her style—witty, lighthearted, and decidedly less dependent on sexualized lyrics than Kim or Foxy—proved popular and marketable. Although valorizing pathology is not a dominant expression in her subsequent work, by her third CD, *Missy E . . . So Addictive* (2001), she began to rely on more violent tropes, such as her "Whatcha Gon' Do," where she threatens to "beat that ass to the ground" and pull out her gun on adversaries. Her commercial releases appear radio friendly; however, Missy appears to have embraced the dominant styles of commercial rap that fixate on the winning formulas for success, as has Eve, who emerged in 1999 as Ruff Ryders' First Lady.

Eve, who hails from Philadelphia, debuted at number 1 on the pop charts in 1999 with her first album, *Let There Be Eve . . . Ruff Ryders' First Lady.* Though the antidomestic violence song "Love Is Blind" was a hit, the album was not decidedly heavy on uplifting social commentary. Songs like "Scenario 2000," "My Bitches," and "We on That Shit," among others, reflected the gangsta bravado tropes that have dominated commercial rap since the mid-1990s. On "My Bitches," Eve, who claims the term "bitch" as a signifier of camaraderie and defiance, shouts out a wide cross section of her "bitches," some of whom stay in school and others who smuggle their men's drugs or refuse to visit men in jail. In essence, the song reflects her own sense of a diverse community of womanhood, not imagined in her lyrics as one-dimensionally ghettoized and dysfunctional. Decidedly sexier in presentation than Missy or L-Boogie, Eve's subsequent albums, *Scorpion* (2001) and *Eve-olution* (2002), similarly engage in the gangsta styles that typify the badman narrative. On "Gangsta Bitches" (2001), Eve joins forces with Chicago rapper Da Brat and Miami-based Trina in an ode to all things gangsta, with a female twist of fashionista style:

> Gangsta clothes, gangsta money, gangsta shows
> Gangsta purse, gangsta shoes, gangsta verse
> We the bitches that the gangstas thirst
> Gangsta bottle, gangsta trees
> Gangsta Brat, gangsta Trina, and gangsta Eve[61]

Eve, like a handful of other female MCs, demonstrates the wide range of diversity among female rappers, sexuality, and gender roles. Inasmuch as their male counterparts are not confined to one style in order to accrue legitimacy, female rappers have carved out their own spaces of authenticity that continue to reflect the dominant impulses of the music market. They can express sensitivity about other people's pain and suffering on some songs while valorizing deadly attacks on adversaries on others. They can offer playful and witty similes and metaphors while injecting their lyrics with deep commentary on the intersectionality of race, class, and gender. Ultimately, the wide range of expression, which inherently rejects the narrow confines and expectations of the female MC, are examples of a peculiar form of male agency. This agency asserts women's abilities to express themselves unfettered by patriarchal assumptions and limitations. It affirms female power and autonomy and challenges male domination, even if it simultaneously upholds hegemonic ideas regarding class. Although these expressions fall short of articulating healing messages of male-female relations or fail to rebuke racism in any substantive way, many core principles of feminism (such as self-expression, resistance to female subjugation, sexual freedom) remain palpable.

Beauty and Objectification of Black Women

Much has been said about the pervasive objectification of women in hip-hop videos. Dozens of articles in scholarly journals as well as the popular press have explored depictions of women in the art, gyrating, dancing, and operating as extensions to male egos.[62] They have been, in fact, presented as veritable proof of the MC's manhood, even if the women in the videos were not really appreciated for anything more than sexual pleasure and status. From Notorious B.I.G.'s "Juicy" to Nelly's infamous "Tip Drill," the scenario is the same: MC raps about how cool he is and how he has all the most beautiful women. Said beautiful women, scantily clad, dance for the attention and pleasure of MC and his boys.

While the objectification of women in hip-hop is clearly problematic, as noted by many observers, it has depicted black women as standards of beauty in ways never before seen in American popular culture. Despite the rare visibility of a Dorothy Dandridge or Lena Horne in selected movies over the course of most of the twentieth century, black women have never been positioned as objects of beauty and desire in popular media to any significant degree. Moreover, in the decades leading up to the Black Power movement, African Americans struggled over self-love and openly ridiculed the notion of black beauty with colloquial sayings, with cosmetics (including popular skin-whitening creams), and in the codes and discourses of various social institutions.[63] Hip-hop, however, as a post–Black Power articulation of black identity, pleasure, machismo, and agency, has positioned black women as the objects of desire, even as (in a general sense) these women are relegated to a subordinate status.

Long before hip-hop, the bikini, the genius of Madison Avenue marketing, or even capitalism itself, people had established their own organic standards of beauty around the globe. For millennia, people have created poems, songs, dances, statues, paintings, even monuments to celebrate the beauty of an elongated neck, lip-disc, muscular torso, small feet, bald head, long hair, or whatever physical standards the group's consensus dictates to be appropriate. Hip-hop falls squarely in this tradition. And as much as the larger (white) American standards of beauty have insisted on the ugliness of a large booty, hip-hop has operated with absolute disregard for this claim. Much as in the aesthetics of large swaths of Africa and its diaspora, a large booty is celebrated as a marker of beauty. From Ghana to Jamaica, Cuba, Brazil, and Puerto Rico,

to Atlanta, New York, Chicago, and Los Angeles, hundreds of songs have extolled the beauty of large buttocks. While this does not mean that these countries are unaffected by European aesthetics of beauty, hip-hop's own standards must be seen as part of a larger gendered aesthetic rooted in African
standards of beauty. This fact is not lost on hip-hop artists themselves.

There is no song more iconic of booty-centric videos than the classic
from Sir Mix-a-lot, "Baby Got Back" (1992). Released in the declining years
of the "Golden Age" of hip-hop, where politically conscious, resistive lyrics
were common, the song established its political stance in the first few seconds of dialogue between two voyeuristic white women criticizing a black
woman from afar:

> Oh, my, god. Becky, look at her butt.
> It is so big. *scoff* She looks like,
> one of those rap guys' girlfriends.
> But, you know, who understands those rap guys? *scoff*
> They only talk to her, because,
> she looks like a total prostitute, 'kay?
> I mean, her butt, is just so big. *scoff*
> I can't believe it's just so round, it's like,
> out there, I mean—gross. Look!
> She's just so . . . black![64]

Sir Mix-a-lot does not equivocate on the standards of beauty and his ode
to the booty. Mix-a-lot rejects the "beanpole dames in the magazines" and
Cosmo magazine's insistence to "the thick soul sister" that she is fat. Still,
like virtually all such videos, the women in "Baby Got Back" are not overweight, chubby, or fat. As the refrain goes, "little in the middle, but she got
much back." Much like the white American male celebration of large
breasts, black men do not see extra size in the butt as dependent on obesity.
Somehow white Americans generally associate a large butt with being fat,
but do not associate large breasts with necessarily being fat. Mix-a-lot and
hundreds of other rappers in the last twenty years have made their prefer-
ences quite clear: fit women with large booties are ideal.

Since "Baby Got Back," hundreds of videos have depicted beautiful black
(and frequently Latina) women as the utmost status symbol for the mack,
pimp, or even the nonmisogynistic cat with game. Mos Def's hit "Ms. Phat

Booty" extols a woman whose "ass is so fat that you could see it from the front." Similarly, Kanye West in "Gold Digger" praises a prediction that his woman will have "an ass like Serena, Trina, Jennifer Lopez." In a medium where rappers brag about having the most valued possessions—a Maybach Benz, Bentley Rolls Royce, Gulfstream private airplanes, jewelry, expensive fashion—it is notable that black and Latina women have been a part of these coveted desires. And while some have argued that the women most desired are light-skinned, a systematic study of videos has never been done. But any look at "Baby Got Back," 50 Cent's "P.I.M.P.," Nelly's "Tip Drill," Jay-Z's "Big Pimping," Lloyd Bank's "On Fire," Juvenile's "Back That Thing Up" or Mike Jones's "Still Tipping" will find a wide range of black women who are nearly universally fit, shapely, but not fat, with large booties and various skin tones, though they all have straight hair. I would not argue that most of these rappers are trying to make a political statement in any systematic way. They simply prefer an Esther Baxter type to a Paris Hilton type. But the new popular celebration of black women's beauty has not been confined to hip-hop videos. A significant corpus of hip-hop and hip-hop-inflected magazines similarly showcases black and Latina women.

King magazine, which promotes itself as "the illest men's magazine ever!" is a black and Latino version of the white men's magazine *Maxim:* cars, sports, entertainment, women. While neither magazine explicitly racializes its demographic, *Maxim* centers its focus on models who are almost exclusively white women, as *King* similarly does with black and, to a lesser extent, Latina women. *King,* which boasts a readership of 500,000, leads the pack of similar (black and Latino) men's magazines, such as *Smooth, Black Men, Fuego,* and *Black Men SSX.*[65] The synergy between hip-hop and these magazines is salient. T.I., The Game, and others have shouted out *King* in songs, and *King* regularly features women who first found professional exposure in hip-hop videos. In fact, some, like Esther Baxter, Jessica White, Ki Toy Johnson, Vida Guerra, and Buffie the Body, have become veritable household names among black and Latino male hip-hop heads. Some, like Esther Baxter, Vida Guerra, and Buffie, have been so wildly popular that they regularly receive huge payments to attend parties, appear in videos, commercials, movies, and even have their own special edition magazines. Baxter, who is brown-skinned, Guerra, who is a lighter-skinned Latina, and Buffie, who is dark-skinned, represent a common spectrum in this space for the conspicuous marketing of beauty and its special attention to the booty.

When *Vibe* held its first annual "Video Vixen" award in 2003, brown-skinned Jeanette Chavis was the winner. The second annual "Video Vixen" award in 2004, which let the people decide by casting ballots, went to dark-skinned Ki Toy Johnson. Esther Baxter took the 2005 newly named "Video Goddess" award, thereby challenging the pervasive comments that hip-hop narrowly celebrates light-skinned women. Beyond these men's magazines, hip-hop magazines similarly highlight these beauty standards.[66]

Hip-hop magazines like the *Source* and *XXL* offer "Dime Piece" and "Eye Candy," sections for video actresses and models in each issue. And the grimy, quasi-hip-hop, street-tales magazine *F.E.D.S.* launched a spinoff, *Sweets,* in 2006 in an attempt to capitalize on the lucrative market that *King* and other magazines have cornered. Strictly speaking, there have never been so many spaces for black female actors and models to find work as in the age of hip-hop. That being said, Paris and other very political MCs note that "black women are more than asses and breasts."[67]

The general narrative in hip-hop scholarship is to reject these images, lyrics, and references to beauty as crude and unloving objectification of women. It is little more than the same sexist impulses that white women have had to deal with in America, some argue. While this may be partially true, as shown in this chapter, female agency must be considered. Many of these women would have never found work in other spaces as models or objectives of desire. And, taken in a historical context, it appears quite bizarre to expect that a culture will not establish its own standards of beauty and art to recognize it. Moreover, one cannot ignore the counterhegemonic thrust of some of this dialogue, even in the midst of the incredibly vulgar and offensive styles of the most misogynistic lyrics. Beauty, some philosophers would say, is by definition exclusive to only a minority of people. That most of us (men and women—of any race) are not drop-dead attractive is what makes those that are particularly notable. And although the dominant standards have been in flux, hip-hop has found a space, oftentimes in the most offensive manner, to embrace elements of African-based standards of beauty. And in typical hip-hop fashion, it is done without apology or explanation. In the final analysis, black women as well as Latina women have enjoyed a celebration as objects of status, desire, and prestige in ways never before seen in the United States. Too often, however, their beauty is celebrated while their humanity is not. They are offered up for the fantasies and egos of men in a larger artistic framework of masculinist discourse.

Feminism from Male Rappers

As mentioned above, men can also be feminists. Scholar bell hooks notes that antisexist men "have a place in feminist movement."[68] The notion that men are integral to ending patriarchy is especially important when considering that men are in the dominant positions to make change. hooks notes that, "since men are the primary agents maintaining and supporting sexism and sexist oppression, they can only be successfully eradicated if men are compelled to assume responsibility for transforming their consciousness and the consciousness of society as a whole."[69] This is more than obvious in the decidedly male-centered world of hip-hop. Men are the majority at the helm of record labels, A&Rs, management, producers, and MCs. With a strong expression of antipathy for women existing in hip-hop songs, it is somewhat remarkable when a male artist offers a challenge to the subordination of women. These challengers, however, are not always feminists in the traditional definition.

Many male rappers have written songs that inveigh against female subordination, from Tupac's "Keep Ya Head up" to Brand Nubian's "Black Woman." Yet, typically, the same artists refer to women as objectified sexual beings or as bitches and hos in other songs. Perhaps one of the most common attempts to reconcile the patriarchal mantra and womanhood is the belief that black men and women are gods and earths. The Nation of Gods and Earths, or Five Percent Nation of Islam (an offshoot of the Nation of Islam) argues that all black men are created in the image of Allah, thereby gods. Brand Nubian, Wu Tang Clan, and Nas refer to black women as "earths" in several songs, extending this ethos into hip-hop. Black women are typically considered esteemed divinities as well, but rarely goddesses. As earths, they represent the foundation of life and beauty. Clearly, this thrust has its limitations for expressing feminist agency. It is largely an extension of patriarchy dressed in the romantic symbolism of nationalist mythology.

Two outstanding cases of male expression of feminism are Digable Planets' "La Femme Fetal" on their debut CD, *Reachin'*, and the Goats's *Tricks of the Trade*. In both cases male rappers explicitly defend the right of women to control their bodies and reproductive rights. Davis writes that "birth control—individual choice, safe, contraceptive methods, as well as abortions when necessary—is a fundamental prerequisite for the emancipation of women."[70] To that end, the all-male Philadelphia-based rap group, the Goats, devoted their first CD to the theme of women's reproductive rights. The CD contains ten skits that tell the story of Chicken Little and his younger brother Hanger Head. The two search for their "Uncle Scam" who is expected to take care of them after their mother was arrested by the "Pro Livins" for attempting an abortion. Along their journey through "Uncle Scam's Federally Funded Freak Show" they encounter the Tattooed Lady, whose tattoos are actually bruises from male assailants. They also visit Rovie Wade, the sword swallower. The carnival announcer declares that "the devil and Clarence Thomas" brought Rovie's performance to the people. Rovie, to their surprise, is actually swallowing a hanger. When asked why, she explains that she would not be swallowing the hanger if she had control of her own body.

On one song, the Goats call prolifers "pied pipers" who are not concerned with the quality of life after birth: "With millions starving they want you to crank out more / Abandon them in diapers to become the real lifers / Doing 5 to 10 for robbing a liquor store."[71] In the CD jacket they provide cartoon pictures of women, including one with "get off my body" written on her torso.

The theme of women's reproductive rights was central to a generally political album that explored the prowar agenda of the Bush 41 presidency, the underfunding of public schools, political corruption, racism, and police brutality. In a typically aggressive hip-hop style, the Goats ridiculed, and offered militant challenges to, the superstructure of racism, imperialism, and patriarchy. The politically charged group never received the commercial success of the Grammy Award–winning Digable Planets, but they did produce one of the most feminist-oriented hip-hop CDs to date.

Digable Planets' "La Femme Fetal" features Butterfly, the lead rapper, who consoles and advises his friend who contemplates having an abortion. She is despondent and depressed that at the clinic antiabortion activists called her a murderer. In response, the rapper explains that

> the fascists are some heavy dudes
> they don't really give a damn about life
> they just don't want a woman to
> control her body or have the right to choose . . .
> because if you say "war" they will send them to die by the score
> supporters of the h-bomb and fire bombing clinics
> what type of shit is that? Orwellian in fact.[72]

Butterfly offers a traditional feminist argument in defense of abortion rights while providing a jazzy melodic backdrop to his political message. Outlining the political platform of archetypal conservatives who claim to be "prolife" yet are typically prowar, pro–death penalty, antiwelfare, and anti–universal health care, he details a classic leftist critique of the contradictions of the use of the term "prolife." Like many other rappers, Butterfly reflects a profound sensitivity to contentious issues in society.

That an all-male group such as the Goats would devote the core thrust of its album to feminist principles helps demonstrate the ways in which hip-hop provides space for articulations of competing ideas (sexism and feminism, for example) while still allowing the artist to claim authenticity in the art. Butterfly's challenge to patriarchy and the contradictions of those who claim to be prolife reflect a common counterhegemonic thrust of hip-hop in the early 1990s. It was a mark of his authenticity to criticize an iconic figure of the power structure like Supreme Court Justice Clarence Thomas. Similarly, commercial rappers since the mid-1990s have typically affirmed their own credibility with sexist tropes, while many underground artists like Jurassic 5 or Dilated Peoples affirm their credibility with broader discourses and styles that are not dependent on misogyny. 50 Cent can affirm his authenticity by rapping about his ability to pimp women (see "P.I.M.P."; 2003), while Paris ("You Know My Name"; 2003) can do so by challenging sexism in the context of revolutionary nationalist politics. Paris reflects what most hip-hop male intellectuals have demanded from the art: "Black women are more than asses and breasts."

Black male writers of the hip-hop generation from Mark Anthony Neal to W. Jelani Cobb and Kevin Powell have been very clear about the constricted notions of black manhood pervasive in hip-hop that celebrate sexism as a normative expression of manhood. These narrow tropes not only undermine women and healthy male-female relationships, but they ultimately undermine the creativity and dynamism of the art itself. Bryon Hurt, filmmaker of the popular documentary *Hip-Hop: Beyond Beats and Rhymes,* which aired on PBS in 2007, shines a light on the misogyny, homophobia, and violence in hip-hop and offers a "loving critique" of the art. Much like other black male writers of the hip-hop generation, Hurt has embraced a larger expression of black manhood that not only avoids degradation of women but actively seeks to view the uplift of black people as inextricably tied to the uplift of black women. Society itself is in peril under a cultural standard that celebrates hatred for women. As writer and poet Kalamu Ya Salam argues, men must understand that "woman's rights are human rights."[73]

Conclusion

The complexities of the gendered discursive qualities in hip-hop are clear. The participation of women in hip-hop has been a dynamic process of contestation, as has been the construction of female images, which must function with hegemonic hypermacho expressions. The badman trope, which dominates hip-hop, has emerged as a central expression of hip-hop authenticity that demands gendered and racialized coding, where black men are the idealizations. Women, therefore, must find space in what is often hostile territory. In doing so, feminist discourses emerge as women challenge marginalization. More specifically, this feminism, like the male coding, is racialized. But too often artists have offered resistive work that fails to qualify as traditionally defined black feminism. Central to the definition of black feminism are two essential components: (1) a self-determined voice that provides agency, and (2) the construction of images that reject sexist controlling images. But, as hip-hop demonstrates, women have long been involved in negotiating ways of expression and agency that reflect the tenuousness of definitions of feminism when applied to hip-hop. It's clear that women, too, can be agents in the promotion of the very negative controlling images that feminists reject. Yet the history of female MCs is a history in which women are incessantly creating self-representation against a backdrop of hypermasculine discourses. The images of women have thereby evolved because of the artistic expression of female rappers who have either embraced or challenged the parameters imposed upon them.

MCs like Lil' Kim and Foxy Brown demonstrate that women can not only be hypersexual on wax but also extol the joys of sexually exploiting the opposite sex. Men for the Ill Na Na and the Queen Bee have been, on more than one occasion, mere props to satisfy their sexual needs and desires. These female MCs likewise portray an image that blends traditional notions of femininity (high heels, skirts) with a brash ruthlessness and sexuality once reserved for male rappers. Are they rebel feminists or opportunistic artists who have little concern about the promotion of pernicious stereotypes of women? They are a little of both.

The market demands demonstrate that haute couture "hootchie" can be profitable. When historically contextualized, one must appreciate their ability to resist the limitations of the female MC. Yet as Lauryn Hill, Missy Elliot, and Eve adroitly show, success for the female MC does not depend on extremes of soft femininity or being a one-of-the-boys "gangsta bitch." Hill in particular, while not embracing an explicit feminist collection of rhymes, proves that women can do it all and do it very well. In the final analysis, women have developed a community of MCs in hip-hop as diverse as hip-hop itself.

In the commercial realm, female rappers have clearly embraced dominant narratives of sexuality, violence, materialism and surreal egotism. Underground female MCs like Bahamadia and, to a lesser extent, Jean Grae have reflected styles that either reject or do not rely on the commercial tropes dominating airwaves. The progression of the female MC is one that is nearly as old as commercial rap itself. Resisting the limitations imposed upon them, early female MCs embraced the dominant styles of rap and infused their own styles with inflections of feminine identity, like sexuality and motherhood. In doing so, they necessarily feminized masculinist discourses and inverted the misogynistic tropes that objectified women and pandered to unhealthy male-female relations. They have embraced some of the core definitions of feminism in the process of creating an identity in hip-hop. Most commercial female rappers, however, also employ terribly problematic tropes in their rhymes. In their attempt to affirm their authenticity, rebel appeal, and agency, female MCs, more often that not, chart styles that remain inextricably attached to dominant ones in rap and manage to celebrate many of the controlling images against which black women have fought for decades. As I mentioned in chapter 1, white supremacists in America have long been drawn to images of black pathology. In fact, they have copiously celebrated black pathology and continue to reward black people who help propagate these images. bell hooks insists that many black men have found meaning by defining black masculinity as being dependent on violence; in doing so, these men have been "reward[ed] . . . for acting like brutal psychopaths."[74] Part of the popularity of the badman trope has been the employment of the badwoman trope and providing a showcase of black female pathology in ways that have been rarely seen in the history of American popular culture. But even in the midst of the most virulent forms of the jezebel figure and misogyny, male and female rappers have continued to voice vituperative challenges to their commercial peers. Some male rappers have demonstrated a sophisticated sensitivity to misogyny while also embracing popular notions of male strength, fearlessness, and egotism. From black nationalist freedom fighters to oversexed gangstas, hip-hop has provided an arena in which women have assumed images as contested as their male counterparts, suggesting that female agency is ever dynamic and complex.

Rebels with a Cause: Gangstas, Militants, Media, and the Contest for Hip-Hop

Helping to initiate the beginning of what many hip-hop journalists have called the "golden age of hip-hop," Public Enemy on "Don't Believe the Hype" (1988) exposed the daunting power of the media's ability to fundamentally chose which artists get exposure and what messages are promoted. "Radio," Chuck D explained, is scared of him because he is "the enemy."

In the classic *It Takes a Nation of Millions to Hold Us Back,* Public Enemy offers biting criticism of prisons, white supremacy, political corruption, and police brutality. Despite its unflinching lyrics and general militancy, couched in a black nationalist framework, the multiplatinum LP would be heralded as a brilliant work and enjoy considerable appeal among a new white hip-hop fan base as well as hip-hop's core community of black consumers. It raised the bar of social criticism and a counterhegemonic style of "blackness" in an age that witnessed hip-hop's rapid expansion into white America. The album became a gold standard for "conscious" rebel music just as N.W.A's *Straight Outta Compton*—also released in 1988—would be the gold standard for gangsta rebel music. Though both gangstas and militants would embrace a somewhat narrow notion of authenticity, they both engaged in a contest over what it meant to be "real" in hip-hop. Being a rebel lends credibility; however, the nature of that rebellion has been contested in the lyrics of scores of songs since the late 1980s. Ultimately, these disparate styles would create a fissure between conscious and gangsta music and eventually between commercial and underground hip-hop.

Rap verbal attacks (generally in a one-way direction at either gangsta or commercial artists) have characterized hip-hop since the early 1990s. But the contest over hip-hop's direction is an older phenomenon. In some respects, this contest has been about keeping hip-hop free from the control of record conglomerates and larger media companies and ostensibly closer to the community that created hip-hop. To a large extent, these exchanges have been highly political in that the art itself is often viewed as a powerful force for political education; witness BDP's *Edutainment* (1990), whose title is a neologism, representing the conflation of education and entertainment. Moreover, many artists correctly argue that this process of education is not necessarily uplifting. People can, after all, be educated to be sexist, racist, and destructive. It has become, therefore, a veritable war within the hip-hop nation to chart the culture's course and shape its social codes, ethics, and destiny.

While this struggle over hip-hop's soul has unfolded, outside critics have lambasted hip-hop for being responsible for a myriad of social ills. Several high-profile politicians, academics, journalists, and activists have held hip-hop culpable for violent crime rates, sexual irresponsibility, poor academic performance, and general social dysfunction. This chapter reveals, however, that these pundits have offered little more than recycled fear of black youth as a social danger. More specifically, anti-rap pundits have pandered to racist and class-based fear of young black people and created untenable arguments to bolster their claims. These attacks have not been ignored by the hip-hop community, which has consistently engaged in vigorous intellectual exchange over its own destiny and that of society at large.

Despite the prominence of some of these hip-hop critics, like Chuck D or KRS-One, hip-hoppers have been largely ignored during the congressional hearings, protests, and boycotts organized by anti–gangsta rap zealots. Many of these hip-hoppers have both defended their art form and attacked those whom they consider threats—external and internal—to the integrity of the art. I argue as well in this chapter that the hip-hop community widely engages in a two-tiered critique of hip-hop and the culture wars. On one front, rappers direct criticism at their hypermaterialistic, violent peers and, on another, they direct criticism at the capitalist, racist society at large that copiously glorifies overconsumption and materialism and facilitates racial subjugation. In addition, hip-hop artists attack sexism and violence in society as well as the misogynist and destructive lyrics of their peers.

Whereas some of the most outspoken critics of rap are prominent right-wingers, critics of hip-hop span a wide political spectrum. Culture-war activists such as C. Delores Tucker, William Bennett, Bill O'Reilly, John H. McWhorter, and Stanley Crouch represent a range of political expressions, not all of which are traditionally considered conservative. Moreover, the discourse cannot be reduced to debates over black cultural expression and white fears of cultural invasion. Nor can it be viewed as the hardscrabble black poor finding voice, resistance, and agency against the black middle class who frowns on "field Negro" expressions. The discourse surrounding hip-hop music is much too dynamic and complex to be simplified with political labeling or class or racial clichés. The nature of these debates is further complicated by the introduction of rappers who have offered a strident and unabashed denunciation of their hip-hop peers who have exploited and bastardized a beloved art form.

Up from the Underground

Hip-hop had its first platinum LP with Run DMC's *Raising Hell* in 1986. In late 1986 the white Beastie Boys's first release, *License to Ill*, became the first rap LP to hit number 1 on the pop charts. Successful hip-hop tours such as the Fresh Fest traveled the country and enjoyed arena booking and thousands of fans. In 1988 BET debuted "Rap City," and MTV followed by launching "Yo MTV Raps" later that year. Both shows, devoted to hip-hop, featured the most popular artists of the time and gave exposure to the genre as never before. The same year two Harvard students, David Mays and Jon Shecter, launched the *Source* out of their dorm room. A one-page hip-hop tip sheet, the endeavor was to become the first national hip-hop magazine. The hip-hop market was expanding in ways that few imagined years earlier. And though the expansion generated millions of dollars, the culture was shifting away from its festive party formulas to more rebel styles.

Extending the boundaries of popular music's standards toward being edgy and culturally rebellious, more MCs explored themes such as violence and sex and employed greater profanity in the late 1980s. In 1985, Philadelphia rapper Schoolly D released the first gangsta rap song, "P.S.K.," which stood for Park Side Killers. Unlike "The Message" (1982) by Grandmaster Flash and the Furious 5, "P.S.K." was an urban tale that offered no cautionary social message. Instead, it was a tale of crime and violence without remorse, unique in its sociopathic message. A year later L.A. rapper Ice T released "Six in the Morning," a song about a day in the life of a gangsta, complete with violence and even the physical assault of a woman. The release of N.W.A's first LP *Straight Outta Compton* in 1988 solidified the emergence of gangsta rap and its nihilistic rebelliousness. In "Gangsta Gangsta" the group celebrated its ability to engage in killing a large number of black people:

> I got a shotgun, and here's the plot
> Takin niggas out with a flurry of buckshots
> Boom boom boom, yeah I was gunnin
> And then you look, all you see is niggas runnin
> and fallin and yellin and pushin and screamin
> and cussin, I stepped back, and I kept bustin.

Balancing the exaggerated violence of N.W.A was the ubermisogyny of 2 Live Crew. In 1989, Miami-based 2 Live Crew released *As Nasty as They Wanna Be,* with the hit song "Me So Horny." In the song "The Fuck Shop," the rappers produced crude lyrics that alarmed many:

> You little whore behind closed doors
> You would drink my cum and nothing more
> Now spread your wings open for the flight
> Let me fill you up with something milky and white
> 'Cause I'm hopin' to slay you, rough and painful
> You innocent bitch, don't be shameful.

These lyrics were a departure from the general thrust of hip-hop's then-festive style; however, they were anchored in the self-aggrandizing storytelling style that had been practiced for decades in the United States.[1] These lyrics demanded that the music remained rowdy, rebellious and culturally unorthodox to young people drawn to edgy sounds.

Despite the emergence of gangsta rap, the dominant style of hip-hop was still festive rap by 1988. The dire conditions, however, of black communities shaped by rising unemployment, declining social programs, police terror, institutionalized racism, crime, and a burgeoning drug trade fomented alarm among young African Americans. The Nation of Islam's reemergence as a national force, the anti-Apartheid movement, as well as a rising popularity in black nationalism, precipitated militant hip-hop in ways that had never existed in American popular music. In 1988, New York City–based Stetsasonic released the radio hit "A.F.R.I.C.A.," which detailed the complicated and dangerous political landscape of Apartheid and South Africa's ruthless policies in Southern Africa. Public Enemy's "Night of the Living Baseheads" detailed the effects of the crack trade and political corruption and sampled Nation of Islam minister Khalid Muhammad. But, as much as dismal urban conditions contributed to the conscious rebel, the role that rap's crossover played cannot be overlooked. The emergence of these militant voices occurred simultaneously with the rise of alarm over "crossover" hip-hop.

In 1988 BET's *Rap City* and MTV's *Yo MTV Raps* exposed a much wider market to rap music and gave greater exposure to the rising tide of commercially successful rappers. These groups provided a new audience a glimpse of a new brand of festive, feel-good, party music. Within two years, however, the two most successful rappers, MC Hammer and Vanilla Ice, typified a watering down of hip-hop and commercial [white] co-optation, many argued.[2] As I discussed in Chapter 2, this fomented a racialized reaction in the form of a new, urban hip-hop expression of blackness. In some respects, this new construction aimed to stifle any co-optation of the art: it was simply "too black" to be commercial or diluted. The rebel also deflected charges of selling out. One could be multiplatinum, have a mostly white, suburban fan base, do movies, make commercial endorsements, and still not be a sellout, as witnessed by Ice Cube and Snoop Dogg's careers. But despite the "too black for co-optation" idea, the very articulation of black authenticity and rebelliousness maintained a healthy and attractive edge for young consumers. While groups like Public Enemy, BDP, and X-Clan served as prototypes for this new blackness, a competing expression took form in gangsta rap with artists like N.W.A, Ice-T, and the Geto Boys.

Ultimately, the axis of hip-hop tilted toward gangsta-dominated tropes by the mid-1990s, giving rise to a new dimension of black militant or "conscious" rap after the meteoric success of West Coast artists Dr. Dre, Ice Cube, Snoop Doggy Dogg, Tha Doggpound, Tupac, and Too $hort. All of these artists went platinum the same time East Coast artists like Brand Nubian, De La Soul, Lords of the Underground, Das EFX, and EPMD were failing to sell a million copies of any CD. The conscious rapper came to be not just critical of corrupt police, the drug trade, prisons, and duplicitous politicians but also hostile to the thugs who had come to dominate hip-hop through tales of violence, misogyny, hypermaterialism, and drug use. From Tim Dog's "Fuck Compton" (1991) to Jeru the Damaja's "Come Clean" (1994), New Yorkers attacked their West Coast gangsta counterparts as "stupid muthafuckas" or "fake gangstas" who "couldn't come to the jungles of the East poppin' that game."[3] Although the most popular image of the hip-hop rebel was no longer one wearing the African medallions and nationalist tricolor, the hostility from mainstream elements continued to take form. Record sales reflected a market more eager to embrace the axiomatic expression of ghetto fairytales of mayhem and pathology than militant narratives of subversive rebellion against white supremacy. In fact, as hip-hop expanded its market appeal, the gangsta tales would become more dominant in crossover hip-hop acts like Snoop Dogg, Dr. Dre, and Tupac, all of whom enjoyed a mostly white suburban fan base. New Yorkers revitalized themselves by adopting gangsta tropes with the most successful New York artist of 1994, the Notorious B.I.G. Others like Jay-Z, DMX, and Nas followed the thug formula with success. With a white consumer base of over 70 percent, most hip-hop fans were not warm to militant tales of white "cavemen," "troglodytes," "crackers," or "devils," as expressed by Brand Nubian, X-Clan, early Ice Cube, and Poor Righteous Teachers. Instead, "niggas," "bitches," "hos," and other derisive and implicitly black reference points had become nearly universal in commercial hip-hop.

Culture Warriors

The "culture wars," defined by Donald Mitchell as "those battles rooted in ideology, religion, class difference, the social construction of racial and ethnic and gender difference,"[4] reached a crescendo in the 1990s. In June 1995,

William J. Bennett, former drug czar of the first Bush administration and head of Empower America, an advocacy organization for "personal responsibility," and C. Delores Tucker, president of the National Congress of Black Women, publicly denounced Time Warner's involvement with "violent and misogynistic" music lyrics. The two condemned the media conglomerate's participation in "filth" that undermined the minds and morality of children.[5] That same month, the speaker of the U.S. House of Representatives, Newt Gingrich, suggested that advertisers boycott radio stations that play "vicious" music. "They could drive violent rap music off radio within weeks," Gingrich predicted.[6] Several weeks later, amid intense criticism from various politicians—most prominently, Kansas Senator Bob Dole—Time Warner announced that it had sold its 50 percent stake in Interscope Records, the label chiefly accused of promoting morally unsound gangsta rap.[7]

The campaign against socially irresponsible music, led by Tucker, Dole, and others, was an extension of the culture wars, which reached new levels of activity in the early and mid-1990s. More than any genre of music, hip-hop has felt the brunt of attack from a wide array of detractors who, for various reasons, have expressed outrage and disdain at what they consider inappropriate cultural expression. While the leading critics of the gangsta rappers gained the spotlight, many observers began to construct a monolithic view of hip-hop as an art form characterized by misogyny and violently hedonistic lyrics.[8] Some heavy-metal groups have been accused of being rap acts because they allegedly embody the violent and crude stereotypes generally associated with gangsta rappers.[9] The very diverse and complex world of hip-hop was thus reduced to a simple, one-dimensional art form devoid of serious political analysis and substantive cultural observations or social responsibility. In the midst of the culture wars surrounding hip-hop, there have remained, however, very articulate and passionate voices of criticism from within the hip-hop community. From rappers to hip-hop magazine editors, many have criticized both the violent, hyper-materialistic, sexist gangsta music and the politicians and culture critics who denounce rap music.

Although early 1990s-era rappers such as De La Soul, KRS-One, Tupac, and Digable Planets eloquently explored in their lyrics such difficult subjects as drug abuse, rape, child abuse, abortion, and even animal cruelty, many other rappers instead consistently affirmed some of the most pernicious stereotypes of hip-hop. Lyrics that glorify violence, drug dealing, and other destructive behaviors provided critics a platform for attack. As hip-hop became more ensconced in the mainstream by the mid-1990s, a nouveau riche style of gangsta rap had begun to dominate hip-hop with as much violence and misogyny as the rap of N.W.A, Ice-T, Geto Boys or Ice Cube, but with decidedly less political commentary.

Jay-Z, Lil' Kim, the Notorious B.I.G., Nas, and other rappers by the mid-1990s helped romanticize the organized crime "mafia style." Frequently dressing like classic Italian mobsters in their videos, these MCs often named themselves after famous Italian or Colombian mobsters and made earnest attempts to be down with La Cosa Nostra. Nas "Escobar" released a 1996 video, "Street Dreams," which was modeled after the 1995 hit mobster movie *Casino*. Snoop Doggy Dogg's sophomore LP was titled *The Doggfather* (1996), and, in his promotional ads, he used a lettering style identical to the movie poster for the original "The Godfather" motion picture. Foxy Brown, in her debut LP *Ill Na Na* (1996), indulged in extreme self-aggrandizement, promoting herself as "the murderess *mami*" and baby girl of the "Firm," a Mafioso-styled family that included rappers AZ and Nas. These mobster lyrics supplanted the gangsta, drive-by style that had pervaded rap between 1992 and 1995.

Jay-Z, in his first solo LP (1996), prided himself on his pimp/mafia/drug-lord style. The opening skit on *Reasonable Doubt* signifies the hip-hop film of choice, *Scarface*, where a mobster arranges a purchase of two kilos of cocaine from Colombians. He later raps about a typical gangsta highlife, complete with expensive cars, hos, and clothes, sipping fine wine and rapping with "a godfather flow." Largely considered a classic, *Reasonable Doubt* inspired scores of imitators who similarly rapped about high-end cars, fashion, "moving product," and killing enemies in order to maintain power. From Ja-Rule to 50 Cent and Rick Ross, such lyrics glorifying crime and rabid materialism have given rap critics a growing following.

Yet these nouveau-riche gangstas did not go unchallenged by their hip-hop peers. The consummate politically charged rap group, Public Enemy, released its fifth album, *Muse Sick N Hour Mess Age*, in 1994, with the strident black militancy that characterized its previous CDs. The group railed against gangsta rappers as "slaves" to the rhythm of the master for their glorification of pathology and destruction at the behest of the white power structure. In that same year, Paris, an Oakland-based rapper, unleashed a lyrical attack against studio gangsta rappers as "fake-ass wanna-bes" who have been enthralled with being gangstas, which he called a "house nigga" mentality.[10] Paris accused these gangsta rappers of being "Uncle Toms" who have been co-opted by racist record companies who could care less about antiblack rappers. Perhaps Paris's most scathing critique of gangsta rappers is his song "40 Ounces and a Fool." In this song, Paris performed an incredibly convincing impression of gangsta rap star Snoop Doggy Dogg who, in 1993, became the only new musical artist to debut at Number 1 on *Billboard*'s pop charts. Paris's pseudo-Snoop calls himself "the man with no conscience" who, with money from the record company, is on his way to the liquor store to help promote drunken debauchery to black people. Paris's parody reflects his disdain for the popularity of gangsta rap and gangsta rappers who, like Snoop, Ice Cube, and others, work for corporate America as salesmen. For example, in malt liquor commercials or in songs such as "Gin and Juice," Snoop's immensely popular song glorified drinking, driving, and smoking marijuana.

Jeru the Damaja (1996) lyrically attacked the "playas" of the rap game, whom he called "too perverted" for pushing lyrics that are "pure narcissism." Rebuking their materialistic drives, he explained that he does not drive a Lexus and does not drink Cristal or Moet; instead, he "keeps it real." The popularity of the "gangsta glam" rap is not to be taken lightly, Jeru implies. In his song "One Day," he discovers that hip-hop has been taken hostage by the opportunistic elements in the industry. In this song, Jeru sees a picture of hip-hop, anthropomorphized as a man, held hostage by a gang of hooded thugs. He can only identify Foxy Brown wearing "fake alligator boots." Bad Boy Records is the one getting hip-hop drunk. When he arrives at the offices of Bad Boy, he is informed that hip-hop has been taken to Los Angeles where Suge Knight, chief executive officer of Death Row Records, will only turn him over to a "real nigga." Jeru retrieves hip-hop the next day.

Many other artists have been equally vitriolic about the rise of hyper-materialistic elements in hip-hop. In fact, to read a list of these artists is to read the who's who of late 1990s underground hip-hop: Mos Def, Common, Jurassic 5, J-Live, the High and Mighty, Blackalicious, the Arsonists, and the Last Emperor.

The Roots, a Philadelphia-based rap group that performs with a live band, unleashed a barrage of rhymes criticizing the gaudy fantasy world of some rappers in their sophomore LP, *illadelph halflife* (1996). In the video

Common has been a political force, lyrical master, and underground hero who has enjoyed critical praise and media exposure, but never a platinum album.

for "What They Do," The Roots parodied the ubiquitous materialism of rappers. With a tip of the hat to De La Soul (who produced a similar video for "Ego Trippin' [Part Two]" in 1994 and performed a cameo in the video), The Roots derided the make-believe world of their peers. The video opens with a shot of a mansion, with a caption that reads, "The Goldstein estate, day rental." In one scene, the lead rapper sits on a bed with three beautiful women. "Yeah, right," the screen reads. Sitting in front of high-priced automobiles, the caption asks, "Can we afford this?"[11]

A Tribe Called Quest (1996) also offered rebuke of these exponents of conspicuous consumption in their LP, *Beats, Rhymes and Life:*

Hip-hop acts posing like fat cats
Lex and the Rolex, Moet and the top hat
Its time to turn the tables on this hip-hop fable
Gat-pulling MCs can never come near
Ninety per cent of all you suckas have filthy LPs 'bitch' this, 'trick' that
Come on, act like you know
I'm that MC who never chose to play the down low.[12]

In the summer of 1996, De La Soul in "Stakes Is High" (1996) also jumped into the fray: "It seems like every man and woman shares the life of John Gotti." Disgusted, they declared that they were "sick of Versace glasses and name brand clothes / sick of swollen-head rappers with their sicker-than raps."[13]

Whereas some artists, like De La Soul and Public Enemy, have consistently provided social and political commentary in their music, others have offered a conspicuously conflictive bundle of messages and imagery in their musical approach. No major artist has straddled social responsibility and glorification of pathology better than Los Angeles–based rapper Ice Cube. Moreover, Ice Cube has been one of the more visible characters in the ongoing culture wars by engaging in spirited and highly controversial disputes on wax. Ice Cube emerged in the late 1980s as a writer and rapper for the pioneering gangsta rap group N.W.A. After his break from the group in 1989, he impressed rap fans nationwide with his platinum debut solo album, *Amerikkka's Most Wanted* (1990). In this album, he addresses several social maladies, including institutionalized racism in law enforcement and sexual irresponsibility, though his strong misogynistic themes remained.

After he came under the influence of the Nation of Islam, Ice Cube's second full-length CD, *Death Certificate* (1991), came closest to a pro-black position that did not denigrate women. His CD, which was the first rap CD to debut at Number 1 on *Billboard*'s pop chart, is divided into the "Death Side" and the "Life Side." The former is the epitome of black people's confusion and ignorance, replete with drug dealing, violence, misogyny, and all sorts of criminal and self-destructive behavior. The "Life Side," however, is "where black people need to go." On this side, he implores black people to resist being co-opted by their oppressors in "True to the Game." He criticizes black people for partaking in their own oppression in "Us," offering a classic Nation of Islam–styled vilification of black people for careless and irresponsible behavior. In "Black Korea," he discusses the tensions between the black and Korean communities in Los Angeles. If these tensions are not mitigated, warns Cube, these Asian-owned stores could be "burned to a crisp." This is not the only song that eerily predicts the Los Angeles Rebellion that would occur a year later. In "I Wanna Kill Sam" and "Horny Lil Devil," he blasts white America for, among other things, kidnapping, enslaving, raping, and oppressing black people for centuries. With such continuous oppression, he warns, listeners should get ready for "Watts Riot, 1991." A year later, Los Angeles exploded, and Ice Cube created a fascinating look at the L.A. Rebellion on his 1992 CD, *The Predator*. Cube's (1992) third CD covered the L.A. Rebellion on four songs and included a sample from an interview with a reporter where Cube explains that, if one studied the Ice Cube "library," he or she would notice Cube's warning regarding the rebellion. On *The Predator*, he blasted his critics, including *Billboard* magazine, which offered an unprecedented denunciation of an LP. *Billboard* charged that *Death Certificate* contained remarks offensive to Jews after a song where Cube offers a verbal assault against his former group N.W.A and its white Jewish manager, Jerry Heller: "How can you call yourselves 'niggas for life,' crew? / with a white Jew telling you what to do?" Being the quintessential gangsta, Ice Cube (1992) responded to his critics bluntly: "Fuck *Billboard* and the editor." Cube's disregard of allegations that he is anti-Semitic and anti-Korean were further demonstrated on an inserted sample from an actual interview in which an interviewer asked Cube about these charges. "Fuck 'em," is the answer, actually sampled from another song, leaving the listener to ponder how Cube really answered the allegations.

Certainly Ice Cube engages in serious social and political commentary and expresses pro-black positions. Yet, throughout his LP, Cube maintains misogynistic styles. In "Don't Trust 'em" Cube warns that "you can't trust no bitch." Women may sexually entice men with the insidious intention of robbery or murder, he warns. Even in the liner notes, he acknowledges "white America's continued commitment to the silence and oppression of black men" and America's cops' "systematic and brutal killings of brothers all over the country." Women (activists or not) who have experienced state-sponsored repression are conspicuously absent. The memory of women killed by the police, such as Eula Mae Love and Eleanor Bumpers, is also absent. So, too, is the memory of black women activists such as Angela Davis, Assata Shakur, Ericka Huggins, and Fanny Lou Hamer.

It is clear that Cube employs a narrow view of black liberation. In essence, it advocates the liberation of black men, not black people. His incessant use of misogynist lyrics and dismissal of women as agents of resistance to oppression are palpable. At the same time, Cube teases his listeners with bits of gender consciousness by proclaiming that he has a black woman for a manager, "not in the kitchen."[14] In 1991, he invited female rapper Yo Yo to a verbal challenge of his sexism. In "It's a Man's World," she criticized him for his wide use of sexist lyrics and, while battling him on the mic, challenged his manhood, even questioning the size of his penis. Whereas Yo Yo presented herself as the "intelligent black woman" who resists sexist lyrics and even challenges the manhood of misogynist rappers, her feminist rhetoric was couched in caustic discourse with Ice Cube, an unabashed male chauvinist. Cube's studio persona ostensibly represents the narrow-minded sexist; however, Cube produced Yo Yo, invited her on his LP, and provided an arena of artistic discourse that would offer a challenge to his lyrics from the vantage of a feminist position. The irony is clear.

Artists such as Ice Cube represent an intimate look at societal pathologies through the construction of first-person narrative. Ice Cube exemplifies what Robin D. G. Kelley explains is rap's fictive badman style, which cultivates outlandish tales of bravado as a stylistic gesture of mic control and artistry. It is not to be taken literally.[15] It is, rather, an effort to outdo any competitor who may attempt to be the toughest on the mic. It is popularly known that in his personal life, Ice Cube divorces himself from his studio gangsta alter ego. In reality, O'Shea Jackson lives in a wealthy, mostly white neighborhood, in a gated home, with his wife and three children. He comes from a two-parent home in a middle-class residential area of South Central Los Angeles; he has never been in prison; he graduated from Taft High School, the wealthiest high school in the Los Angeles Unified School District; and he immediately went to college. He left college to pursue his music career with N.W.A in 1988.[16] Ice Cube, as sexist gangsta rapper, assumes a carefully contrived studio persona. His real-life identity as a law-abiding, millionaire producer, actor, and director, with a black woman manager, provides a challenge to his own artistic expression.

Rappers, as noted above, are not the only ones in the hip-hop community who are at once critical of both anti-rap crusaders and the gangsta glam hedonism of some artists. Every major hip-hop magazine has voiced opposition to the popularization of drugs, misogyny, and drinking that pervades rap. Selwyn S. Hinds (1997), music editor of the *Source,* the most successful music magazine in monthly newsstand sales, wrote an open letter to C. Delores Tucker offering a critique of her campaign against "scarecrows" in the hip-hop industry. Hinds explains that "our culture reveres figures of violence" such as military heroes or fictional action heroes. Although he admits that music has the power to influence behavior, he argues that deeper issues than Snoop Dogg's lyrics cause violence. He does not support misogynist music, but he encourages his writers to critique it. He blasts Tucker for "morally condescend[ing] when the cameras beckon." Moreover, she fails to "acknowledge that misogyny is a sickness that has plagued America for all 200 plus years of her existence, not simply the last 10 or so dominated by hip-hop." In the final analysis, he writes, "I find you both worrisome and confusing" as a "private citizen embarking on a witch hunt" under a "veil of righteousness" that is unable to disguise a troubling "hypocrisy."[17]

External Attacks

Conservative political commentator and former Supreme Court nominee Robert H. Bork emerged as an outspoken critic of rap music in 1996 when he asserted that rap is a reflection of the moral declension of the United States. Rap, he claimed, helps push America "towards Gomorrah": "It is difficult to convey just how debased rap is," he noted. He blamed the popularity of such "degenerate" music on "modern liberalism," which is enamored of "radical individualism" and other values that are fundamentally hostile to American freedom.[18]

For anti-rap crusaders like Bork, rap is a monolithic genre of crude "noise with a beat," little more than a "knuckle-dragging sub-pidgin of grunts and snarls, capable of fully expressing only the more pointless forms of violence and the more brutal forms of sex."[19] His insistence that rap lyrics are witless diatribes of barbarism reflects his ignorance of the music or a disingenuous agenda. In fact, many rap songs grapple with issues of contention in society, imploring listeners to assume greater social responsibility.[20]

Such crude lyrics provided arsenal for those who, like Bob Dole and C. Delores Tucker, attack gangsta rap. In a May 1995 speech, presidential candidate Bob Dole blasted similar lyrics and record companies for promoting such music. These companies, Dole argued, must be attacked for the "marketing of evil through commerce." He condemned businesses that benefit "from extolling the pleasures of raping, torturing and mutilating women, from songs about killing policemen and rejecting law."[21] While Dole centered much of his attack on record companies (mainly Time Warner) for promoting gangsta rap, Tucker emerged as an outspoken critic of individual rappers as well as their companies.

For Tucker, the artists bear the brunt of the responsibility for such lyrics. A leader of a women's organization, the National Congress of Black Women, she has been particularly sensitive to antiwoman lyrics.[22] In 1995, she warned that the sexist violence in these songs should not be dismissed. Sexist and violent gangsta rap, she insisted, has produced a cultural standard of cool among youth that glorifies criminality: "The rap talks about the life in the ghetto and makes it sound so good and so real," Tucker explained. "It puts people in the position of the gangster. Everyone accepts it and puts themselves in the video because of the misconception that [being a gangster] is the only way to be somebody."[23] Tucker has not equivocated on her stance that gangsta rap breeds self-destruction among the youth who listen: "[Children] are walking time bombs and gangsta rap is the origin of these time bombs. They are recruiting more and more young children. The cost to community is just too great."[24]

In defense of their art, some rappers directly addressed Dole and Tucker in their songs. In the tradition of rappers who are critical of the typical, unimaginative, and simplistic lyrics of the average MC, Ras Kass released his first CD (1996) with a mission to imbue hip-hop with higher levels of consciousness and creative dexterity. Writing his lyrics in the midst of the fierce attacks on hip-hop and increased social-program cutbacks initiated by the 104th Congress, Ras Kass introduced some astute observations of politics and music. He inveighed against the simple-minded gangsta rapper but simultaneously acknowledged the market for such rappers. Though radio stations and video programmers are also culpable, true lyricists in hip-hop are ignored by the public because listeners cannot relate, he said. "Elevating," he complained, is treated like "elevator music." Despite his efforts to introduce a substantive discussion of politics backed by impressive rhymes and beats, the simple lyrics about killing, pimping, and drug selling invariably win a larger crowd. Mediocrity, he insists, is his nemesis, but "ridicule is the burden of genius." The industry, he explained, is part of the larger capitalist order, which is a game of "pimps and hoes." Money, not moral responsibility, makes the world go around.

Despite his cynical look at the politics of hip-hop, Ras Kass displayed his unyielding appreciation for it throughout his CD. In fact, his love of hip-hop inspired his attempt to salvage it and defend it against its detractors whose sincerity he doubts. Calling out Dole and Tucker, he warned that he was not scared of their attacks. What the world needs, he argued, is less "free cheese" and more white-collar jobs. He also criticized their emphasis on gangsta rap while "white powder" brokers were "getting over." Here, Ras Kass criticized the inequities of the justice system in meting out punishment for drug-related offenses. Crack convicts—mostly black—automatically receive much harsher sentences than those who convicted for possession of similar amounts of powder cocaine, who are mostly white.[25] Cocaine, of course, is needed to produce crack. Ras Kass's lyrics also reflect his disdain for political pundits who assume the role of moral crusaders but do little to address the fundamental causes of gangsta rap lyrics or who are reticent to address other types of injustice in society. As he observed, people would rather work than receive welfare, if given the opportunity. But note that Ras Kass specifies the desire for jobs that provide livable wages, not entry-level positions at fast-food restaurants. In a similar vein, female rapper Yo Yo explained that "rappers are a product of America. Attack the world rappers live in, not the words they use to describe it."[26]

The most controversial rapper of the mid-1990s, Tupac Shakur, caught the ire of many anti–gangsta rap exponents before his death in a drive-by shooting in 1996. One of the most successful rappers in the industry, Tupac

Shakur was a complicated rebel who, like Ice Cube, straddled the worlds of black nationalist resistance and nihilistic thuggery. By his fourth CD, *All Eyez on Me,* Tupac's political fervor had dropped off considerably from that in his first CD, *2Pacalypse Now* (1991). Still, he was keen on offering social commentaries to the public. In 1996 he blasted C. Delores Tucker for trying to "destroy" him. That same year he stated that President Bill Clinton and Senator Dole were too old to understand the complexities of the "rap game." Tupac implied that the generational chasm is one cause of the misunderstanding of hip-hop on the part of anti–gangsta rap crusaders: "If these people actually cared about protecting the children like they say they do, they'd spend more time trying to improve the conditions in the ghettos where the kids are coming up," Shakur said of Tucker, Dole, and others.[27]

While these conservatives blamed rappers for causing violence, KRS-One reminded them that "America was violent before rap." This rather obvious observation seems to have been lost on critics who appear to create to a "those-were-the-days" myth of yesteryear good times. Compared to the history of the initial invasions of North America by Europeans in the sixteenth century, through wars against Indians, over two hundred years of brutal slavery, another hundred years of mob violence in cities, lynching, terrorism, and codified white supremacy, Bork's complaint that rap brings America closer to barbarism appears absurdly comical. In fact, in 1996, the year that Bork made claims about violence and rap music, the national homicide rate was 24 percent lower than when the first rap song was played on the radio.[28] Not beholden to the facts, Bork offered only the most visceral yelps of alarm about the new black art form, warning of a profound cultural threat to the larger social order.

The New Danger of the Twenty-First Century

Following the 1996 presidential election, the culture wars declined in visibility. Though MCs were becoming more vocal critics of their gangsta peers as commercial hip-hop styles constricted into total gangsta styles, external attacks were not as visible until Eminem's meteoric rise. In fact, perhaps no individual rapper has been as maligned by as many cultural crusaders as Eminem. Criticized by various groups for sexist and homophobic lyrics, Eminem endured protests and pickets after his first commercial release, *The*

Slim Shady LP (1999). Sued by various family members and others, Eminem had become a unique bad-boy rapper who developed a style that was self-effacing, rebellious, and comically surreal. Despite his offensive lyrics, Eminem responded to his (mostly white) attackers by accusing them of racism. In his highly political "White America" (2002), he correctly pointed out that he is far from being the first homophobic or sexist rapper. To be sure, it is conspicuous that organizations found Eminem cause for alarm when artists from underground/conscious types like Common, Black Star, Ras Kass, to commercial or thug rappers like Jay-Z, Nas, Lil Jon, or 50 Cent have universally employed homophobic lyrics and most have referred to women as bitches and hos. Ultimately, these lyrics were less a problem for critics like Tipper Gore and Lynne Cheney until whites began listening to the songs, Eminem insists.

Displaying a particular sensitivity to the power of race in cultural politics, Eminem insisted that these attacks as well as his success were partially due to his being white: "If I was black, I woulda sold half." Inasmuch as Eminem's being white brings attention to him, various majority white activist groups saw Eminem as one of their own in ways that they did not view DMX, who similarly uses "faggot" or "bitch": "See the problem is / I speak to suburban kids . . . who look just like me."[29] Fundamentally, white America sees Eminem as one of its own and implicitly expects different behavior from him. Other multiplatinum artists such as Tupac, 50 Cent, DMX, and the Notorious B.I.G. have constructed rhymes that appear as vulgar, if not more so, than those of Eminem. The Notorious B.I.G.'s crass lyrics on "Ready to Die" (1994), "Dead Wrong" (1996), and "Niggas Bleed" (1997) are, in effect, less offensive because such pathological expressions are virtually expected from the black ghetto, where pathology is assumed to be a veritable norm. The outcry at Eminem must be read as more than the power of verse. It is, at its most fundamental level, a visceral display of the shifting nature of racial discourse in the arena of cultural politics and the cultural wars. Eminem demonstrates profound insight when he details the "hypocrisy" of white America in its reaction to him and his art.

Further contradictions are evident in the conflict between conservative Fox News journalist Bill O'Reilly and rapper Ludacris. In 2002 O'Reilly publicly denounced an endorsement deal between Atlanta-based rapper Ludacris and Pepsi. Calling Ludacris a "thug," O'Reilly encouraged his listeners to petition Pepsi to drop the rapper. Shortly after the anti-Ludacris campaign, Pepsi dropped the artist. Hip-hoppers pointed to the clear in-congruence with the television host's reticence on the sex and violence on his own network or with the music recorded by Ozzy Osborne who also inked an endorsement deal with Pepsi around the same time as Ludacris.[30] When O'Reilly settled a sexual harassment lawsuit from a subordinate co-worker in 2004 who reportedly had taped recording of O'Reilly engaged in graphic talk of sex, Ludacris responded, "I'd be lying if I didn't say it brings a smile to my face. These are words that I say and this mother f**ker is say-ing the same words that I say and is criticizing me?"[31] Like other rappers, Ludacris managed to mock his critic in his hit song "The Number One Spot" (2004) telling O'Reilly by name to "kiss the plaintiff and the wifey."

Beyond endorsement deals, other critics have joined a general conversa-tion accusing hip-hop of fomenting dangerous and irresponsible behavior and undermining civilization itself. Conservative cultural critic Bernard Goldberg argues that not only is gangsta rap "ignorant [and] soul-deadening," it is "tearing down" America.[32] Others have focused on the spe-cial danger that hip-hop represents to black people.

(Black) Barbarians at the Gate

One of the most vitriolic critics of hip-hop is John H. McWhorter, who sees African American culture as being crippled by a special "separatist" and "victimology" sensibility that finds origin in the Black Power movement of the 1960s.[33] Black people have, he argues, embraced "defeatist" notions that undermine their very desire and will to excel: "If you look at what black people considered important to talk about 75 years ago, they were inter-ested in talking about progress and uplift and what they could achieve de-spite the obstacles," he notes.[34] Currently, McWhorter claims, nothing rep-resents the disruption of the black community's core values of uplift more than hip-hop. Sounding similar to critics who attacked jazz as dangerous "jungle music" leading to the likes of marijuana smoking and rape, McWhorter fumes over rap music that "is seriously harmful to the black community." Unlike the inspirational music created by African Americans until the 1970s, McWhorter laments, "hip-hop creates nothing."[35] As evi-dence of this danger he refers to his seeing a group of young black males in Harlem who had "rap ingrained in their consciousness" as displayed in their "antisocial" behavior. He insists that, "by reinforcing the stereotypes that long hindered blacks, and by teaching young blacks that a thuggish adversarial stance is the properly 'authentic' response to a presumptively racist society, rap retards black success."[36] Like the dozens of other anti-rap critics, McWhorter fails to offer any evidence of hip-hop danger beyond his empirical example from Harlem and general references to lackluster academic performance, which is conveniently never measured against any historical baseline. Are readers to believe that prior to hip-hop there were no groups of crude young men who were adversarial to authority? Was there no black-white academic achievement gap before hip-hop or Black Power?

For McWhorter, hip-hop grows from the same terrible, miserable historical moment and political/cultural impulse that gave the world Muhammad Ali, Kwanzaa, and African American Studies: the Black Power era. He conjures tales of bygone days of the good life characterized by black responsibility, moral awareness, hard work, family values, and peaceful living. The black protest era, he bemoans, "spelled the demise of old standards of responsibility." Instead, the black freedom movement gave rise to those who celebrated what he terms "hating whitey for its own sake." This, in turn, led to black people burning down "their own neighborhoods as gestures of being 'fed up.'"[37] He fails to mention that most of these cases of civil unrest were the immediate responses to police brutality against the black community. For him, it was simply blind hatred and defiance to well-meaning and honest white police officers.

Ultimately white people—the "do-gooder" liberal ones—also share culpability for black failure, he explains. The 1960s liberalism and the welfare state have affected black behavior so much that young black females in the twenty-first century "had babies in their teens because there was no reason not to with welfare waiting to pick up the tab." Again, McWhorter conspicuously provides no data to substantiate his argument that black teens have actually increased rates of childbirth since the mean ole liberals bamboozled black folks in the 1960s.[38]

By making broad historical references to create straw men to apologize for white supremacy, McWhorter conveniently obfuscates our understanding of the complexities of class, race, and their relationship with hip-hop. McWhorter's terribly ahistorical ramblings invent a fictive world of Black America before the civil rights movement that really was not as warm and romantic as he would lead us to believe. America was no bastion of freedom and fairness. Millions of Americans were not allowed to vote in 1950. They were not allowed to serve on juries, run for office, be Southern law-enforcement officers, or attend any flagship public university in the South. In decrepit and terribly underfunded schools, millions of children languished in hostile school systems that treated black people's history as they treated black children: with contempt and antipathy. In no school system were student expenditures or resources ever found to be equal between white and black schools. White schools always received more. Black people lived in an incredibly hostile climate that saw them as a "problem," not as fellow citizens privy to the same rights, respect, and freedoms enjoyed by whites.[39]

But African American critics of hip-hop are not confined to the right. Perhaps no comments about the plight of the hip-hop generation have been as controversial and publicized as those of a May 2004 National Association for the Advancement of Colored People (NAACP) gala speech from comedian Bill Cosby. Among other things, Cosby posited a decline in values among African Americans, leading to crime, high school dropouts, and teen pregnancy. Also condemning the popular hip-hop fashion of baggy, low-hanging pants, Cosby lamented a lost generation: "You wouldn't know that anybody had done a damned thing [during the Civil Rights movement]. Fifty percent drop out rate, I'm telling you, and people in jail, and women having children by five, six different men." Unlike the years' of Cosby's youth, black children of today have little healthy family structure, he insisted to applause and laughter. "In the old days," he noted, "you couldn't hooky school because every drawn shade was an eye."[40]

Clarence Page, a syndicated columnist, agrees with McWhorter and Cosby when he writes that a 2004 study on low-income black youth finds troubling evidence that hip-hop negatively influences young people by promoting a narrow and problematic notion of black authenticity: "The standards of 'black authenticity' promulgated in hip-hop culture are not only too narrow but downright dangerous." Page insists that prior to the Black Power movement's demands to be "authentic," black people did not dichotomize blackness and social or educational responsibility. "The 'authentic black,'" he writes, "came to define a person who did not 'sell out' to bourgeois middle-class standards, the same values that enabled our families to prepare us for college in the first place."[41] Similarly disturbed by the threat that hip-hop poses for the survival of black people, Juan Williams expresses exasperation at the damaging effects of the art on black youth: "The real question is how one does battle with the culture of failure that is poisoning young people—and do so without incurring the wrath of critics who say we are closing our eyes to existing racial injustice and are 'blaming the victim.'"[42] Bob Herbert likewise warns of the deleterious consequences of hip-hop on American society. When four aspiring Boston hip-hop artists were murdered in December 2005, he noted that they were "among the latest victims of the profoundly self-destructive cultural influences that have spread like a cancer through much of the black community and beyond." Joining Page, McWhorter, Williams, and other journalists who blame hip-hop for crime, educational failure, and general pathology, Herbert refers to soul legend Sam Cooke for inspiration: "I'll paraphrase Sam Cooke: A change has got to come. Reasonable standards of behavior that include real respect for life, learning and the law have to be re-established in those segments of the black community where chaos now reigns."[43]

Herbert's use of Sam Cooke speaks to the profound generational divide that characterizes much of the criticism found among most African Americans engaged in these culture wars. Cooke and his era of soul music represented a sentimental value for the generation before hip-hop. In the memory of that generation, the 1950s and 1960s represent an era of public respectability, restraint, values, and moral sensibilities that extolled education, work, community, and family. Hip-hop, in contrast, represents sexual irresponsibility, criminal behavior, disrespect, and anti-intellectualism. In essence, it endorses and foments a culture of failure. Herbert joins others in conveniently avoiding the data that show that, by many measures, the hip-hop generation is actually quantifiably better off than any other generation of black folk, including those of Sam Cooke's era.[44]

Cosby, Williams, Tucker, and Page represent an older generation of African Americans (all were born before 1955) who matured before the advent of hip-hop, never attending high school parties with the hottest MCs who were spitting rhymes over a booming sound system. The ominous piano riff from BDP's "The Bridge Is Over," Pete Rocks's horn sample from "T.R.O.Y.," or Biggie's "Big Poppa" most likely represent nothing sentimental for them. They did not have the sonic backdrop of hip-hop to remind them of their first dates, parties, concerts, graduation, prom, or other milestones in life, the way African Americans born after 1965 did. Their cultural distance from hip-hop may complicate their ability to find special sympathy for the art, even as they are confronted with some of its most vulgar elements. But for the hip-hop generation, critics like Kevin Powell, W. Jelani Cobb, Joan Morgan, Davey D, and Bakari Kitwana attempt to find space for the art's redemption, even as they critique it. As Chris Rock says, "As much as I love hip-hop, it is becoming harder to defend." But many do, and one way to do that is to examine the data. How does hip-hop undermine the quality of life for black youth? What proof do these critics use? Some argue that studies have found that exposure to violent rap music has been found to negatively influence perceptions of black people.[45] But even violent rap music cannot explain away the vast institutional structures of white supremacy that pervade America.

While Williams, Page, and Herbert have openly acknowledged the structural forces of racism, for McWhorter and other conservatives, structural racism simply has no real power over black folk, who are simply enthralled with proving their racial sincerity through victimhood. To them, hip-hop only makes matters worse. Never mind that when education is controlled for, whites outearn blacks, Latinos, and Asians from high school dropouts to college graduates and professional-degree holders. Ignore Department of Justice data that reveal that whites get more lenient sentencing as first-time offenders for the same crimes as blacks and Latinos in every region of the country. Disregard the fact that white males are grossly overrepresented at the upper echelons of newsrooms, corporate boards, judgeships, and other professional arenas of power. Ignore studies that show that with identical job applications those with "white names" are 50 percent more likely to get a call back than those with "black names." Patterns of discrimination are also found in home loans, police traffic stops, police shootings of unarmed citizens, and medical treatment. You will not hear McWhorter, or right-wingers like Michelle Malkin or Armstrong Williams talk about these pervasive patterns of discrimination, which reflect the intractable nature of racism that undoubtedly affects the quality of black life. Instead, McWhorter insists that any lack of equality is a result of black people's culture, white liberals, and agitators who "destroyed the survival skills poor black communities had maintained since the end of slavery."[46] Conservatives are known for their apologist positions that defend a system that has never been a meritocracy. What is particularly fascinating about McWhorter is his clumsy use of history to make his argument.

The Hip-Hop Generation: Young, Educated, and Black

There is no doubt that black people are disproportionately poor, are in prison, or achieve academically below that of whites. But despite the alarms of those who argue that commercial hip-hop's pathological messages have deleteriously affected black people on any macro level, *there is no evidence.* In fact, if one looks at life expectancy, income, educational attainment, poverty rates, teenage birthrate, and infant mortality rates, *the hip-hop generation is the most affluent generation of black people in U.S. history.*[47] When the twentieth century came to a close in 2000 the annual average unemployment rate for black people dropped to a historic low of 7.6 percent. Home ownership, education, and income were the highest on record. The poverty rate for African Americans was the lowest in history. The poverty rate for African Americans—which in 2006 stood a few points higher than its 2000 historic low—at 24.4 percent is twice that of the national average. It is, however, significantly lower than the 41.8 percent of 1965, an era that existed before McWhorter laments the leftists who "encouraged the worst in human nature among blacks and even fostered it in legislation" with welfare.[48] His let-them-fend-for-themselves agenda is the worst kind of conservatism, one that results in the sort of extreme poverty, squalor, and despair that were more pervasive before the expansion of the welfare state. But, more important, he intimates that a welfare state that cares for society's most needy is mutually exclusive with personal responsibility by inventing a mythic past of relative comfort.

The most striking data for the soothsayers of doom centers on educational achievement and black people. Despite the declarations from critics that insist that hip-hop (or affirmative action) has dumbed down black youth with "anti-intellectualism" and fear of being called white, African Americans in the hip-hop generation are the most educated generation of black people in U.S. history. When the first hip-hop video was produced in 1979–1980, the black graduation rate from high school hovered at slightly over 70 percent. After the production of thousands of rap songs, videos, dozens of hood movies, and millions of pairs of baggy jeans sold, the rate for African Americans between eighteen and twenty-four years of age who earned a high school diploma or equivalency degree stood at a record 85.6 percent, compared to 91 percent for whites and 65.7 percent for Latinos. Interestingly enough, only a month after Cosby's 2004 speech at the NAACP convention, a U.S. Census report offered this headline about high school graduation rates compiled from the Department of Education: "Non-Hispanic White and Black Graduates at Record Levels."[49] Similar gains were made in higher education. From 1985, with the release of Run DMC's *King of Rock* album, to 2004 the number of African Americans earning four-year bachelor's degrees more than doubled. As a percentage of all bachelor degrees, the increase was from 5.9 percent to 9.4 percent in the same period. From the year the first hip-hop DJ, Kool Herc, turned five in 1960 to Kanye West's multiplatinum *College Dropout* in 2004, there was more than a six-fold increase in the percentage of blacks with college degrees. In 2004 a higher percentage of African Americans earned law, medical, and other professional and graduate degrees than any point in history. The number of black people who earned doctorates doubled between the release of N.W.A's *Straight Outta Compton* in 1988 to 2005, when their Compton homeboy The Game released his multiplatinum debut album, *The Documentary.* More specifically, African Americans represented 7.1 percent of all doctorates earned by U.S. citizens in 2004; this is the highest rate in history—and a 9 percent increase over the previous record year, 2003. Although black women are well over half of blacks in college, 2004 was a record year in the enrollment of black men as well. Simply put, though the historic gap between black and white educational attainments remains, as of spring 2006, it is the smallest in history.[50]

Similar data dispel notions that hip-hop's incredibly violent lyrical landscape actually foments real violence in the lived experience of African American (or other) youth. Violent crimes such as murder, rape, and assault, as well as robbery and arson, declined among whites and blacks as rap lyrics became more violent in the 1990s. In fact, the black-on-black murder rate has plummeted since the release of the first hit rap song in 1979. When the decidedly nonviolent festive party song "Rapper's Delight" hit airwaves in 1979, there were 37.5 black homicide victims per 100,000 black people in the United States. Over 90 percent were killed by other blacks. In 2004, after twenty years of gangsta rap and thousands of references to killing "niggas" in hip-hop, the black homicide rate plunged over 45 percent to 19.7 per 100,000. In New York City in 1990, at the height of the conscious or party rhymes of Public Enemy, Brand Nubian, Digital Underground, EPMD and A Tribe Called Quest, 2,262 people were murdered; most were black and Latino males.[51] By the time raps about killing and misogyny had become

Figure 4.1. Number of African Americans Earning Master's Degrees, 1985–2004

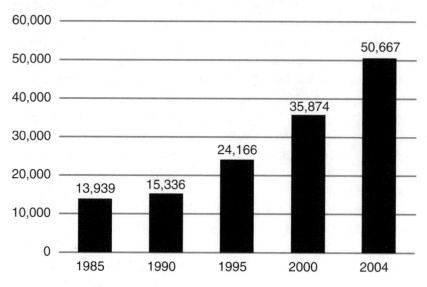

Source: U.S. Department of Education.

standard in hip-hop and super thug 50 Cent narrowly missed the mark of having the most successful album of 2005 (settling for second place, after Mariah Carey), the number of people murdered in New York City fell a staggering 75 percent to 539, a rate similar to that city's murder rate in 1963.[52] Most dramatic of all is that the black homicide victim rate in 2004 is actually lower than any rate going back at least to the 1940s.[53] The fact is that, not only do they graduate at higher rates than those in the teen years of Cosby, Page, and Herbert, black people are safer now than when Cosby et al. were teenagers. Though not as dramatic, the national rate of reported cases of forcible rape dropped 14 percent from 36.8 victims per 100,000 in 1980 to 31.7 in 2005.[54] This is not solely attributed to higher arrest rates, since young people (those twelve-to-eighteen year olds coming of age and not already in jail) also committed less crime across the country. Violent crime among those between twelve and eighteen years of age dropped 50 percent from 1992 to 2000.[55]

Despite the highly sexualized lyrics of hip-hop, the black birth rate for fifteen-to-nineteen year olds in 2004 was the lowest in the more than fifty years in which records have been kept. In fact, they dropped more than a

Figure 4.2. Homicide Offending Rates per 100,000 People, 1980–2000

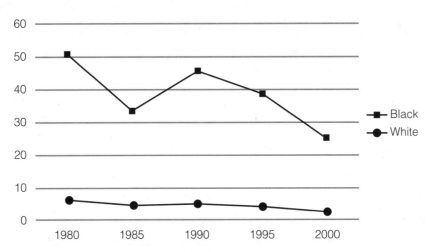

Source: Homicide Trends in the U.S. (Washington, D.C.: Bureau of Justice Statistics, 2004); http://www.ojp.usdoj.gov/bjs/homicide/tables/oracetab.htm.

third since 1980, when Lil' Kim was just entering kindergarten. Black infant mortality has also reached its lowest rate on record.[56] Despite Cosby's complaint about the rise of rates of unwed black women and "having children by five, six different men," nonmarital births among black women have dropped to a record low in 2004, 67.2 per 1,000 births. In contrast, the rates were 95.5 and 81.1 in 1970 and 1980, respectively.[57]

Although commercial hip-hop is marked by incredibly misogynistic lyrics, the most ambitious recent study of African American youth found that young black males express less chauvinistic opinions than other males in the study. The University of Chicago–based study, "The Black Youth Project," released in 2007, found that among black, white, and Latino males, black males are more likely to believe that men and women should equally share childcare and household work. Black males were second only to black females in believing that "there is a lot of discrimination against women in this country." In fact, African American and Latino men—at 36 percent and 37 percent, respectively—were significantly more likely to believe that women face a lot of sexism. White males endorsed this statement at a rate of 7 percent. At 74 percent, young black males were also most likely among males to believe that hip-hop videos "portray black women in bad or offensive ways."[58]

Figure 4.3. Births to 15–19-Year-Old Females, per 100,000 Females

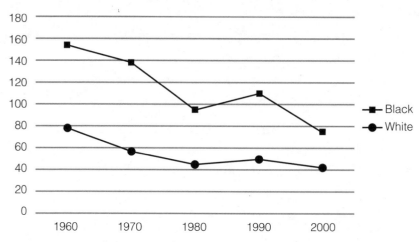

Source: National Center for Health Statistics, Table 3. Crude Birth Rates, Fertility Rates, and Birth Rates by Age of Mother, According to Race and Hispanic Origin: United States, Selected Years 1950–2000, *Health United States, 2004 with Chartbook on Trends in the Health of Americans* (Washington, D.C.: Government Printing Officer, 2004), 109; ftp://ftp.cdc.gov/pub/Health_Statistics/NCHS/Publications/Health_US/hus04tables/Table003.xls.

Finally, though hip-hop has been denounced as a cause of black youth irresponsibility and disengagement from education and even civil involvement, black political participation for eighteen-to-twenty-nine year olds has also reached record highs. In 2004, hip-hop mogul Diddy initiated the "Vote or Die" campaign to encourage electoral participation among young Americans. While the voting rate increases were starkly high for all youth voters, these increases were led by black voters who produced the largest increase in turnout among any group. In fact, their turnout rate was second only to whites by a thin 2.5 percent—49.5 percent to 47 percent of white and black citizens respectively. While 2004 was relatively successful, eighteen-to-twenty-nine-year-old black voters voted at higher rates in the 2002 midterm elections than any similar black age cohort in U.S. history. In fact, African American young people were more likely to vote in 2002 than young adults of any other race or ethnic group in the country.[59]

These findings, of course, confirm that hip-hop generation African Americans are not nearly as gullible, impressionable, or uncritical as critics imply. Nor are they rejecting the standards of earlier generations in favor of

This cartoon ridicules the hip-hop generation of African American youth as materialistic and uninterested in voting and civic involvement. Yet only a few weeks before this cartoon was published, African Americans between the ages of 18 and 24 voted at rates higher than whites, Latinos, and Asians of the same age cohort.

barbarism. At the most basic level, these data reveal that the detractors of hip-hop have denounced the vulgarity of rap as socially dangerous without any real evidence. In fact, there is a direct negative correlation with the rates of homicide, teenage pregnancy, and violent, hypersexual lyrics in hip-hop and a positive one with educational attainment.[60] This does not mean, of course, that ambition, personal responsibility, or educational performance among young black folk cannot be improved. Indeed, these data are not mutually exclusive with this proposition, any more than discussing the presence of structural racism is mutually exclusive with endorsing hard work or personal responsibility. But what is significant about these data is that, while they are encouraging, they also confirm the disparities between whites and blacks in quality-of-life indices. By nearly every major positive index, blacks lag behind whites, while blacks lead whites in nearly every negative index. These data also demonstrate that larger forces are at work in determining the rise and decline of crime rates. The violent crime rate was at a thirty-year low in 2003, which nearly matched a thirty-year low in the unemployment rate and poverty rate.[61] Crime rates are generally connected to poverty rates. To blame black cultural production (no matter how offensive) for violence helps to absolve powerful macro forces and policy makers from responsibility for creating conditions that foment crime. New York City witnessed a more violent crime rate in the mid-1960s, when popular music consisted of doo-wop groups and rock-and-roll artists like Elvis, Bill Haley, Sam Cooke, and the Temptations. Without graphic video games, movies, or tales of beat downs or drive-by shootings on the radio, gangs have thrived in the streets of Philadelphia, Boston, and Chicago since the late nineteenth century. The violence of American West or American South in the nineteenth century is legendary. A thriving economy, expansion of education, and lower poverty rates prove more effective in decreasing crime rates than attacking rap music.

Review of government data refutes claims that African Americans have fallen from some pristine past of social stability, responsibility, and educational success because of hip-hop or any other factor. The data instead show a steady improvement in the quality of life, by most measures, for African Americans. And while there are more black people in prison, this is not so much for a higher crime rate as it is for harsher penalties for convictions. Conservatives have managed to co-opt the old African American ideals of personal responsibility and hard work, notions that were tapped by the

1995 historic Million Man March and created much of its appeal. The same ideals exist in all major black nationalist efforts. Anyone familiar with black nationalism knows that nationalists have no shortage of criticism for white supremacy, even as nationalists endorse "nation building" through hard work, self-determination, and personal responsibility. What black nationalist (or integrationist) leader has ever denounced work, the "family," or personal responsibility? The values of personal responsibility are not, and have never been, the exclusive claims of the Right, claim artists like The Roots, Immortal Technique, Mos Def, Dilated People, or Paris.

Conclusion

Without doubt, the misogyny, debauchery, hypermaterialism, and antisocial nihilism in rap lyrics should be open to criticism. These attacks on hip-hop, however, need to be contextualized and examined with greater sophistication. What may appear to be a sincere concern for the well-being of America's youth is often a guise of a more sordid and insidious attack on black youth culture and its ability to critique, analyze, and provide commentary on society. What do these critics say about any models of positive cultural influences? The implication in these clarion calls on the danger of hip-hop culture is that there are alternative positive cultural examples to be had. What about white youth, and their relatively higher standards of living and lower levels of crime and poverty? They similarly consume hip-hop and are, in fact, its chief consumers. How can one explain their patterns of consumption without the concomitant alleged pathologies? That right-wingers such as Rush Limbaugh, Bill O'Reilly, Robert H. Bork, and others genuinely feel remorse and concern for the plight of poor, inner-city, black youth is questionable, considering their positions on job-training programs, crime laws, educational funding, civil rights, and various social services for the urban poor.[62] Their attacks on rap appear to be little more than a guise for the traditional right-wing rhetoric of intolerance and race baiting. Critics have simply ignored the data revealing the incredible strides that young black people have made under considerable challenges. These anti-hip-hop crusaders have carelessly and disingenuously demonized a generation of black youth as endorsing criminality, anti-intellectualism, laziness, and immorality. Many critics have shown an inability to transcend the narrow parameters of a discussion centered on poverty, crime, and pathology, as described by some rappers. They resort to a simplistic pandering to fear and ignorance, resulting from limited understanding and vast generation gaps.

Ultimately, the attacks on black cultural production are a convenient measure for feigning concern for the interests of blacks, Latinos, and the poor while engaging in no meaningful efforts to improve the communities in question. In fact, white supremacists have always held black cultural production with deep contempt. From blues to jazz and rock, black musical forms have been called alternatively base, primitive, crude, and socially dangerous.

While some may want to charge that whites or the black middle class have been hostile to hip-hop, hip-hop's appeal transcends class and racial lines. What some may want to interpret as a class chasm is a generational one, where (like rock-and-roll and jazz before it) hip-hop has become synonymous with (black) youth culture, much to the chagrin of older folk— black and white. Although Bill Cosby and Stanley Crouch may voice their hostility at some types of rap, there is no doubt that their children listen to hip-hop. In fact, one study found that 97 percent of black youth listen to hip-hop.[63] A typical seventeen-year-old African American living in an affluent section of Lithonia, Georgia, is about as likely to listen to rap as his counterpart in the poor Vine City section of Atlanta. Their sixty-something grandparents, however, are probably not waiting for the next Ying Yang Twins or Mike Jones CD to drop. In 1988, working-class and poor African Americans with grandchildren were probably not quoting Eazy-Z from "Gangsta Gangsta" any more than middle-class black (or white) grandparents.

The consumers of hip-hop are overwhelmingly white and middle class, reflecting the demographics of young people in America. Black consumers of hip-hop transcend class lines from the poor to upper middle class. Any visit to any prestigious university will find privileged young people (of any race) able to engage in spirited debates about the merits of the latest hip-hop beef or who qualifies to be the hottest new rap artist. Except for its first, precommercial years, hip-hop has never been peculiar to the black working class or poor. From the Sugar Hill Gang to Run DMC, De La Soul, Ice Cube, Prodigy, Diddy, Kanye West, and Lil Jon, middle-class MCs have remained intrinsic to expressing a range of hip-hop's core expressions. Additionally, as hip-hop spread, it resonated with African American youth, despite class, region, or gender. By the early 1990s, its ambitious penetration into white youth culture had become largely successful.

The politics of rap consumption and criticism cannot be viewed in simplistic terms of clichéd assumptions about race and class. Still, this does not mean that many critics did not operate out of a context that was particularly colored by race and class. Often culture critics have demonstrated pronounced hostility to black youth culture in particular.

Many hip-hop artists have offered strident and subversive messages in their rhymes, evoking outcries from conservative critics and others who have argued against the rising tide of radical politics. And though critics have attacked artists for their leftist and more militant expressions, most of the earliest criticism was levied against artists who were violent, misogynistic, and otherwise sociopathic in their rhymes. By the late 1990s, however, criticism against these rappers was muted as institutional forces moved to circumscribe the exposure of radical artists, who were moved further to the margins of commercial hip-hop. The counterhegemonic rebel then became best represented in the quintessential thug rapper, who was criticized by traditional rap critics, as well as others in hip-hop. In fact, progressive politics and lyrics among many hip-hoppers shifted from criticizing societal crises at large to critiquing their peers, creating in some respects a more divided hip-hop. These divisions are not along clichéd geographical lines as much as they are along artistic styles of expression, typified by arguments over "realness" and commercialism.

While many have celebrated violence and sociopathic rhymes, they have not gone unchallenged by their peers, who have similarly resisted absolving political, economic, and social forces for creating and maintaining poverty. For many of these hip-hop artists, the fight has been on two fronts: (1) against the rappers who reify dangerous stereotypes and (2) against the problematic impulse to fixate on the meaning of the rhymes and not on the conditions that create the rhymes. Economic and educational structural forces influence crime rates more than rap lyrics. But even this understanding does not deter hip-hoppers from denouncing their peers for pandering to racist images of black and Latino people.

Unfortunately, rap appears much more monolithic in mainstream media coverage and as portrayed by the most prominent critics of rap, due in no small measure to the market dominance of gangsta rap. The hip-hop

community, in the face of attacks from conservatives and liberals, has reacted with strong critical analysis. Although it is far from monolithic, the
hip-hop nation has demonstrated no tolerance for Bill O'Reilly, John
McWhorter, or Robert H. Bork. Instead, critics of gangsta rap and sexist
and criminal glorification have given a very articulate, fresh voice to hip-
hop aficionados who appreciate hip-hop but are uncomfortable with the
messages of some of their peers. Writers for major hip-hop magazines and
several prominent artists have recognized the vulgar nature of some lyrics.
Some artists like KRS-One ("Love's Gonna Get 'Cha" [1990]; "Free Mumia"
[1995]), Kanye West ("Crack Music" [2005]), and The Game ("Hate It or
Love It" [2005]) have demonstrated that rappers have a right to expression
and simultaneously confront the deeper causes of gangsta rap lyrics and the
political agenda of anti-rap crusaders, thereby giving a new dimension to
the discourse within the cultural wars.

5

Locked Up: Police, the Prison Industrial Complex, Black Youth, and Social Control

So if America is majority white, then the prisons 'Another Country' like James Baldwin / Blacks and Latinos all in the system.
   Talib Kweli, "The Human Element," in *The Unbound Project* (2000)

The rapid expansion of the prison industrial complex has been a salient feature of hip-hop narratives since the late 1980s. In a wide range of approaches, the hip-hop community has scrutinized this multibillion-dollar industry, which encompasses the superstructure of the justice system (police, courts, laws, etc.), in general, and the prison industry in particular. Inasmuch as hip-hop is a broad expression of politics, the ways in which rappers have engaged the prison industry is complex, reflecting perspectives including romantic notions of authenticity to radical narratives of prison abolition. While the hip-hop community has not been monolithic in addressing the prison industry, narratives referencing prisons have become more common among rappers of all persuasions—gangstas as well as radical progressives. Additionally, community-based hip-hoppers and hip-hop fans have initiated various antiprison campaigns across the country, at times intersecting with the artistic efforts of commercial artists.[1]

   The earliest references to prisons in hip-hop emerged simultaneously with the initial rapid expansion of the prison industry in the late 1980s. This rise was coterminous with the crack scourge that swept the country, resulting in a spiraling murder rate and a sharp rise in other violent crimes. This era was marked by a recession that significantly affected postindustrial cities as well as rural areas. Many small towns demanded new prisons, which could employ hundreds in largely depressed economies. The policies of the Reagan and first Bush administrations endorsed rapid expansion of prisons as a means to control a fast-growing crime rate while affirming the spirit of "law and order" that had become a conservative slogan since the late 1960s. While conservatives advocated for prison expansion, they also pushed for privatization of the prison industry, generating millions for private businesses. In 1993 the Clinton administration began to extend these projects with great aplomb. The prison industry had become one of the fastest growing sectors in a recession economy, with profound racial implications. In 1990 it was reported that one in four young black men was in the penal system.[2] Coupled with incarceration were high murder rates, which claimed the lives of thousands of black men each year, prompting social scientists to dub them an "endangered species."[3]

Out of this context emerged the earliest organic responses to the exploding prison industry and its nexus with crime and race. While some artists offered cautionary tales of youth led astray, others rapped about prison bids as badges of honor and street credibility. Still others condemned the prison industry as an extension of a larger racist effort to control and exploit poor people of color. At times, rappers produced songs that were mixtures of all three perspectives. Although it is less apparent in the romantic tales of prison life giving credit for authenticity, these songs generally depict prison as inimical to the well-being of the black community and inherently racist. In this chapter I explore the ways in which this sensibility reflects the organic historicizing that artists undertake in their effort to explain current events. These narratives do not view prisons as isolated from other state apparatuses that have functioned to marginalize, discriminate against, and oppress people of color and the poor. In addition, the ways in which gangstas and so-called conscious rappers copiously address police and prisons reflect hip-hop's larger obsession with the nebulous notion of a racialized authenticity.

In the thirty years of hip-hop's development, the art has spanned the spectrum of social commentary. At the close of the twentieth century, songs attacking the plague of drugs and black-on-black violence have given way to criticism of the prison industrial complex and the criminal justice system in general. In an era of unprecedented black affluence, prisons remained an arena of stark exception to the improved quality of black life. It also became the focal point of a new activism among members of the hip-hop generation.

Prison as Social Control

The general consensus in the United States is that prisons are an important institution of civilized society, removing dangerous elements from the general public, extending safety, and ensuring the greater good in the process. Further examination, however, reveals the incredible chasm created by how the justice system has enforced law, resulting in a legal system that disproportionately incarcerates people from poor communities, particularly those that are of color. For African Americans, prison proved anathema in the earliest years following the Civil War.

Immediately following the Civil War, former confederate states passed repressive racist laws barring blacks from voting, serving on juries, holding public office, or having access to equal education and employment. Collectively known as "black codes," these measures developed out of concern over the control of black labor and included vagrancy acts that allowed the arrest of scores of thousands of black people and forced them to work for the state as quasi slaves. Though the federal government curtailed these black codes during Reconstruction, they grew in virulence after Reconstruction's end in 1877. As a source of intensive labor exploitation, the state forced freed people (largely men) to build roads, railroads, and bridges, as well as to engage in plantation labor under terribly inhumane conditions.[4] Wealthy landholders—many of whom were former enslavers—enjoyed cheap plantation labor through convict leasing with the state. The draconian laws that permitted the courts to incarcerate anyone they determined to be "vagrant" were very profitable measures. They were also a powerful extension of the state's ambition to exact formalized social control and domination in a form that approximated slavery. This and other legal policies operated as a corollary to vast informal modes of social control and white hegemony. Public beatings and lynchings were other extralegal means to exert white supremacy over the black population.

In the face of such bold subversion of the constitutional and basic civil rights of American citizens, the federal government remained silent as the New South industrialized and exported millions of tons of cotton, sugar, and other goods on the backs of black labor. At a rate of one person every two days, black people were lynched across the country, although primarily in the South. In justifying such harsh punitive policies, racists insisted that black people were violent, pathological, and dangerous. The only way to maintain control of the lot was to demonstrate white dominance via various actions, including the occasional spectacle of white-on-black violence that swept through early twentieth-century black communities. Though the prison industry then was somewhat primitive compared to today's system, it was an important example of the early efforts to control, exploit, and profit from black people through punitive measures.

Though whites were also imprisoned, they generally avoided punishment for crimes committed against blacks. In fact, despite the thousands of black people murdered by whites in lynch mobs up to 1952, no white person was ever convicted of murder or manslaughter in any case of lynching.[5]

Black expressive culture has always reflected the cultural, political, and social conditions out of which it emerged. In the context of social control, blues and early R&B songs occasionally discussed the wrath of white supremacy and prisons in particular. Though generally more surreptitious than its rebel-styled progeny in hip-hop, blues music provided several songs that discuss prisons. Ma Rainey's "Chain Gang Blues" (1925) was one of the earliest recordings referencing prison, followed by Blind Lemon Jefferson's "Hangman's Blues" (1928), Blind Boy Fuller's "Big House Bound" (1938), Bukka White's "Parchman Farm Blues" (1940), Big Maceo's "County Jail Blues" with Tampa Red (1941), and Lightnin' Hopkins's "Jailhouse Blues" (1946). These songs provided some insight into the horror experienced by rural black folk who could, at nearly a whim, be sentenced to some of the harshest and most inhumane forms of penal control developed in the industrialized world. Outsourced as labor, placed into chain gangs, and used for building bridges, roads, and dams, prisoners were veritable slaves for the state. The torture, hot boxes (inmates forced to sit in metal boxes with deadly temperatures), public flogging, rape of black women prisoners, and primitive living conditions were identical to life under slavery in the United States.

By the 1950s prisons proved to be very important in maintaining social control and repressing the growing black freedom movement. Thousands of civil rights activists were imprisoned throughout the country, primarily in the South. Voices protesting the imprisonment of black leaders surfaced in newspapers or in public speeches. But these protests did not deter law-enforcement agencies from arresting blacks who advocated for democracy. Grassroots workers like Fannie Lou Hamer, Ann Moody, and Willie Mukasa Ricks were beaten and even tortured in jails for attempting to register to vote or organize the black poor. Martin L. King, Jr., penned his most celebrated expression of social, spiritual, and political justice while jailed in Birming-ham, Alabama in 1963. The threat of death, beating, or imprisonment loomed large for the scores of thousands of black people and others willing to resist white supremacy during this era. Some prisons were filled to capac-ity and beyond as protesters eagerly accepted jail time as a badge of honor for resisting injustice. Indeed, even prisons proved to have limitations in their efficacy. By the mid-1960s, the black freedom movement adopted even more confrontational measures with white supremacy as Black Power ad-vocates took root in communities across the country.

Numerous imprisoned black radicals, generally considered political prisoners, experienced celebrity status during the Black Power era. Huey P. Newton, cofounder of the Black Panther Party, was the first to enjoy celeb-rity as a prisoner in the United States, after he was charged with the murder of a police officer. "Free Huey" buttons, posters, and T-shirts and rallies on college campuses and at courthouses across the country revealed a sharp departure from traditional methods of protest over the imprisonment of black leaders. Similar protests emerged in favor of Angela Y. Davis, a young philosophy professor accused of supplying arms to conspirators in a failed courtroom escape attempt. The popular, grassroots support for others like George Jackson, the Black Panther 21, Bobby Seale, and Ericka Huggins provided an early axiological framework around which current resistance to incarceration and the general prison industry would form. In particular, African American activists saw the prison industry as inextricably con-nected to the various apparatuses that systematically oppressed black peo-ple. This was not new, of course, but the level of resistance and criticism had been enhanced by political action and more sophisticated organization. Ad-ditionally, activists saw the release of several high-profile prisoners—in-cluding Huey Newton, Bobby Seale, Ericka Huggins, and many others—even as some are doomed to a life in prison or worse. Despite the continued incarceration of black activists, the sensational releases clearly proved inspi-rational to activists nationwide.

Hip-hoppers of the late 1980s obviously operated from a different cul-tural and political worldview than those of the Black Power era. However, like their predecessors, they were intimately connected to the world around them. Their art, therefore, reflected the concerns, issues, and sensibilities of the moment, while it was also anchored in a black expressive culture that came of age in the era of Black Power. Many of these artists were also the children of activists, for example, Tupac, Chuck D, Professor X of X-Clan, and others. In this respect, the style of protest was decidedly militant and confrontational in ways that the social commentary and protest in the work of earlier musical artists like Marvin Gaye, James Brown, and the Impressions were not.

Part of the stylistic differences in protest in music is simply a result of the brash style and unapologetic rebellious character that typifies hip-hop. It is not that Marvin Gaye, Curtis Mayfield, or James Brown did not curse or make off-color racial comments in private, but such widespread use of profanity or taboo race talk was alien to popular music. Moreover, it was assumed that socially unacceptable language restricted radio play, record sales, and exposure. Finally, as rappers lyrically explored the world around them, prisons necessarily loomed large as reference points for the cult of authenticity. As conditions continued to improve for African Americans throughout the 1990s, the salience of the prison industry was even starker. Indeed, prisons appeared to be a prominent blight on the world of black and brown people, generating considerable attention, criticism, and activism.

A Sign of the Times

Music cannot be separated from the social, political or cultural context from which it develops. Indeed, the contours, nuances, and personality of hip-hop music reflect the world that gives birth to the music. More specifically, the conscious rap that ascended to popularity in the late 1980s was a direct result of the desperate conditions of black communities in the 1980s. Crime, joblessness, drugs, and police abuse all converged to foment what many would consider "positive," "conscious," "message," or "black nationalist" rap. Similarly, as conditions improved in black communities, protests in rap moved to the margins, giving way to a return to hedonistic styles and a new glamorized gangsta trope.

In the midst of President Ronald Reagan's "trickle-down" economics, massive tax breaks for corporations and the rich gutted social services, limiting social security benefits, and simultaneously doubling the expenditures for the military industrial complex throughout the 1980s. The tax rate for the richest Americans was cut from 68 percent in 1981 to 28 percent by the time Reagan left office.[6] Tax incentives for U.S. corporations to relocate factories abroad accelerated deindustrialization across the country. From Detroit, to Gary, to Chicago, and to Los Angeles, millions of manufacturing jobs were lost. The black unemployment rose to a staggering 18.9 percent by 1982, two years before a cheap, highly addictive form of cocaine first appeared in inner cities. Fueled by the lucrative drug economy, limited employment opportunities, and weak social networks, gangs vied for control of a multimillion dollar industry. Marked by a deadly rise in the crack cocaine trade, black communities witnessed alarming rates of violent crime. Thousands of young black people were killed across the country. In fact, 11,488 black people were murdered in 1990 at a rate of 37.6 per 100,000. The white murder rate was six times lower at 5.4 per 100,000 in 1990. That same year in New York City alone 2,262 people were murdered. Most of those murdered in New York City were black and Latino men and boys.[7] At this time, pro-black lyrics, Afrocentric (read as "conscious") fashions, and demands for peace developed as a direct response to the sense of social alarm in black communities.

The dismal reports on black teenage pregnancy, imprisonment, poverty, drug abuse, disease, criminality, and decreasing life expectancy precipitated a shift toward black nationalism among many African Americans in the late 1980s. In academia, black social scientists and others convened conferences and published research on the dire state of African Americans.[8] Many black college students, partly inspired by the anti-Apartheid activities of the era, as well as the sense of urgency, affirmed African identities and employed a trope historian Robin D. G. Kelley calls "freedom dreams": a utopian vision of freedom located in idealized Africa lands.[9] Afrocentric speakers, such as Dr. Jawanza Kunjufu, Dr. Frances Cress Welsing, and Ashra Kwesi, were in high demand on college campuses. Books such as *They Came before Columbus, The Iceman Inheritance, Stolen Legacy,* and *The African Origin of Civilization* were required reading for the young Blue Nile– and Egyptian musk–wearing brothers and sisters with chew sticks and newly discovered African roots, names, and fashions. Natural hair in the form of dreadlocks, twists, and other styles had become fashionable for the first time since the Black Power era, and black youth adorned T-shirts with the visages of Malcolm X, Nelson Mandela, and Marcus Garvey.

Hip-hop similarly reflected this new consciousness. In the midst of reports on the insalubrious nature of being black in America, musical groups like Brand Nubian, Public Enemy, and KRS-One warned about the dangers of drug dealing and substance abuse. Collectives of rappers, such as the

Stop The Violence Movement and the West Coast Rap All-Stars, denounced black-on-black violence. From African medallions to the rise in the popularity of Louis Farrakhan, many viewed black nationalism as a viable expression of dissent and resistance to white supremacy and black self-destruction. Many rappers saw their art as a tool of resistance and political expression. As Brother J of X-Clan rapped in 1990, "While society gets stronger and stronger, my race gets weaker and weaker / maybe I can make a difference through a mic and a speaker."[10]

In the mid and late 1980s many hip-hoppers engaged in various forms of activism. Decidedly liberal, most of the activism was limited to supporting the extant mainstream organizations in the black community. In 1984 and 1988 hip-hoppers like Melle Mel, DJ Macnificent, Afrika Bambaataa and the Universal Zulu Nation performed on behalf of the presidential campaigns of Jesse Jackson and mayoral campaign of David Dinkins, who became the first black mayor of New York in 1989. Boogie Down Productions worked with the National Urban League in various antiviolence campaigns in coalitions that typified the liberal and reformist style of eighties political activism in hip-hop.

Though much of this resurgence of black cultural nationalism had not yet matured into independent and sophisticated political mobilization, rappers were beginning to specifically address particular issues. In 1990 X-Clan initiated the Blackwatch Movement for youth to address some of the fundamental concerns of the black community, particularly peace efforts. From drug abuse and inadequate schools to sexism and health care, no major concern went ignored by hip-hoppers. No issue, however, has been as central to the discourse of hip-hop radicalism and its collective self-expression as the prison industrial complex. From conscious rappers to nihilistic thugs, from commercial to underground, and from every region in the United States, prisons would be a prominent trope in hip-hop. A reading of prisons reveals how essential they have become to expressions of authenticity and credibility as well as a cause for alarm and protest.

Prisons and the Cult of Authenticity

In general, hip-hop in late 1980s had established two distinct camps of authenticity, which are best represented by their archetypes—Public Enemy and N.W.A. Both groups expressed unorthodox styles of rebellion and bad-man style, couched in an urban, postindustrial context of young black male identity. Public Enemy's black nationalist style and sensibility pulled from the black radical tradition, making conscious references to icons of black militancy, while N.W.A adhered to a caustic style of street-level violence and pathos. For both groups, prisons were anathema, as a form of political repression for one and as a threat to street-level criminal enterprise for the other. Subsequent hip-hop artists through the first decade of the twenty-first century would express influences from one or both of these camps.

The first major reference to prisons as an extension of racist social control was Public Enemy's seminal album *It Takes a Nation of Millions to Hold Us Back* (1988). The CD jacket featured the group behind bars and standing on an American flag. Unabashed in its militancy, the song "Black Steel in the Hour of Chaos" raised the bar of critical race discourse and the prison industry as it explained how the song's protagonist was arrested for refusing to join the "army or whatever" for a government that "never gave a damn about a brother like me." Chuck D provides a racialized account of the state penitentiary, which operates like "a form of slavery." In this song, he is arrested because of his politics, which is "fucking up the government"; the black community provides an oasis of freedom for a group of inmates—53 in all—who conspire to escape. Ultimately, the escape is successful, with the help of the S1Ws, the "Security of the First World,"—Public Enemy's own security force—which arrives and sprits them away.

Taken in context, this song is particularly powerful. The album provides references to several icons of black resistance who have been widely considered political prisoners, including Huey Newton, Bobby Seale, and Eldridge Cleaver. In "Rebel without a Pause," Chuck D calls himself a "supporter of Chesimard." The reference is to Assata Shakur (nee Joanne Chesimard), former Black Panther and member of the Black Liberation Army who was arrested in 1973 for charges of killing a New Jersey State trooper. Sentenced to life in prison in a weak case, she escaped in 1982 and found exile in Cuba. In "Prophets of Rage," Chuck D swipes at British Prime Minister Margaret Thatcher for her unwillingness to endorse the release of Nelson Mandela, who was the world's most famous political prisoner at the time. While Chuck D provides commentary on the role of prisons in undermining the black freedom movement, he is also critical of law enforcement for operating as agents of the state and assiduously arresting black people. More specifically, the radical narratives of this album point to the Federal Bureau of Investigation and the Central Intelligence Agency as inimical to black people's freedom. In "Louder than a Bomb" and "Party for Your Right to Fight," the references to phone taps, former FBI director J. Edgar Hoover's racism, and federal surveillance revisit the systematic campaigns waged by the FBI's infamous COINTELPRO (Counter Intelligence Program) against the Black Power movement. Though the album makes several references to the role of prisons and the larger justice system in curtailing black freedom, the text recognizes the role of prisons in repressing dissent and gives little consideration to the sorts of crimes that have led to the incarceration of most black inmates. Congruent with the politics of the Nation of Islam—which provides inspiration for Chuck D—Public Enemy does not offer biting criticism of poverty as a factor in precipitating crime. This perspective, however, would come to dominate the critical discourse in hip-hop surrounding the prison industrial complex and the black community. Though it would be expressed by rappers of all persuasions, gangsta rappers would be the first to offer the narratives of imprisonment for drugs and other offenses. This was a departure from the articulation of prisons as an institution of repression of radical political action characterized by Public Enemy.

Although N.W.A's discourse on prisons was very different than that of Public Enemy's, the former group discussed prisons in a context that was, in many ways, more relative to the state of black imprisonment. No musical artist (of any genre) has discussed the prison industrial complex as effectively, broadly, or with such sagacity and perspective as N.W.A cofounder Ice Cube. N.W.A's *Straight Outta Compton* (1988) gave the world a new perspective of street-level violence, gang culture, defiant swagger, and confrontational style. While the group has been heralded by some as an example of postindustrial subversion couched in counterhegemonic deconstructions of power and identity, the group was not solely about resistive politics. The lyrics of the first LP offer a cross section of braggadocio, placed in street-level standards of cool within a badman narrative. On "Gangsta Gangsta," MC Ren, Dr. Dre, Ice Cube, and Eazy-E rap about beating a "nigga for nothing at all," shooting into a crowd and seeing "niggas running, and falling and yelling and screaming." The song opens with Ice Cube informing the listener that he "never shoulda been let out the penitentiary." Ultimately, after the drive-by shootings, beatings, and homicides, Cube is returned to jail, wearing "county blues." Ice Cube is the only protagonist in the song who lands in

Public Enemy's classic 1988 album cover best represents the black nationalist "conscious era" of hip-hop's critique of the prison industrial complex as an extension of repression of revolutionary and militant politics.

jail. Overall, the song provides little in the way of radical social commentary or subtle criticism of the prison industrial complex, beyond the implication that prisons simply fail the public by letting criminals like Cube's character back on the streets. The characters in the song offer no redeeming features; they express no particular consciousness of poverty or of racial oppression in a hostile white world. Instead, they revel in badman tales of violence and misogyny. In fact, six times the rappers call women "bitches." This is more than any rap song from any other group at the time. Ultimately, this reference to prisons as social control bolsters the conservative demand for increased punitive measures to incarcerate criminals.

Though "Gangsta Gangsta" appears far from subversive, the video for
N.W.A's "Express Yourself," directed by Rupert Wainwright, reflects the black
nationalist consciousness that had come to dominate hip-hop in the late
1980s. Among other scenes, the video depicts N.W.A members behind bars
while images of a white police officer/minister/slave overseer (all played by
the same actor) suggest a historic continuity with white supremacy. In fact,
the video opens with a white overseer on a horse striking a whip at enslaved
black boy who stops picking cotton in defiance to the enslaver. When the
young boy attempts to throw a rock at the overseer, the black adults restrain
him. That same white man is then incarnated as a police officer on a horse
raising his baton at black citizens. The subtext here is a powerful recognition
of organic resistance to oppression, particularly salient among the youth,
while simultaneously offering criticism at the more cautious steps assumed
by adults. The scene where the white minister is placed behind bars, as is a
white businessman, is presented as triumphant. In another segment of the
video, Dr. Dre (the architect of the beats) enjoys being president of the United
States with the tricolor flag of black nationalism in the White House (renamed the "Black House"). A picture of Malcolm X, brandishing a rifle, is
prominently featured on the wall behind President Dre. "Free South Africa" is
inscribed on the Malcolm picture. Another photo of Martin L. King, Jr., bal-
ances the Malcolm photo. Yet despite this, the video concludes with Dr. Dre
walking toward the electric chair with flashes of the same white man who operated as enslaver, minister, and police officer before Dr. Dre is electrocuted.

Though the video for "Express Yourself" reflects some racial consciousness and resistive politics absent in most rap videos, it fails to evoke the op-
timism of a triumphant ending for the oppressed. It is, in fact, a triumph for
white supremacy when the final image is of the rebel Dre being killed by the
state. The lesson does not portend the likelihood of successful resistance
but instead warns that resistance to white supremacy can be deadly. The
bouts with law enforcement in "Fuck tha Police" and the video for "Straight
Outta Compton," however, demonstrate a much more optimistic sense of
resistance to racist law enforcement.

In the video for "Straight Outta Compton," also directed by Rupert Wainwright, N.W.A members roam the streets of Compton and run when police
arrive with sirens and lights. Chased down, they are all placed in a police van,
except Eazy-E, the group's leader, who taunts the police from a car moving
along side the van. Without explanation, the group is released from police

custody and the video concludes with them gesturing dismissively at the police as they retreat. The subtext of this video suggests less of radical politics, à
la Public Enemy, and more of street-level criminals angered by police intrusion. The lyrics offer a bold valorization of gang violence, including boasts of
having "a crime record like Charles Manson." Eazy-E proudly exclaims his
lack of compassion for those slain in the streets: "So what about the bitch who
got shot? Fuck her! / You think I give a damn about a bitch?" Ultimately,
N.W.A offered a new level of shock value in the lyrics that at the time were
crasser than anything to date. In terms of unpacking the politics of this song
and its video, there is little to suggest that the hostility expressed toward the
police was little more than anger at law enforcement's intent to circumscribe
N.W.A's criminal behavior. Moreover, the video shows no intimate connection with the people of the community, who are absent (unlike the festive and
resistive community-based style of "Express Yourself"). It offers, instead, a dys-
topian view of urban space, devoid of coherent or organized resistive politics.

Of all the songs, "Fuck tha Police" offers the most explicit and powerful
expression of resistance to the justice system and police brutality. In "Fuck
tha Police" the power relationships are reversed when N.W.A puts the police department on trial and Cube testifies against racial profiling (before
the term was popularized in the 1990s) and police brutality. Not following
any method of subtlety, Cube exclaims his willingness to "go toe to toe"
with a cop and produce a "bloodbath of cops dying in LA." In the finality,
Judge Dr. Dre declares the cop guilty:

> [Dre] The jury has found you guilty of being a redneck,
> white-bread, chickenshit motherfucker
> [Cop] But wait, that's a lie! That's a goddamn lie!
> [Dre] Get him out of here!
> [Cop] I want justice!
> [Dre] Get him the fuck out my face!
> [Cop] I want justice!
> [Dre] Out, right now!
> [Cop] Fuck you, you black motherfuckerrrs!

The demands for justice from a racist police officer appear ironic, but ultimately cathartic to many listeners who are familiar with the pervasive nature
of police brutality and a biased justice system.

Without systematic studies from social scientists and others, N.W.A (as with most African Americans) understood the historic legacy of white supremacy and its contemporary power. Law-enforcement officers, however, took offense at the song.

In 1988 FBI Assistant Director Milt Ahlerich wrote to Ruthless Records criticizing *Straight Outta Compton* for promoting "violence against and disrespect for the law enforcement officer."[11] Legally unable to order the song banned, Ahlerich stated that the FBI "took exception" to the group's violent lyrics. The FBI made no comment about the charges of police racism and brutality that fomented such antipolice themes.

Ice Cube broke from N.W.A in 1989 after a dispute with payment and the business tactics of manager Jerry Heller, who along with Eric "Eazy-E" Wright, controlled Ruthless Records and the group. Ice Cube sought the production of the New York–based Bomb Squad, who was responsible for producing Public Enemy's work. His exposure to various New York artists and the Nation of Islam–influenced members of Public Enemy in particular significantly influenced Ice Cube's creativity and perspectives on the role of art in political discourse. His first solo LP, *Amerikkka's Most Wanted* (1990) was celebrated as a brilliantly executed work. The *Source* awarded it its highest rating, the coveted "five mics." In fact, it was the only LP from a non–New York artist to receive five mics in the first ten years of the magazine's publication. Though Ice Cube would maintain his gangsta rapper sensibilities in the album, each protagonist in his songs who engaged in crime against the black community suffered consequences. He was also clear about racism in the justice system on "Amerikkka's Most Wanted." He concludes:

> I think back when I was robbin' my own kind
> The police didn't pay it no mind
> But when I start robbin' the white folks
> Now I'm in the pen wit the soap-on-a-rope
> I said it before and I still thought it
> Every motherfucker with a color is most wanted.

Here, the implication is that black-on-black crime is of little concern to authorities. The zeal with which black criminals who target whites are arrested reflects racism in law enforcement and in the application of the law. Cube does not romanticize robbery as much as he spins a demonstrative tale of systematic patterns of discrimination to a catchy beat and radio airplay.

Ice Cube's sense of political expression and discussion of the prison industrial complex in his music only intensified as black nationalists established near hegemony in hip-hop. While Brand Nubian, X-Clan, Public Enemy, Poor Righteous Teachers, Rakim, KRS-One, and others were from the New York area, Ice Cube forged the gangsta rap–style dominant in California with the nationalist rebels of the East. His second full-length solo album, *Death Certificate* (1991), did not equivocate on its rebel-with-a-cause sensibilities. This was extended on his subsequent solo releases *The Predator* (1992) and *Lethal Injection* (1993), which were not only decidedly nationalistic and hostile to white supremacy but commercially successful as well, making him the only solo hip-hop artist to earn platinum sales with his first four LPs.[12] Cube addressed every major form of urban pathology explored by social scientists, from teen pregnancy and unemployment to failing schools and hospitals. However, nothing was as dominant a theme as police brutality and prisons. In fact, his third LP opens with "The First Day of School," which depicts the processing of new prisoners, including a strip search. Unlike the protagonist who dies after getting shot in a drive-by while selling drugs ("Alive on Arrival" [1991]), those who killed or shot police officers universally escaped punishment. In most examples police proved themselves to be racist brutes, providing context to his antipolice lyrics:

(Two cops yelling to a subdued black man)
Cop: We're gonna do you like King!!
Man: What goddamn King?
Cop: Rodney King, Martin Luther King and all the other goddamn kings from Africa!

This scene is disrupted when a black man yells, "Look out motherfucka!" and gunshots ring out. The implication is that the officers are shot in defense of the subdued black man.[13]

On some tracks, Ice Cube employs first-person narrative to take the listener inside the prison industrial complex, including its colloquialisms, complex social codes, racial politics, and prison gangs, such as the California-based Black Guerilla Family, White Pride, and (Latino) North Side. Beyond the descriptive tales of prison life, Ice Cube offers very sharp scrutiny of the prison industrial complex in several songs. In "My Summer Vacation" (1991) Cube questions the efficacy of reform for a prisoner sentenced to fifty-seven years: "No chance for rehabilitation / look at the motherfuckin years that I'm facing." Similarly, he explores the futility of prisons in "Lil Ass Gee" (1993) and "What Can I Do?" (1993), where protagonists are drawn to drug selling by poverty and greed, only to have a life of limited employment options due to felony convictions. While these cautionary tales inveigh against the romantic gangster life, they also indict the prison industry as an extension of white supremacy's attempt to control and exploit black people. In "What Can I Do?" he explains that whites have broken "every law known to man to establish America. But [they'll] put you in the state penitentiary; [they'll] put you in the federal penitentiary for breaking these same laws."

The protagonists who directly confront and challenge the police in Ice Cube's songs and videos universally emerge triumphant. At the end of the video for "Today Was a Good Day" (1992) Ice Cube finds himself surrounded by a massive police force that converges on his home, guns drawn and a helicopter circling. Despite demands for him to surrender, Ice Cube casually walks inside his home, where over a dozen police rush in after him. "To be continued . . ." reads the conclusion of the video. The video for "Check Yo Self" (1992) resumes the story, finding bodies of policemen lying on the floor of Ice Cube's home, apparently slain by Cube, who is arrested and sent to jail, where he eventually escapes with the help of a black woman correctional officer, intimating her racial allegiance and resistance to the injustice of the prison system, as well as Ice Cube's appeal with women. Melding the black nationalist politics of the East Coast's major artists and the street-level gangsta tropes of the West, Cube offered a unique style of politicized gangsta rap, similarly explored by Oakland-based Paris and Tupac and Los Angeles–based Da Lench Mob. Years later, Immortal Technique and dead prez would also promote themselves in a style that is described by the latter as "revolutionary but gangsta."14

Ice Cube's participation with Da Lench Mob and their *Guerrillas in the Mist* (1992) extended this critique of the prison industry. In fact, this album begins with a monologue on the history of capital punishment in America, including state-sponsored killing by methods such as pressing with weights, stoning, hanging, decapitation, firing squad, and hanging someone until they rot to death from starvation or dehydration. The monologue ends with a reference to the August 14, 1936, killing of Rainey Bethea, which was the last public execution in the United States. A black man accused of raping a white woman, Bethea was hanged in front of a crowd of 20,000 whites. A witness explains that the assembled crowd drank lemonade and "had a good time" as the man was killed.[15] Inserting this monologue offers a documentary-like style that is didactic and rich in conveying the brutality of capital punishment, as screams resonate in the background of the commentator's message. The insert evokes an ominous sense of despair that also provides context for black distrust of the criminal justice system.

"Lost in the System" is a first-person narrative of the trials of a black man who fails to pay traffic tickets and is convicted and ultimately goes on a tour of the most infamous prisons in California, including Folsom, Soledad, San Quentin, Chino, and Blythe. Like the general thrust of Ice Cube's work, racism in the criminal justice system dominates the narrative of prison industry:

> Since I'm black and I'm supposed to be wrong
> the prosecution wasn't very long
> Start stackin' months on me like hotcakes.[16]

Ultimately, these lyrics from the West Coast reflect the sort of folk perspective that early blues songs did for African Americans in the South during the early twentieth century. California's booming prison industrial complex witnessed exponential growth and a market for billions of dollars for local economies. Mandatory minimum sentencing, three-strikes policies, and a recession guaranteed an expanding base of inmates, most of whom were of color. Studies demonstrated that in California whites received more lenient sentences than blacks and Latinos convicted of the same crimes as first-time offenders.[17] The institutionalized nature of racism from the arrest, to the trial, and to the conviction have been creatively covered in dozens of songs, revealing that rappers provide new meaning and insight into the dimensions of the prison industry.

Gangstas and Prisons

Around 1992, the axis of hip-hop shifted toward West Coast gangsta rap and away from the militant expressions of hip-hop jeremiads with the release of Dr. Dre's immensely popular *The Chronic.* But even in the discourse of being a thug, prisons were an important backdrop. As hip-hop's black nationalist radicalism influenced gangsta rappers like Ice-T and Ice Cube, who performed much more explicit tales of killing police officers than any East Coast militant, criticism of hip-hop continued to grow. Ice-T formed a heavy metal group, Body Count, which released its first LP, *Body Count,* to a maelstrom of protest in 1992 over the song "Cop Killer." As a pioneering gangsta rapper, Ice-T's new work was heavily associated with rap music, and under pressure from police groups, politicians and others, he was forced to drop "Cop Killer" from his LP. Soon thereafter he was eventually dropped from his label, Time Warner.[18] In 1991–1992, Ice Cube similarly experienced protests against his lyrics, including an unprecedented editorial attack from *Billboard* for lyrics considered offensive to Jews and others. Perhaps there is no better example of the hierarchal value placed on life than when Time Warner forced Interscope Records, which in turn forced its subsidiary Death Row to make Dr. Dre remove a line from his classic *The Chronic* that was antipolice. The line, "Mr. Officer, I wanna see you layin' in a coffin, sir" was considered unacceptable by the corporate elites, who did not object to Dre's lyrics about killing black people or his expressed contempt for black women. In September 1992, Vice President Dan Quayle denounced Tupac's music, claiming that "it had no place in our society." Quayle was partially responding to charges that Tupac's song "A Souljah's Story" incited Ronald Ray Howard to kill a Texas state trooper.[19]

Following nationally coordinated protests to court cases and pressure from music labels, the violent thrust of hardcore rappers shifted focus from killing the police to killing other black people. Politicians and police groups did not express alarm when Snoop Doggy Dogg boasted that "I never hesitate to put a nigga on his back!" Moreover, as violent narratives about killing black people (generally known as "bitch ass niggas," "punk motherfuckas," or "buster ass marks") expanded, rap songs explored the prison complex, but largely as a code of honor or a thug rite of passage.

Among the gangsta rappers who vied for street credibility, shout-outs to "niggas on lock," "my niggas up north," and "niggas doing bids" became a staple on albums. From Jay-Z to Lil' Kim, Trick Daddy, The Game, and Fat Joe, acknowledging imprisoned comrades has become a marker of authenticity that suggests familiarity with both the streets and those who have fallen victim to them. Running from the police and attempting to avoid conviction for living the thug life have similarly evolved into a trope of street credibility. It is therefore ironic that many self-defined thugs have come to celebrate their peers in prisons as well as to view incarceration as honorific examples of dedication and valor to a nebulous expression of black realness.

In one of the earliest of such thug prison songs, Snoop Dogg's "Murder Was the Case" (1993) depicts Snoop going to prison and provides a descriptive tale of prison violence but little in the way of resistive political expression. Similarly, Freeway and Beanie Sigel even rap in prison in videos reflecting a sort of raucous festive style, as does DMX in the video for "Where the Hood At" (2003). In most gangsta tales of prison, thugs are fearful of the police in ways not expressed by the black nationalists of the early 1990s. Running from the "po-po," "jakes," "one-time," and "5-0" strikes a contrast even with N.W.A's earliest articulation of the gangsta rebel. In dozens of videos, hard-core gangsta rappers who write fictionalized stories of grandiose success as drug dealers, murderers, and ruthless criminals run like rabbits from the police. From MC Eiht's "All for the Money," to Mobb Deep's "Shook Ones" and to Wu Tang's "Can It All Be So Simple," running in constant fear from the police has emerged as a staple of the "realest niggas." The trope had become so cliché by 1996 that the Roots derided it in their satirical video "What They Do." Without doubt, the alleged courage and toughness of the thug appears untenable in their constant fear of white authority. In an ironic attempt at defiance and street credibility, these thugs have made images of bug-eyed black men fearfully running from white men as a new standard of cool.

Some gangsta rappers who had previously expressed radical black nationalist leanings, such as Tupac and WC, moved closer toward gangsta tales in the ways in which prisons and police were referenced. Though he recorded commercially for a short five years (1991–1996), Tupac is the most prolific and successful commercial artist in hip-hop. In the short time before his murder in 1996, he spanned the political gamut from a street-based, autodidactic advocate of black power who denounced white supremacy and black-on-black violence to a hedonistic gangsta who boasted of his ability to slay "niggas," use drugs, and flee from the police. Though his first commercial release, *2Pacalypse Now* (1991), was his most militant exploration of police and prisons, he managed to funnel similar polemic references to the criminal justice system throughout his career. In "Runnin'" (1995), Tupac and the Notorious B.I.G. (aka Biggie Smalls) develop a tale of criminality, drug dealing, and murder leading to police pursuits. Neither rapper accepts arrest without a fight or flight. While 'Pac runs from the police "all night," Biggie muses:

> Run from the police picture that, nigga I'm too fat
> I fuck around and catch an asthma attack
> That's why I bust back; it don't phase me
> When he drop, take his glock, and I'm Swayze
> Celebrate my escape, sold the glock, bought some weight
> Laid back, I got some money to make.

Although Biggie engages in a fight-the-police (rather than flee) narrative, his gangsta tropes do not necessarily point to police corruption, brutality, or other police malfeasance. Here the police are simply pursuing criminals, not harassing innocent citizens or political revolutionaries. Fundamentally, the song falls into the category of the many others that reinforce "law-and-order" rhetoric by bolstering notions of black criminality, giving no critical examination of the police or offering broader counter hegemonic analysis. Tupac, however the thug, would offer subtle commentary throughout his celebration of gangsta life. In several songs Tupac describes his own internal conflict about being a thug as he bemoans his attraction to the brutality of the streets, which only extends suffering and anguish to those who are already most oppressed. In many of his songs, prison looms as a machination of a larger racist system that houses those who were raised in poverty and enticed by materialism, violence, and greed. In "My Block (Remix)" (2002) Tupac explores the troubled and unglamorous world of the thug life, which leads to prison or death:

> The underlying cause of my arrest, my life of stress
> And no rest forever weary, my eyes stay teary
> for all the brothers that are buried in the cemetery
> Shit is scary, how black on black crime legendary
> But at times unnecessary, I'm getting' worried
> Teardrops and closed caskets, the three strikes law is drastic
> And certain death for us ghetto bastards
> What can we do when we're arrested, but open fire
> Life in the pen ain't for me, 'cause I'd rather die.

Beanie Sigel's 2005 album represents a contrast to the earlier black militant association with prisons. According to his gangsta narratives, Sigel finds himself arrested, not for revolutionary politics, but for brutalizing black people.

Here, Tupac references California's three-strikes law and the utter hopelessness of those threatened with spending a life in prison for a conviction of a third felony. Similar references have been made by several California rappers, including Ras Kass, Snoop Dogg, and Xzibit. Westside Connection's "Three Time Felons" (1996) is a boastful celebration of street credibility and gangsta life where Mack 10, Ice Cube, and WC brag that they only hang with thugs who already have three strikes. Indeed, the threat of spending a life in prison will not deter them from their commitment to gangbanging. This is, of course, a sharp contrast to WC's and Ice Cube's early work about black uplift and killing neo-Nazis and other white supremacists.[20]

The departure from radical black nationalist rebel music in prison and police references is most evident in the gangster tales told since the mid-1990s. In 1997 Notorious B.I.G. bragged that federal agents tapped his phone because he was flagrant about his criminal activities. Unlike X-Clan's or Public Enemy's references to phone taps, Biggie was not being sought for being a black revolutionary engaged in the militant struggle to free black people from white supremacy. He was making "niggas bleed" and living the gangsta glam life, instead. Trick Daddy's "Thug Holiday" (2002) typifies the narrative that at once valorizes those "thugs" in prison while simultaneously celebrating a criminal ethos and a timidity of the police: "But when I think about it, what would I be without my gun / How could I get away from the po-po's if a nigga couldn't run." Beanie Sigel weaves a narrative of incarceration in "What Your Life Like" (2002), where the self-described "realest nigga" affirms his street credibility in violent tales of gangsterism and graphic prison tropes:

> Niggas wanna know if Beanie Sigel life is real
> Nigga, twenty-five to life is real
> I get a body, take me right to jail.

Sigel offers no romantic tales of beating down correctional officers, escaping, or rebelling. Instead, he positions his toughness on simply surviving hellish circumstances, which include beatings from officers. This and most thug narratives of prison are tales of limited remorse and instead frustration at incarceration. Moreover, they typically endorse acceptance of their situation instead of resistance to the larger criminal justice system—whether they recognize it as racist or not. Though vocalizing a bold and brash bad-boy style of machismo, thugs generally look over their shoulders in fear of the police. Sigel, Trick Daddy, WC, and others develop styles that glamorize criminal behavior and are afraid of the police who thwart the very activities that give thugs credibility.

Beyond some obligatory reference to public housing or poverty, these songs generally fail to address the challenges faced by the urban poor in a racist criminal justice system, instead offering a neominstrelsy of pernicious stereotypes of young black people. These images popularize and endorse the expansion of the prison industrial complex in both their subtlety and the uncritical ways in which the general public embraces myopic representations of black authenticity. The fear that many Americans have of young black men is endorsed, articulated, perpetuated, and tolerated by most of hip-hop's thug community. In the midst of the 1990s, even as violent crime rates declined, the economy expanded, and conditions for African Americans improved, black people were being incarcerated in record rates. Indeed, housing the black and brown poor behind bars has become big business in America.

Political Prisoners

By the mid-1990s the explicit style of black nationalist rap had declined as gangsta rappers took center stage. A handful of self-described thug rappers maintained some semblance of social critique and expressions of an affinity to the black freedom movement. Tupac and Nas, in particular, represent this model. In the video for "Trapped" (1993), Tupac raps behind bars with "Free All Political Prisoners" written on the walls behind him. He also scrutinizes the efficacy of prisons: "Too many brothers daily heading for the big pen / niggas commin' out worse off than when they went in." As he defiantly challenges police authority in the video, Shock G assures Tupac that "they can't keep a black man down." Though no major East Coast artist since Public Enemy ever offered as direct a challenge to the police in graphic tales of killing them and escaping from prison, Nas offers a "freedom dream" of freeing all political prisoners in "If I Ruled the World" (1996). For other inmates, he promises to "open every cell in Attica, send them to Africa."[21] Both Tupac and Nas express solidarity with political prisoners as well a general code to "the streets" as a way of affirming their authenticity while simultaneously intimating political consciousness. In 2003, Ja Rule released *Blood in My Eye,* named after the book of the same title by George L. Jackson, the Black Panther field marshal and political prisoner who was killed by guards in a California prison in 1971. Though Ja Rule even models his cover art after the cover art of Jackson's 1972 book, the CD offers no explicit homage to the revolutionary icon of prison-based resistance. It is instead a celebration of all things gangsta: murder, misogyny, and pathos.

Though some rappers make reference to political prisoners as a group, no specific political prisoner has enjoyed as much attention as Mumia Abu Jamal from the hip-hop community. Channel Live's 1995 song featuring

KRS-One, "Free Mumia," was the first song solely about Mumia Abu Jamal, the most celebrated person on death row, an award-winning journalist, and a former Black Panther convicted of killing a police officer. Viewed by many to be a flagrant case of trumped up charges against a radical, Mumia is widely considered a political prisoner by many hip-hoppers. In several songs, references to Mumia are little more than cursory statements that expose the listener to the case, such as "3 The Hard Way" (1996) by Bahamadia, "K.O.S. (Determination)" (1998) by Black Star, and "Caution" (2000) and "Proper Propaganda" (2002) by Rakka Iriscience, of Dilated Peoples.[22] Mike Ladd and others on "Social Policy Derelicts" (2000) rap that "Mumia Abu Jamal must have justice / Hateful judge Sabo must have a death wish." Here rappers make reference to Albert Sabo, the Pennsylvania judge who sentenced Jamal to death and more people to death row than any sitting judge in the country. Some songs are more substantive, even offering details to the case, such as "911 Mumia" (2000), which includes verses from several rappers on behalf of Mumia and justice in the criminal justice system. In "Human Element" (2000), Talib Kweli takes offense when a white socialist asks him if he knows anything about Mumia. After a second thought Talib reconsiders his reaction: "But, yo, on the other hand, you tell some brothers Mumia's on death row, and they think he's making records with Suge Knight." In "TV Guide" (2002), Ras Kass provides a monologue with Mumia Abu Jamal at the conclusion of the song, where Jamal discusses the role of the government and media in marginalizing radical discourse through palliative programs, shows, and news. Taking a cue from Mumia's point, in "Freedom" (2002) Chali2na of Jurassic 5 notes the timidity that many people have over engaging in resistive politics with the prison industrial complex or with substantively assisting the case of Mumia:

> Got people screamin' "free Mumia Jamal"
> But two out of three of ya'll will probably be at the mall
> I'm heated wit ya'll, the defeated will fall
> Incomplete and unsolved when the word freedom's involved.[23]

These many songs reflect the hip-hop community's awareness of and sensitivity to the role that prisons play in circumscribing dissent. The breadth of engagement with the Mumia case also demonstrates the creative consciousness of rappers who range from quasi-gangsta rappers (Ras Kass), to underground (Jurassic 5), to so-called conscious (The Roots, Black Star). Despite the attention given to Mumia among many rappers, many other rappers have brought attention to the broader populations within prisons and the systematic bias that brought them there.

Prisons, Class, and Race

A number of rappers express the same radical Left position of scholars like Angela Y. Davis, Manning Marable, and others who have explored the criminal justice system's policies, which have had deleterious consequences on the black and Latino poor. dead prez has launched salvos against the police and prison industrial complex in over a dozen songs. In "Window to my Soul" (2003), the group displays a clear analysis of the profit motive for the prison industry, which relies primarily on incarcerating poor people of color:

> Who benefits? The police, lawyers and judges
> The private-owned prison industry with federal budgets
> All the products in the commissary tell you who profit
> It's obvious and it's going too good for them to stop it.

Black Star adroitly dissects the intersection between crime, profit motive, and prisons in "Thieves in the Night" (1998): "Creating crime rates to fill the new prisons they build / over money and religion there's more blood to spill / the wounds of slaves in cotton fields that never heal." Like early Ice Cube and Public Enemy, Mos Def anchors his narrative into a continuum of racial subjugation traced back to slavery. By placing the prison industrial complex into historical context, its connections to various methods of social control and economic exploitation appear even more salient. Similarly, Mike Ladd explains that "prison is cheap labor" in a country where "incarceration is the national flavor."[24] Some artists have created thematic albums with skits around specific topics, and, as prisons became a more prominent issue of contention, Spearhead in 2002 created the first such album around the prison industrial complex.[25]

Spearhead's 2002 LP *Stay Human* protests the prison industry in general and the death penalty in particular, making creative references to the roles of class and race in the criminal justice system. The Bay Area group interweaves a story of "Sister Fatima," a community activist sentenced to death for the murder of a prominent couple. The governor justifies the death penalty during an interview between songs. Fatima, who is also interviewed, states her innocence and argues that she is only guilty of advocating radical politics. After her highly publicized execution, the real murderer emerges and brings authorities to the bodies, proving that Fatima was indeed innocent. This fictional account of the failure of the death penalty to prevent an innocent person from being executed is particularly powerful as DNA evidence exonerates dozens who have been condemned to death across the country. In fact, at least 25 people have been found innocent *after* their executions.[26] Though the LP has several lighthearted dance and club-friendly songs, Spearhead does not equivocate on the death penalty, insisting that it is at most hypocritical: "The government says that killing's a sin / unless you kill a murderer with a lethal syringe," Michael Franti raps. The LP references corporate control of the media, political corruption, and the importance of activism in a style that condemns white supremacy while simultaneously endorsing multiracial coalition building in ways not typical to many in hip-hop.

Of course, the diversity of hip-hop artists offers a diversity of perspectives and approaches to critiquing police and the prison industry. As mentioned above, many have explored the pervasive racial and class bias in the application of the law. The stark contrast to a majority black and Latino prison population in a majority white country is referenced creatively by Talib Kweli, who creates a pun, simile, and metaphor as well as a literary allusion to a famous James Baldwin novel when he raps, "So if America is majority white, then the prison's 'Another Country' like James Baldwin / Blacks and Latinos all in the system."[27] dead prez also brings attention to the black and brown majority in America's prisons in "Behind Enemy Lines" (1999), which includes background conversations in Spanish and English among prisoners. This song also views prisons as institutions to hold political prisoners as well as those who are criminals. The reference to the three-time killer "Kenny" provides context to Kenny's pathology, making reference to his Vietnam vet father's drug addiction, as well as a life of poverty and family dysfunction. The implication, of course, is that no one is born a criminal. Indeed, there is a clear consciousness among rappers of the interconnection between poverty and crime. Franti of Spearhead explains that "it's a crime to be broke in America" in his discursive explorations of the prison industrial complex. He raps, "They lockin' brothers in the poorhouse who can't afford Morehouse." Franti's reference to the prominent black college reflects his analysis that considers the nexus of class and race in the prison industry. He extends his discussion:

> The punishment is capital
> for those who lack in capital
> because a public defender
> can't remember the last time
> that a brother wasn't treated like an animal.

In a similar vein, Talib Kweli explains, "Niggas don't sell crack cause they like to see blacks smoke / niggas sell crack 'cause they broke." The Notorious B.I.G., Jay-Z, KRS-One, Clipse, 50 Cent, Tupac, and many others have explored this poverty-as-incentive-to-sell in first-person narratives, and drug dealing leads to increased likelihood of violence in these songs. In fact, studies show that controlling for class, there is no significant difference in violent crime rates between black and whites.[28] Furthermore, while poor people are more likely to commit certain types of crimes (car theft, armed robbery, burglary, drug selling), very little effort has been made to decrease the conditions that give rise to poverty as a strategy to combat crime.

Prison Expansion, Race, and Big Business

By the early 1990s, the country was in the middle stages of a rapidly expanding prison industry. In the late 1980s, a stubborn recession and the crack cocaine epidemic had led to a growing crime wave that provoked many lawmakers to call for harsher punitive measures for drug-related crimes. In 1986, Congress responded by passing the Anti-Drug Abuse Act that gave mandatory minimum sentences to crack convicts. Partly inspired by the 1973 New York State Rockefeller Drug Laws, these new measures mandated that anyone convicted of having 5 grams of crack cocaine must be sentenced to five years in prison. Possession of ten times that amount of powder cocaine resulted in the same minimum sentence. Though not explicitly racist, the effects were clear: nearly 90 percent of crack users were black; an estimated 90 percent of powder cocaine users were white. Blacks were sent to jail in much higher rates than whites who were also convicted of drug crimes. Across the country the same patterns were reflected in the implementation of these new laws as well as by the racialized campaign against drugs. Moreover, in the popular imagination of America, drug users were black. A 1995 survey published in the *Journal of Alcohol and Drug Education* revealed that 95 percent of respondents envisioned a drug user as black. Police raided black homes, stopped and searched black motorists, and arrested them at rates much higher than whites. In fact, research conducted by the U.S. Commission on Civil Rights revealed that African Americans constituted 14 percent of all drug users but constituted 35 percent of those in drug arrests, 55 percent of those convicted of drug-related offenses, and 75 percent of those imprisoned for drug-related crimes.[29]

The role of prisons and the police in exercising social and political control has been well documented and examined by scholars for decades.[30] But the chasm in racial makeup between those who used drugs and those who were penalized for using drugs grew increasingly palpable in the 1980s and 1990s. The assiduous pursuit of criminals was, in many respects, a highly racialized venture where law-enforcement officers operated with the tacit consent of the wider public to arrest, try, convict, and imprison (black) criminals. The national patterns are more evident in certain cities. For example, 80 percent of New York City's drug users were white in 1989; however, 92 percent of those arrested in drug busts were black or Latino.[31] The zealous pursuit of black criminals allowed many white users to escape capture, but even when whites were found guilty of drug-related offenses, they enjoyed much lighter sentences than black and Latino counterparts convicted of the same crime, even as first-time offenders. In 1996, New York Governor George Pataki's administration released a report that revealed that blacks and Latinos were sentenced to 4,000 more prison sentences for jail time a year over whites convicted of the same crime. The non-profit Sentencing Project confirmed this finding when it reported that same year that black and Latino first-time offenders in the two most populous states, California and New York, were given harsher sentences than whites convicted of the same crimes. With all things being equal, whites were much more likely to receive drug counseling, parole, and lenient sentences than blacks and Latinos.[32] In fact, black youth who are first-time offenders are six times more likely than white first-time offenders of the same crime to be sentenced to prison. For drug offenders, black male youth are a staggering forty-eight times more likely to be sentenced to prison for the same crime than are white male youth first-time offenders.[33]

The reasons for the rapid imprisonment of black people are many. Clearly racism plays a predominant role, as indicated by the black and white sentencing patterns for the same crimes. Poverty, too, is a central factor for increasing the chance of arrest. Black and Latino people are over five times more likely to be poor than whites. Another reason developed when violence swept U.S. cities in the late 1960s, fomenting demands from black and white citizens for greater anticrime initiatives. Many of these "anticrime" initiatives were realized in the rhetoric of prison expansion and respect for law.

Though "law-and-order" rhetoric developed as a campaign slogan for conservatives in the 1960s, the term transcended partisan lines as Democrats attempted to affirm that they were tough on crime. In fact, more black people were imprisoned under the administration of President Bill Clinton than under the administrations of Reagan and Bush the elder combined.

In 1994 the neoliberal policies of President Bill Clinton helped to extend the prison industrial complex with the Violent Crime Control and Law Enforcement Act. This crime bill allocated $7.9 billion for states to build more prisons, and it expanded the list of criminal offenses. These policies helped accelerate the number of inmates in prisons from 503,586 in 1980 to 1,962,220 in 2001, nearly a 400 percent increase. About two-thirds of those arrested were incarcerated for nonviolent drug offenses. The mandatory minimum sentence for crack possession meant that black imprisonment rose at a particularly sharp pace. In 1995, the number of black people in prisons surpassed the number of whites for the first time in U.S. history. In fact, black men in the United States by 2001 were incarcerated at a rate 8.4 times higher than black men in 1993 South Africa, which at the time officially and explicitly upheld white supremacy.[34]

The increased punitive measures also focused on the death penalty, dropping the age at which children could be tried as adults to below fourteen years old. Despite sharp criticism from many opponents of executing children, the United States remained steadfast. In fact, throughout the 1990s the United States refused to sign the UN Convention on the Rights of the Child partly because it would prevent the execution of children, a policy it once shared with only a handful of countries: Iran, Pakistan, Kuwait, and Taliban-controlled Afghanistan. This convention has become the most widely ratified human rights treaty in history. By 2003, over 190 countries

Figure 5.1. U.S. Incarceration Rate, 1975–2001 (prisoners per 100,000 population)

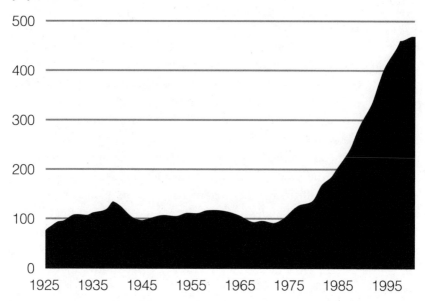

Source: Sourcebook of Criminal Justice Statistics 2001, http://www.prisonpolicy.org/ graphs/incrate19252001.html.

had ratified it; the only country besides the United States that did not sign was Somalia, which lacks a central government.[35] The crime bill also expanded federal death penalty offenses from two to sixty.[36]

Across the country, the death penalty has proved grossly biased against people of color and the poor. In fact, in states with long histories of white-on-black violence, whites have enjoyed leniency when murdering blacks, while blacks are greatly penalized for killing whites. In Florida, a black man convicted of murdering a white person is forty times more likely to be sentenced to death than he would be for being convicted of killing a black person.[37] Thousands of black people have been murdered by whites in the past 150 years in Texas, Florida, and Georgia, but from the end of slavery in these states to August 2003, no white person in any of these states has ever been executed for the murder of a black person.[38] Additionally, of the over 800 people executed in the United States since the reinstatement of the death penalty in 1976, over 80 percent were convicted of killing whites,

Figure 5.2. U.S. Incarceration Rates by Race, 2004

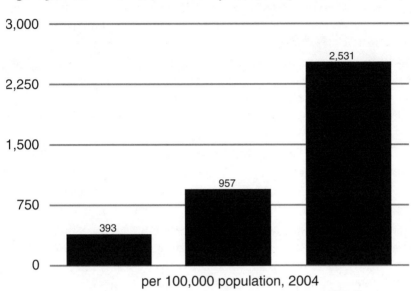

Source: Prison Policy Initiative, http://www.prisonpolicy.org/graphs/raceinc.html.

who constitute around 50 percent of annual murder victims. Of those executed, nearly all were poor at the time they were arrested.[39]

Since the late 1980s, several studies have widely documented institutionalized forms of police monitoring. Patterns of systematic stopping of black motorists, known as "driving while black," have been found in studies across the country, and rappers have made comment. Houston-based rapper Chamillionaire, in his 2006 hit "Ridin," provides a resistive narrative to driving while black and police harassment:

> Thinkin they'll catch me in the wrong, they keep tryin (Keep tryin)
> steady denyin that it's racial profilin
> damn about them not feelin my attitude
> When they realize I ain't even ridin dirty
> Bet you'll be leavin with an even madder mood (Hahaha)
> Then I'll laugh at you then I'll have to cruise.

Although Chamillionaire is a southern rapper discussing police harass-ment, the racial discrepancy in criminal sentencing is smaller in the South than in any other region. In terms of regional patterns of sentencing dispar-ities, the level of justice system bias has been most pronounced in the West, where blacks received sentences that were on average 13 percent longer than those of whites. The rate was closest to parity in the South, where sentences were 3 percent higher for blacks than for whites.[40]

Several times a year as well, there is a case of an unarmed black person being killed by police. The majority of these cases occur outside of the South and are relatively frequent in the bicoastal centers of hip-hop: New York and Los Angeles. In New York alone three major cases between 1998 and 2000 have struck a chord in the hip-hop community and the larger black commu-nity: Abner Louima (tortured and sodomized with a plunger by police) in 1998; Amadou Diallo (shot at least forty-one times by police, hit nineteen times as he stood in the vestibule of his home, unarmed and innocent of any crime) in 1999; Patrick Dorismond, a twenty-six-year-old security guard (shot dead after an argument ensued between him and an undercover officer asking Dorismond for marijuana in 2000; no weapons or drugs were found on his body). Several other unarmed and innocent citizens of New York City have been shot and killed by New York City police since 1998. None has been white. The most notable recent case has been Sean Bell, a twenty-three-year old who was killed by police in a hail of fifty shots on his wedding day in No-vember 2006 when Bell left a club during his bachelor party. These cases, al-though extreme, cannot be taken as entirely aberrant in the New York Police Department (NYPD). Under Mayor Rudolph Giuliani's administration, scores of thousands of black and Latino citizens were detained by police. In 1997–1998, the NYPD reported that its street crimes unit detained 45,000 people, most of whom were released when no criminal violation could be found. Critics estimate that the number of those detained was many times higher and denounced the intrusive police state tactics of the NYPD. The ex-ecutive director of the American Civil Liberties Union noted that, of those detained by the police, "virtually everybody is innocent and virtually every-body is not white."[41] Similar systematic efforts to control blacks and Latinos without consideration of guilt or innocence have been found nationwide.

These data were not lost on those communities most affected by police and the prison industrial complex—African American and Latino youth. By the close of the 1990s, the hip-hop community, bolstered by such sharp social commentary, had developed a very sophisticated antiprison movement that spanned the country. The Ella Baker Center for Human Rights in the California Bay Area has been effective in utilizing hip-hop youth to organize against police brutality and prison expansion. In 2000, thousands of young people were mobilized in an effort to prevent the passage of Proposition 21, which would facilitate criminal prosecution of children and expand the criminalization of various activities. For example, graffiti would include a mandatory minimum sentence of a year in prison under the new law. Ironically, some graffiti artists used their talent to express opposition to Proposition 21 on city buses across the state. A "No More Prisons" campaign operates in twenty-six cities, and three different collaborative CD projects have attacked facets of the criminal justice system.

The only album focused solely on prisons is *No More Prisons* (1999), which brought together artists, such as dead prez, Sister Asia, and Daddy-O, to collaborate on efforts to help promote critical discourse and substantive policy reforms regarding the prison industry. This project included information on the expansion of the prison industry and the simultaneous decline in educational funding. The liner notes explain that "since 1987, total spending on prisons has increased by more than 30 percent, while higher education has been cut by 18 percent." The CD also provides data on racial and class bias in the criminal justice system. Proceeds were used to assist the Prison Moratorium Project, an effort to stop prison expansion.

The Unbound Project Vol. 1 (2000) is directed at the case of Mumia Abu Jamal, showcasing commercial and underground artists on songs about Mumia, the death penalty, police brutality, and prisons. *Hip Hop for Respect* (2000) is a collaborative effort initiated by Mos Def and Talib Kweli as an expression of resistance and protest to the shooting of Amadou Diallo in particular and police brutality in general. As Talib explains in the liner notes, the hip-hop generation must express outrage because the focus of police terror is typically a member of that group. Moreover, the album was designed to "demand respect, hip hop style." Talib states, "Hip-hop is the last folk music . . . it is uncompromising, unflinching, and straightforward." The proceeds from the project go to the Hip Hop For Respect Foundation, a nonprofit organization that fights against police brutality nationwide. Artists such as Pharoahe Monch, Rah Digga, Cappadonna, Kool G Rap, and Common deliver powerful verses that reflect the anger and outrage at incessant attacks on black life by the police. Their sagacity is evident throughout, even on verses that did not make it into the song, such as Ras Kass's strike at the capitalist motivation behind prison construction: "Even American Express is building prisons, 'cause genocide is big business."[42]

Though around fifty artists were involved in the project, it was not without its share of hurdles with labels over clearance and other legal wrangling. Each rapper worked for free, but as Talib notes, some labels were not too eager to engage in the project:

> If this was gunbussing, drug dealing, how-many-niggas-can-I-kill rhymes, this joint would have been out for our people to soak in a long time ago. But when we talk about defending ourselves and direct our energy toward the real enemy, not each other, then there is a hesitation on the part of these corporations that get rich off of our culture to put out positive music. Everyone wants to stay away; it's too political.

The question of record company disinterest in promoting radical or progressive social commentary is an old one. The reluctance to push music that promotes radical politics seems obvious to those who see record labels as bastions of greedy conservative interests. But since the late 1980s there has been the consistent presence of artists whose artistic message is anathema to white supremacy or conservative and right-wing politics: Ice Cube (who has gone multiplatinum with lyrics like "I'm killin' more crackers than Bosnia-Herzegovina"), dead prez, the Coup, KRS-One, Spearhead, and many others. Rakaa Iriscience of Dilated Peoples, which has worked in antiprison and Free Mumia programs such as Refuse and Resist, insists that, while their label would prefer "beats by Dr. Dre and an R&B singer on every track," their group has creative freedom: "We do what we want to do."[43] Still, artists like Paris and Ice-T have resigned from labels because the labels have opposed lyrics intimating the killing of politicians or police.

Another concern is market demand and radio play. These antiprison/antipolice brutality collaborative albums have never had radio hits or heavy video rotation. Their messages, however, have not been entirely muted in the music industry. Artists also rely on other elements of hip-hop to promote politics. In cities across the country, "No More Prisons" graffiti campaigns have emerged among hip-hop graffiti artists. In 1999 the book *No More Prisons,* by William Upski Wismatt, was released at the same time as the similarly titled CD, the first such collaboration between a book and hip-hop album release.[44] The leading hip-hop magazines, *XXL* and the

Source, have even issued special issues on the prison industrial complex and the hip-hop generation, revealing the degree of attention this critical issue has received from the community most affected by prison policy.

In addition to their work in collaborative efforts, groups such as the Coup, Dilated Peoples, and Black Star have donated their talent in concerts protesting prison expansion. In late 2003, dead prez reported that group members were arrested and beaten by officers in New York City. In response to this confrontation, the group announced its plans for a lawsuit against the NYPD as well as promotion of the People's Self-Defense Campaign, a program of the Malcolm X Grassroots Movement, designed to organize against police brutality.[45] Critical Resistance, a nonprofit organization opposed to prison expansion, works with youth and hip-hop contingents.

The prison industrial complex, with its wide-reaching power, has become an indelible part of black and Latino youth consciousness as they forge creative outlets in hip-hop. As the case with other issues of contention, hip-hoppers respond to the prison industrial complex in a variety of ways that reflect a wide range of political and cultural practices and sensibilities. Data from across the country for decades have reflected the inveterate nature of racism in the criminal justice system on every level, from arrest, trial, and sentencing to prison treatment. The rise in the prison industrial complex in the last 2 decades of the twentieth century also reflects the historical tendencies of bias and racialized policy making. Though the rhetoric of "law and order" remains popular among conservatives and many neoliberals, their narrow notions of law and order remain suspect. Poverty, widening class divisions, institutionalized discrimination, and other forms of inequality are not explicit concerns for those who demand "order" in America. Rarely, if ever, do pundits address the conditions that give rise to crime, such as poverty, although most inmates lived in poverty when they were arrested. Few specifically address education, although over half of all state prison inmates are illiterate.[46] The fear of violence cannot explain the rapid rise in the prison population, since over 70 percent of those sentenced to prison in the 1990s were nonviolent offenders. Particular crimes (those predominantly committed by poor black and Latino perpetrators) have been identified to receive the harshest punitive measures.

Despite the institutionalized nature of this bias, the fanciful tales of murder and mayhem that are so pervasive in hip-hop must be addressed. The acceptance of the thug and the gangsta as a standard of hip-hop authenticity is inherently problematic, especially as gangstas and thugs typically prey on other poor black and Latino people. Few offer any resistive expression toward white supremacy. There must be concern about the degree to which all people, even people of color, embrace pernicious stereotypes of black and Latino criminality, further extending the power of the prison industry complex. Studies show that African Americans and Latinos are in fact eager to develop harsh penalties for crimes, partly because they are more likely to be victims.[47]

The issue, however, of the power and function of criminalization must be effectively addressed on various fronts. Hip-hop has long engaged in discussion of the exigencies of the prison industrial complex; however, the art is not monolithic in its approach. Its diversity offers a range of cultural expressions, some of which are quite subversive and resistive to white supremacy and other forms of oppression. The obvious interest of music conglomerates to mute or peripheralize these voices is clear, but in the final analysis, artist agency must be considered as well. Moreover, the ways in which black youth have internalized problematic "controlling images" that reduce blackness to pathological expressions of crime and misogyny must be examined. "Keepin' it real" then becomes a tragic bastardization of hip-hop's original mission to subvert crime and youth violence.

Epilogue

Hip-hop has been an ever dynamic force with potential for social change, for better or for worse. The question, however, is the degree and nature of that influence. In 1994 in Bloomington, Indiana, I witnessed local Hoosier youth wearing the gangsta uniform with which I was familiar growing up in South Central Los Angeles: flannel shirts, sagging "khakis" (Dickies brand pants of any color), and Chuck Taylor Converse brand basketball shoes. Some even went as far as to wear blue or red bandanas, signifying Crip and Blood gangs, respectively. During one altercation with a local "BGC" ("Bloomington Gangsta Crip"—as we jokingly called them), a young man aggressively asked, with outstretched arms, another youth if "you got beef, muthafucka?!" Fortunately, the other youth had no beef. The drama immediately reminded me of the DJ Quik song "Jus Lyke Compton":

> I don't think they know, they too crazy for their own good
> They need to stop watchin' that "Colors" and "Boyz in the Hood"
> Too busy claimin' Sixties [an LA-based Crip gang], tryin to be raw
> And never ever seen the Shaw [Crenshaw Blvd in Los Angeles].

There was no denying the influence of hip-hop on that spring day in America's heartland. But my imaging a reconfigured scene without hip-hop brought the same hot-headed youth to mind, only in a different cultural display. In my reimagined scenario, the BGC was rocking a mullet, Iron Maiden concert T-shirt, tight jeans, Vans brand sneakers, yelling "Come on, asshole! You wanna piece of me?! Fuckin' aye!!" The behavior was the same, only with different cultural inflections.

175

Hip-hop had become a way in which cultural displays of youthful rebellion, antiauthoritarian behavior, and cool had been packaged. It was an articulation of cool that was evident in hip-hop-styled semiotics that were, in fact, synonymous with African American (male) youth culture. Long before the first pair of baggy FUBU jeans were sold, there were antiauthoritarian youths. Whether it was the 1930s Zoot Suit culture, the 1950s leather-jacket rock-and-rollers with cuffed jeans and white-Ts, the 1960s longhairs, or the 1990s hip-hoppers, youth culture has been a convenient whipping boy for cultural critics who look to find easy sources of blame for social ills. The overwhelming majority of listeners of gangsta rap do not jump into "low-lows" (low-rider cars), load "straps" (guns), and look for some enemies to shoot, just because Snoop did it in a song.

Like jazz in the 1920s or rock and roll in the 1950s, hip-hop has been maligned, attacked, and blamed for various social and cultural dangers to American youth. Like those vilified art forms of the last century, hip-hop has gone mainstream, despite the "haters." It has become a dominant music to the majority of the country's youth. Like the young people of the 1920s and 1950s, those of the hip-hop generation have not en masse devolved into barbarians or sociopaths. Critics continue to blame hip-hop for various ills without credible evidence. African Americans of the hip-hop generation have graduated from high school, college, graduate, and professional schools at rates higher than any generation of black people in U.S. history. As elections in 2002 and 2004 demonstrate, they also vote at rates higher than any similarly aged black generation in history. The black murder rate in 2004 declined to rates lower than any year since at least the 1940s.[1] The black teen birthrate is the lowest in documented history. Along with the increases in these positive indices is the visibility of black artists who have gained unprecedented control over their cultural work, celebrating industriousness and conspicuous consumption.

Though not examined directly in the book, since it is not central to the thesis of hip-hop's struggle over racialized authenticity, the impact of hip-hop in a capitalist economy is notable. There has been, in fact, an incredible expansion of commercial opportunity for members of the hip-hop generation beyond rapping. Indicative of the expansion of black commercial opportunity is the rise of hip-hop moguls. In fact, the only nonathlete African Americans to appear on various lists of wealthiest Americans under 40 are hip-hop business tycoons: Sean "Diddy" Combs ($346 million net worth),

Shawn "Jay-Z" Carter ($340 million net worth), Damon Dash ($200 million net worth), Ice Cube ($145 million net worth), Curtis "50 Cent" Jackson III ($100 million net worth), Cornell "Nelly" Haynes, Jr. ($60 Million net worth), and Jermaine Dupri (also $60 Million net worth). There are also those who are over forty years old: Russell Simmons ($325 million net worth) and Andre "Dr. Dre" Young ($150 million net worth), among others. Collectively, the top ten wealthiest people in hip-hop are worth over $2 billion.[2] Unlike the hyperexploited black musicians of earlier generations, hip-hop entrepreneurs, for better or worse, have embraced capitalist principles with zeal, boldness, and business savvy.[3] Their stories, which all begin when they are in their twenties without a college diploma, are replete with shrewd negotiating practices, hard work, and the determination typically thought to be lacking among many hip-hoppers.

When they could not get signed to a label Jay-Z, Damon Dash, and Kareem "Biggs" Burke formed Roc-A-Fella Records in 1996. After Jay-Z's *Reasonable Doubt* went gold, major companies approached the twenty-something black men with what Dash called "nigga deals" that assumed their ignorance and gullibility. Rejecting offers that did not grant them the control or profit that they found appropriate, they held out until they negotiated a lucrative 50–50 partnership with Def Jam Records, giving Roc-A-Fella ownership of half of its master recordings. That same year, Percy "Master P" Miller's No Limit Records entered into a distribution deal with Priority Records, where he negotiated complete control of his label's master recordings and 85 percent of his label's sales. This was an unprecedented venture between an independent label and a major distributor, a feat that white artists had never been able to accomplish. The result was that Master P was the first hip-hop mogul to reach $300 million in net worth.[4] Cash Money Records ventured into a similar deal in 1998 with Universal Records. From Ruthless, Rap-A-Lot, and So So Def, to Bad Boy, Roc-A-Fella, and Aftermath, artist-owned independent ventures have characterized a scale of control over cultural production unseen in any other genre of music. From real estate and film, to restaurants, sports teams, and even oil refineries, these moguls have been ambitious with their investments. From fashion houses like G-Unit, Sean Jean, and Rocawear, young black men have reaped millions in ways that no generation of black fashion designers have. They have given initial opportunities to dozens of video directors like Hype Williams, Bille Woodruff, and F. Gary Gray. Some have found success in big movie productions. In 1998, Gray had the biggest movie budget ever for a black director with "The Negotiator." Gray went on to direct such mainstream hits as "The Italian Job" (2003) and "Be Cool" (2005). From writers, producers, choreographers, managers, lawyers, and security, hip-hop generation professionals have enjoyed unprecedented access to the music industry's billions, by employing their own. There is even a cottage industry of hip-hop-inspired fiction books. In 2005 50 Cent founded G-Unit Books in his effort to enter the lucrative market. Of course, many from Fat Joe, Jay-Z, 50 Cent, and Russell Simmons to David Banner and Trick Daddy have created community service programs for young inner-city folk. From the No More Prisons movement, to voting campaigns and antipolice brutality efforts, hip-hop has been central to the mobilization of young people in grassroots activist arenas.

These stories do not mean that hip-hop is not without its challenges. Many artists are being terribly exploited in hip-hop. Like any genre of music, few artists ever get rich, of course. Stories abound of artists who remain in debt and unhappy in the industry that celebrates capitalist success and consumption. Many have complained of being cheated by their young black hip-hop bosses. Apparently the infamous "Industry Rule #4080" that record companies are shady applies regardless of color.[5] Contrary to the widely held belief to the contrary, no rappers have been slain because of any rivalry on wax.[6] Still, there is the tragic thuggish behavior of some rappers and their entourages at award shows and other venues. Too frequently, efforts to accrue street credibility find wealthy adults willing to risk jail time to "keep it real," resulting in beatings, stabbings, champagne bottles to the head, and shootings. But few critics of the hip-hop generation make any effort to consider the incredibly complex political economy of hip-hop. While it extols pathology in its verse, it has witnessed a generation of African Americans who enjoy the highest standard of living in history. It has created a vibrant community of diverse grassroots activists, intellectuals, visual artists, spoken word–influenced poets, entrepreneurs, and a range of professionals who have never enjoyed as much access to the employment and resources created by the commodified cultural work of black people.

While hip-hop's mainstream shows very little in the way of leftist subversive radicalism, it is not without glimpses of political consciousness. In fact, under the administration of President George W. Bush, increases in subversive expressions are common among the most mainstream of artists, including Jay-Z, Eminem, Ludacris, Kanye West, and Lil' Wayne, all of whom have criticized the Bush administration for the war in Iraq, the handling of Hurricane Katrina victims, and other issues.[7] These sorts of political expressions are uncommon among mainstream R&B and pop musicians whose format typically encompasses love ballads and festive tracks.

The hip-hop media have also been quite substantive and relevant in many ways. The hip-hop magazine *XXL* is the most popular music magazine in U.S. newsstand sales, outperforming *Rolling Stone, Vibe* and *Spin.* Hip-hop's literary presence has given rise to other widely read publications, accounting for millions of readers of the *Source, Murder Dog, Elemental,* and other publications. Most readers are under thirty-five. Current events relevant to black and Latino life in America are covered with sophistication. Stories on conflict diamonds, the crisis of AIDS, voting, potable water in developing countries, Latin American migration into the United States, and African civil wars are covered in most hip-hop magazines and (thanks to the efforts of superstars Jay-Z, Kanye West, Diddy, and others) also in hip-hop videos and songs. Between the advertisements for rims, booty videos, and jewelry are articles on the prison industrial complex, international manifestations of hip-hop, police brutality, the military industrial complex's effects on black and Latino people, and other issues rarely covered in the more politically tepid *Ebony.*

Against the backdrop of these promising characteristics, however, the arena of commercial hip-hop is constricted by the markets' fixation on black pathos in hip-hop music. Whether called the "badman," "bad nigger," or "real nigga," the commercially successful artists in hip-hop universally adopt narrow expressions of racialized imagery that valorize hypersexuality, misogyny, and violence. No other popular medium has represented the black image in such myopic ways, even as black people lay claim to more creative control in hip-hop than in any other popular medium. Still, as explored here, these artists are not without their critics, some of the most virulent of whom are rappers themselves. Many in hip-hop have vilified the gangsta as a tired, revised zip-coon minstrel figure that reifies the most troublesome expressions of white supremacy. These "real niggas" have been ridiculed as "real cowards" for their celebration of black death and fear of white racist authority. But, as Jay-Z has noted, the market is open for only narrow expressions of hip-hop: "I dumbed down for my audience to double my dollars."[8] The mogul, whose worth is over $340 million, insists that he would rather rhyme like lyrical masters and politically conscious MCs like Common or Talib Kweli, but he has instead made artistic and political sacrifices to acquire the resources to benefit the community.

Ultimately, the vulgarity and constriction of artistic expression in mainstream hip-hop may be troubling for many, but, as data show, it has not led to the rise of criminality or educational collapse on any macro level. Sure, the educational attainment gaps between white and black youth have been maintained, but, as noted earlier, that gap has become the smallest in history. This forces us to consider the ways in which fans of hip-hop are not so impressionable, gullible, or, simply put, stupid that they are unable to distinguish between art and reality. Hip-hop, for its critics, is somehow unique from the thousands of movies, television shows, and books that tell violent stories. According to critics, hip-hop is somehow uniquely special in its ability to influence its fans to become violent. Interestingly, hip-hop's expansion beyond the United States is often political in ways that it was once in the early 1990s.

The international manifestations of hip-hop are considerable. In the last decade, as hip-hop expanded its appeal considerably, there have emerged local communities of "heads" in the far reaches of the world. Ghanaian hip-life, Panamanian- and Puerto Rican-inspired reggaeton, South African kwaito, and other hip-hop/local hybrids have made indelible marks on glocal (global/local) youth culture and political expressions. In Kenya, over half of the indigenous languages have recorded rap songs. In Malawi and Uganda, local artists rap about AIDS and sexual responsibility. In Brazil, rappers address the grotesque disparities between rich and poor, life in the favelas and racism. African immigrants in Spain rap about police corruption and racism, as do Turkish rappers in Germany. In Poland, poor Poles address poverty and political apathy in hip-hop rhymes. Southern Italian rappers, calling themselves "Sons of Hannibal" ground their own sense of legitimacy and affinity with hip-hop by declaring their own African ancestry as descendants of the African soldiers of the third-century B.C. conqueror Hannibal who marched his troops on Rome, nearly defeating the powerful empire. In Cuba, young people enjoy a state-sponsored hip-hop festival in August after years of unsuccessful government efforts to repress the spread of the culture. When asked how they can get away with criticizing the Cuban government so openly, one political rapper smiled and said that his rhymes are "not criticizing the government. I am only discussing how we can *improve* the government."⁹ Though international hip-hop is decidedly more political than its U.S. forms, not all international types are explicitly political and resistive to government corruption or racism.

In Venezuela, the group Los Vagos y Maleantes ("Bums and Thugs") is straight gangsta, even killing an occasional "nigga" in Spanish verses. In fact, the word "nigga" appears in many instances of non-U.S. hip-hop. I came across a hip-hop party poster in Santo Domingo, Dominican Republic, that offered "niggaz" a higher entrance fee than "girlz." The poster was otherwise in Spanish. In the small Indian Ocean country of Mauritius, a local group of Creole rappers debuted with "Negre por la Vie" ("Black for Life") and celebrated shout-outs to "my muthafuckin' niggas" but otherwise rapped in Mauritian Creole.

From the well-developed hip-hop community of France, to Japan's "Nip-Hop," to Australians and New Zealand Maoris, hip-hop has become a veritable global movement. Ultimately, hip-hop's power as a political force depends on the people who comprise these glocal communities. From the efforts of grassroots workers to stop the expansion of prisons, to the academic conferences and panels on misogyny, feminism, voting, and activism, hip-hop's scope is broad and deep in America and abroad. It remains ever dynamic and full of potential to celebrate life or valorize killing. It can be good and bad and everything to everyone. Fifteen years from now may be witness to a remarkable formal force of global reckoning for serious political and social change with hip-hop at the center, or it could be a global force of new celebrations of rims, booty, and whatever high-end drink is the latest fad. Hip-hop, as we know, remains as unpredictable as ever.

The hip-hop landscape in the United States may never be mirrored exactly in other places. There are obviously vast differences in economic, political, and cultural institutions in the United States that make finding exact overlap with other nation's hip-hop expressions difficult. In the United States, the focus of this book, we find a powerful cultural expression that has not only shaped the identity of a generation of African Americans but has influenced the culture of others as well.

NOTES

Introduction

1. Rakaa Iriscience, personal communication, February 11, 2002.

2. Tricia Rose, *Black Noise: Rap Music and Black Culture in Contemporary America* (Hanover, N.H.: Wesleyan University Press, 1994).

3. The historical narrative of hip-hop has been extensively documented by a wide range of scholarly and journalistic accounts. For the most detailed study of its origins and early years see Jeff Chang, *Can't Stop Won't Stop: A History of the Hip-Hop Generation* (New York: St. Martin's Press, 2005). See also Rose, *Black Noise;* Nelson George, *Hip Hop America* (New York: Penguin, 1998); Cheryl L. Keyes, *Rap Music and Street Consciousness: Rap from Its Earliest Roots to the Present Day* (Urbana: University of Illinois Press, 2002); Murray Forman, *The 'Hood: Race, Space and Place in Rap and Hip-Hop* (Middletown, Conn.: Wesleyan University Press, 2002).

4. Jim Fricke and Charlie Ahearn, *Yes Yes Y'all: Oral History of Hip-Hop's First Decade* (New York: Da Capo Press, 2002), 44–55; DJ Macnificent, personal communication, March 22, 2002.

5. Though the dominant narrative of hip-hop insists that the four elements emerged among African Americans and Puerto Ricans in the Bronx, graffiti, the oldest element, had a large number of white participants with no contact with the musical components of the culture. In fact, in all-white areas such as Canarsie or Bensonhurst in Brooklyn, white graf artists actually wrote white supremacist pieces on walls in efforts to prevent integrated neighborhoods in the early 1970s. It was not until the mid-1980s that virtually all graffiti artists of what became known as a "hip-hop style" had direct contact with the other three elements of the art. DJ Macnificent, personal communication, March 22, 2002; Davey D, "Is Hip-Hop Black Culture?" FMV Hip Hop Newsletter, ca. 1999, http://www.daveyd.com/flipscriptmulti.html.

6. The most comprehensive collection of work on hip-hop comes from Murray Forman and Mark Anthony Neal, eds., *That's the Joint! The Hip-Hop Studies Reader* (New York: Routledge, 2004). This ambitious volume includes essays on the history, lyrical structure, dance, visual art, and political and cultural implications of the art of hip-hop in an easy and practical way.

7. This is an unconventional use of the term "Other" in reference to racializing processes. I attempt to use the term from a black vantage point. Typically, people of color (or some marginalized white ethnic group) are considered to be the "Other," which clearly reflects the dominant perspective; e.g., "flesh-colored" crayons or bandages were

assumed to look like white people's flesh. For black people, however, the Other was certainly not themselves. Whiteness was a contrast even to how black people were self-perceived. Whites, were, in fact, not only hostile and oppressive, they were rendered Other in the collective black imagination of eighteenth-century America and beyond.

Chapter 1. The Minstrel Reprise: Hip-Hop and the Evolution of the Black Image in American Popular Culture

1. Asterisks in original; see Topher Sanders, "Phonte: Holding Hip Hop Accountable," http://www.allhiphop.com/features/?ID=899.

2. There is a very impressive body of work on this phenomenon. For an exploration of the development of these stereotypes, see Melvin Patrick Ely, *The Adventures of Amos 'n' Andy: A Social History of An African American Phenomenon* (1991; repr., Charlottesville: University Press of Virginia, 2001); Sam Dennison, *Scandalize My Name: Black Imagery in American Popular Music* (New York: Garland, 1982); Eric Lott, *Love and Theft: Blackface Minstrelsy and the American Working Class* (New York: Oxford University Press, 1993); Donald Bogle, *Toms, Coons, Mulattoes, Mammies, and Bucks: An Interpretive History of Blacks in American Films* (New York: Continuum, 1994); Ed Guerrero, *Framing Blackness: The African American Image in Film* (Philadelphia: Temple University Press, 1993); Janette Faulkner and Robbin Henderson, eds., *Ethnic Notions: Black Images in the White Mind* (Berkeley, Calif.: Berkeley Art Center, 1982); Tommy L. Lott, *The Invention of Race, Black Culture and the Politics of Representation* (Malden, Mass.: Blackwell Publishers, 1999); Mel Watkins, *Stepin Fetchit: The Life and Times of Lincoln Perry* (New York: Vintage, 2005).

3. Imani Perry, *Prophets of the Hood: Politics and Poetics in Hip Hop* (Durham, N.C.: Duke University Press, 2004), 10.

4. Crazy Legs, quoted in "B-Boying," *Vinyl Exams* (CD; New York, Sony Music, 2000); DJ Macnificent, member of Zulu Nation, personal communication, March 27, 2002. Imani Perry provides a very sophisticated discussion of the ways in which hip-hop is an African American art form. See Perry, *Prophets of the Hood*, 9-37.

5. Quoted in Perry, *Prophets of the Hood*, 16.

6. Lhamon, in his book *Raising Cain*, argues against the general narrative that identifies 1843 as the date of the first minstrel show. Though performers were not called "minstrels" at the time, that style of entertainment had been around since at least 1815. W. T. Lhamon, Jr., *Raising Cain: Blackface Performance from Jim Crow to Hip Hop* (Cambridge, Mass.: Harvard University Press, 1998), 56-57.

7. John Strausbaugh, *Black like You: Blackface, Whiteface, Insult and Imitation in American Popular Culture* (New York: Tarcher Penguin, 2006), 62. I use the term WASP—white Anglo-Saxon Protestant—as a literal reference to that group, without conflating affluence with its identity, since, strictly speaking, most WASPs have never been affluent.

8. Alexander Saxton, The Rise and Fall of the White Republic: Class Politics and Mass Culture in Nineteenth-Century America (New York: Verso, 2003), 109, 165. For an exploration of these historical phenomena and the development of these stereotypes, see Ely, *The Adventures of Amos 'n' Andy;* Lhamon, *Raising Cain.*

9. Lhamon, *Raising Cain*, 6.

10. Ibid., 44–45, 118.

11. Collins argues that black feminism demands that women reject "controlling images" of a racist patriarchal system. These images are those that attempt to undergird white supremacy and sexism. The Jezebel and Mammy are, at times, expressed by black women artists who are rewarded for behavior pleasing to those in power. See Patricia Hill Collins, *Black Feminist Thought: Knowledge, Consciousness, and the Politics of Empowerment* (New York: Routledge, 2000).

12. Ely, *The Adventures of Amos 'n' Andy*, 206–215. See also Watkins, *Stepin Fetchit;* Champ Clark, *Shuffling to Ignominy: The Tragedy of Stepin Fetchit* (New York: iUniverse, 2005).

13. James Edward Smethurst, *The Black Arts Movement: Literary Nationalism in the 1960s and 1970s* (Chapel Hill: University of North Carolina Press, 2005); Mark Anthony Neal, *Soul Babies: Black Popular Culture and the Post-soul Aesthetic* (New York, 2002); William L. Van Deburg, *New Day in Babylon: The Black Power Movement and American Culture, 1965–1975* (Chicago: University of Chicago Press, 1992).

14. For a more detailed and substantive consideration of this phenomenon, see William L. Van Deburg, *Black Camelot: African-American Culture Heroes in Their Times, 1960–1980* (Chicago: University of Chicago Press, 1997), esp. 23–61; William R. Grant IV, *Post-soul Black Cinema: Discontinuities, Innovations and Breakpoints, 1970–1995* (New York: Routledge, 2004); Neal, *Soul Babies*.

15. Mark Reid, *Redefining Black Film* (Berkeley: University of California Press, 1993), 25–26.

16. Neal, *Soul Babies*, 24.

17. For a good examination of the effects of Black Power on the cultural, political, and psychic landscape of America, see Van Deburg, *New Day in Babylon;* Jeffrey O. G. Ogbar, *Black Power: Radical Politics and African American Identity* (Baltimore: Johns Hopkins University Press, 2004); Peniel Joseph, *Waiting 'Til the Midnight Hour: A Narrative History of Black Power in America* (New York: Henry Holt, 2006).

18. Chang provides a wonderfully detailed look at the local political economy of the Bronx that gave birth to hip-hop. See Jeff Chang, *Can't Stop, Won't Stop: A History of the Hip Hop Generation* (New York: St. Martin's, 2005).

19. Afrika Bambaataa, personal communication, April 2002.

20. Felicia M. Miyakawa, *Five Percenter Rap: God Hop's Music, Message, and Black Muslim Mission* (Bloomington: Indiana University Press, 2005), 21.

21. Boogie Down Productions, "My Philosophy," in *By All Means Necessary* (CD; Jive Records, 1988).

22. Robert F. Worth, "*Nigger Heaven* and the Harlem Renaissance," *African American Review* 29, no. 3 (Fall 1995): 461–473.

23. Joe William Trotter, Jr., *The African American Experience*, vol. 2, *From Reconstruction* (Boston: Houghton Mifflin, 2001), 420; Jacquelyn Y. McLendon, *The Politics of Color in the Fiction of Jessie Fauset and Nella Larsen* (Charlottesville: University Press of Virginia, 1995).

24. W. E. B. Du Bois, "Negro Art," *Crisis*, June 1921; reprinted in *W. E. B. Du Bois: A Reader*, ed. Meyer Weinberg (New York: Harper & Row, 1970), 239.

25. Alain Locke, *The New Negro: Voices of the Harlem Renaissance* (1925; repr., New York: Atheneum, 1992), 15.

26. Ibid., 12–15.

27. Martha Jane Nadell, *Enter the New Negroes: Images of Race in American Culture* (Cambridge, Mass.: Harvard University Press, 2004), 34–39.

28. Ibid., 33.

29. Public Enemy featuring Ice Cube and Big Daddy Kane, "Burn Hollywood Burn," in *Fear of a Black Planet* (album; 1990).

30. X-Clan, *To the East Blackwards* (album; 1990).

31. See Nadell, *Enter the New Negroes*, 74.

32. Langston Hughes, "The Negro Artist and the Racial Mountain," reprinted in *Modern American Poetry: An Online Journal and Multimedia Companion* to the *Anthology of Modern American Poetry*, ed. Cary Nelson (New York: Oxford University Press, 2000), http://www.english.uiuc.edu/maps/poets/g_1 /hughes/mountain.htm.

33. Nadell, *Enter the New Negroes*, 70–71.

34. Ibid., 72–73.

35. This is, to some degree, an extension of the valorization of what some militants of the Black Power era termed the "lumpenproletariat." This romantic notion of the "poorest of the poor" on one level functioned to validate some of the most oppressed communities, assigning them certain affirmation and symbolic power that was inherently resistive and counterhegemonic. However, it also functioned to destabilize some black organizations by tolerating reckless (so-called lumpen) behavior. For a more substantive discussion on lumpenism and the Black Panther Party see Ogbar, *Black Power*. See also Chris Booker, "Lumpenization: A Critical Error of the Black Panther Party," in *The Black Panther Party Reconsidered*, ed. Charles E. Jones (Baltimore: Black Classic Press, 1998).

36. Murray Forman, *The 'Hood Comes First: Race, Space, and Place in Rap and Hip-Hop* (Middletown, Conn.: Wesleyan University Press, 2002), 29.

37. See Chapter 5 for an elaboration of the racially discriminatory patterns of the criminal justice system. Matthew Davis, "The World's Biggest Prison System," *BBC News*, April 7, 2006, http://news.bbc.co.uk/2/hi/americas/4858580.stm.

38. Janeé Bolden, "Controversial MC NYOIL Vents: 'Anybody That Rhymes about [Selling Drugs] Is a Dummy,'" December 18, 2006, *SOHH.com*, http://www.sohh.com/articles/article.php/10493.

39. Ibid.

40. Marcus Gilmer, "The Controversy of Race in Spike Lee's *Bamboozled*," *Not Coming to a Theatre Near You*, http://www.notcoming.com/features.php?id=9.

41. Kevin Powell, *Who's Gonna Take the Weight? Manhood, Race, and Power in America* (New York: Three Rivers Press, 2003), 140.

42. bell hooks, *We Real Cool: Black Men and Masculinity* (New York: Routledge, 2004), xii.

43. W. Jelani Cobb, "We Still Wear the Mask," http://playahata.com/hatablog/?p=1654.

44. This refers to U.S. domestic sales. See "List of Best-Selling Albums in the United States," *Wikipedia*, http://en.wikipedia.org/wiki/List_of_best-selling_albums_(USA). Child rappers Lil' Bow Wow, Lil' Romeo, and Lil' Wayne have gone platinum during this era with a largely target audience of teens.

45. Stanley Crouch, *The Artificial White Man: Essays on Authenticity* (New York: Basic Books, 2004), 10.

46. Powell, *Who's Gonna Take the Weight?* 148; Bakari Kitwana, *The Hip-Hop Generation: Young Blacks and the Crisis in African-American Culture* (New York: Basic Civitas, 2002), 205.

47. Demetria Lucas, "Shock and Awe," *Source,* November 2006, 24–25.

48. "The Best of 2006—MTV News," http://www.mtv.com/#/news/.

49. Mos Def, quoted in "Instinctive Travels," *Source,* June 2005, 93.

50. For greater details see www.stopcoonin.com.

51. Bryan Monroe, "The Culture of Disrespect: From *The Message* to the Conversation," *Ebony,* July 2007, http://www.ebonyjet.com/features/featured_articles.aspx ?id=4532.

52. Mark Anthony Neal, "Critical Noir: Songs of the Sad Minstrel," *AOL BlackVoices,* http://blackvoices.aol.com/entmain/music/critn010604/20050112.

53. The Perceptionists, "Black Dialogue," in *Black Dialogue* (CD; New York: Definitive Jux, 1995).

54. "Game On: The Roots Have Made Their Best Record Ever—But Will Anyone Hear It?" *Philadelphia City Paper,* August 17–23, 2006, http://www.citypaper.net/articles/ 2006–08–17/cover.shtml; see also FAQ: ?uest Answers Your ?uestions, http://www .okayplayer.com/theroots/Questfaq.htm.

55. Nadell, *Enter the New Negroes,* 16.

56. Ibid., 69.

57. This is rooted in Antonio Gramsci's theories of social and political control. See Strinati Dominic, *Introduction to Theories of Popular Culture* (New York: Routledge, 1995), 165.

Chapter 2. "Real Niggas": Race, Ethnicity, and the Construction of Authenticity in Hip-Hop

1. Historically, the most virulent and violent forms of white supremacy have been zealously maintained by white southerners. White southern politicians, law enforcement officials, and civilians from the colonial era to the 1960s openly and proudly engaged in the violent subjugation of black people through repressive laws, public beatings, rape, arson, lynching, arrests, and torture. Every southern state passed laws that denied black people access to voting, equal education, and sundry public accommodations. These laws were repealed in the 1960s after a prolonged struggle that met with massive resistance from white southerners. A young black producer and executive, Timbaland, has underwritten Sparxxx's career, adding to the rapper's legitimacy and visibility. To date, no significant protest or criticism of Sparxxx has emerged from within or without the hip-hop community.

2. Bonnie Mitchell and Joe Feagin argue that people of color in the United States have developed and maintained their cultural practices as a means to resist oppression in a state of internal colonialism. See their article "America's Racial-Ethnic Cultures: Opposition within a Mythical Melting Pot," in *Toward the Multicultural University,* ed. Benjamin

Bowser, Terry Jones, and Gale Auletta Young (Westport, Conn.: Praeger Publishers, 1995). See also William Van Deburg, *Black Camelot: African-American Culture Heroes in Their Times, 1960–1980* (Chicago: University of Chicago Press, 1999), 24, 57, 231; see also John W. Roberts, *From Trickster to Badman: The Black Folk Hero in Slavery and Freedom* (Philadelphia: University of Pennsylvania Press, 1990), 174–180.

3. There appears to be some dispute over the origins of *bomba* and *plena* music from Puerto Rico. Some scholars and participants have argued that the two styles have developed from different traditions: the *bomba* from West Africans and the *plena* from Tainos and Spanish. Others have argued for a mutual African base and degrees of European or Taino influence. According to one source, "The *plena* arose at the beginning of the 20th century in the sugar-growing areas along the southern coast of the island. The varied musical expression of the slave population, the peasantry, *jibaro* and the national elite make up the direct context for the birth and growth of the *plena*. Besides having its musical and social roots in our West African heritage, *Plena* was also influenced by *jibaro* (Spanish-Arabic) music, the native Taino Indians, and the music of the European-style salons, in addition to the music of displaced freed slaves [*sic*] who traveled to Puerto Rico from English-speaking Caribbean Islands seeking work. As the rural workers moved to San Juan and other urban areas in the recent past, the *plena* became a part of the urban cultural life, performed for entertainment at informal social gatherings." Beyond the reliance on drumbeats, *plena* also encompasses lyrical elements, including call-and-response and improvised social narrative, similar to rapping's "freestyle" of improvisational wordplay. See "Plena," at *Music of Puerto Rico: Know Us by the Songs We Sing,* http://www.musicofpuertorico.com/en/genre_plena .html. See also Ruth Glasser, *My Music Is My Flag: Puerto Rican Musicians and Their New York Communities, 1917–1940* (Berkeley and Los Angeles: University of California Press, 1997); Juan Flores, *From Bomba to Hip-Hop: Puerto Rican Culture and Latino Identity* (New York: Columbia University Press, 2000); and Frances R. Aparicio, *Listening to Salsa: Gender, Latin Popular Music, and Puerto Rican Cultures* (Middletown, Conn.: Wesleyan University Press, 1997).

4. Robin D. G. Kelley, *Yo Mama's Disfunktional! Fighting the Culture Wars in Urban America* (Boston: Beacon Press, 1997), 38.

5. Aïda Croal, "Eminem: Legitimate Heir or Thief in the Temple?" formerly at *Africana.com,* retrieved December 12, 2000.

6. Marvin J. Gladney, "The Black Arts Movement and Hip-Hop," *African American Review* 29, no. 2 (Summer 1995): 291.

7. It must be understood that the popular use of the term "black" in this context refers to African Americans, although many Latinos are also black. Toure's use of the term reflects the colloquial meaning that situates Puerto Ricans outside the conventional definition of being black. For a historical discussion of an Afro–Puerto Rican identity, see Roberto P. Rodriguez-Morazzani, "Beyond the Rainbow: Mapping the Discourse on Puerto Ricans and 'Race,'" *Centro: Journal of the Center for Puerto Rican Studies* 8, nos. 1 and 2 (1996): 128–149. Winston James, "Afro-Puerto Rican Radicalism in the United States: Reflections on the Political Trajectories of Arturo Schomburg and Jesus Colon," *Centro* 8, nos. 1–2 (1996): 92–127; and Toure, "The Hip-Hop Nation: Whose Is It?" *New York Times,* August 22, 1999.

8. The decision to place someone on the cover of the *Source,* the leading music magazine in newsstand sales nationally and the most revered hip-hop magazine, is not necessarily determined by record sales. In fact, the Beastie Boys and Kid Rock, who are white rap acts, have outsold virtually everyone ever to grace the covers of any hip-hop magazine. They, however, have never appeared on the cover of any hip-hop magazine. Still, nonmusicians such as Malcolm X and Mike Tyson have managed to appear on the cover of the *Source.* The general level of relevance to hip-hop (as opaque a notion as it is) seems to determine who appears on the cover. Moreover, journalists with their "ears to the street" often assume the task of differentiating between "pop" acts with a tenuous grounding in the hip-hop community and more legitimate acts. Clearly, the notion of "legitimacy" and "relevance" are highly subjective, as are artistic observations in general, further obviating the understanding of authenticity.

9. "Blackness," as used here, may be better expressed as a genetic and cultural relationship to Africa. Aware that race is socially contrived, I generally rely on the person in question to be his or her chief determiner of his or her "race." As blackness in the United States is understood differently than it is in most other parts of the world, I use the term "black" in reference to Latinos with some hesitation. A Latino, of course, can be of any race. Many African Americans who have declared themselves black and were viewed as black, such as former congressman Adam Clayton Powell or (in an extreme case) Walter White, executive secretary of the National Association for the Advancement of Colored People, would never have been considered such elsewhere. This does not, however, exclude them from being "black people," as it was understood in their own cultural and social context. Without doubt, the term suggests particular historical, social, political, and cultural experiences that have been significantly determined by the highly racialized traditions of the United States. To deny one's right to self-definition is problematic. Similarly, a light-brown-skinned, curly-haired person from Cuba may never have viewed herself as black or have been considered such until arrival in the United States. I argue that she still reserves the right to be simply Latina, Cuban, "*mulatta,*" or any other designation.

10. Graffiti and b-boying have been suffused with the talent and artistic input of non–African Americans since their beginnings. In fact, Taki 183, one of the earliest graffiti artists to achieve notoriety, was a white teenager from the Bronx. Subsequent "kings," or graffiti master artists, such as "Zephyr," "Seen," and "Cope2," have also been white. The mostly Latino Rock Steady Crew is the most popular crew of b-boys and b-girls in the world, while Crazy Legs, a Puerto Rican, is perhaps the most popular b-boy, featured in several films and documentaries.

11. See Nelson George, *Hip-Hop America* (New York: Penguin, 1998), 57.

12. Eithne Quinn, *Nuthin' but a "g" Thang: The Culture and Commerce of Gangsta Rap* (New York: Columbia University Press, 2005), 92–99; see also Van Deburg, *Black Camelot;* Roberts, *From Trickster to Badman.*

13. Noam Chomsky, *Reflections on Language* (New York: Pantheon, 1975), 133.

14. Several journalistic pieces have lauded N.W.A's *Straight Outta Compton* (CD; 1988) as a seminal work, one of the greatest hip-hop albums ever produced, and a number of academics have viewed the group as more than a simple gangsta rap act bent on nihilistic barbarism. Robin D. G. Kelly, Tricia Rose, and Teresa Martinez all contend that

the group is conscious of white supremacy and that the group's art operates as a resistant to a system of institutionalized oppression and marginalization.

15. See Chapter 3 for a more elaborate discussion of the bad nigger trope and its historical development.

16. Eithne Quinn offers an extensive and sophisticated treatment of gangsta rap in *Nuthin but a "g" Thang.*

17. The overwhelming majority of gang conflicts are intraethnic, although rare conflicts erupt between black and Latino gangs. There is also an Asian gang presence in the city that primarily rivals other Asians and surrounding Latino gangs. In contrast to street violence, prison conflicts are significantly determined by race. For a brilliant study of Los Angeles gang culture, see Susan A. Philips, *Wallbangin': Graffiti and Gangs in L.A.* (Chicago: University of Chicago Press, 1999).

18. The Latino community in Los Angeles County represents about 44 percent of the total population. About two-thirds of the Latino population is Mexican, followed by El Salvadorian and other Central American groups. Although a sizable number of Africans were enslaved in Mexico up to the early nineteenth century, there has been a remarkable "erasure" of the African presence through assimilation and collective state-sponsored efforts. Unlike with Caribbean Latinos, the African influence in dance, music, and phenotype is substantively less visible—if visible at all—among Mexicans and most other Central Americans, though small communities of African Mexicans remain today. For information on Latinos in Los Angeles, see the U.S. Census Bureau, "State and County Quickfacts: Los Angeles County, California," http:// quickfacts.census.gov/qfd/states/06/06037.html. For greater detail on the African presence in Mexico, see Colin A. Palmer, *Slaves of the White God: Blacks in Mexico, 1570–1650* (New York: Oxford University Press, 1976), and Ben Vinson III, *Bearing Arms for His Majesty: The Free-Colored Militia in Colonial Mexico* (Stanford, Calif.: Stanford University Press, 2001).

19. As noted above, Latinos were the cofounders of hip-hop but had a marginal presence in the elements of rap and turntablism. Latinos have been most visible in break dancing and graffiti art.

20. It was not until a 1996 beef with Ice Cube that anyone called attention to the fact that the group's members were not Mexican: "Everybody in the ghetto, know what you're doin' / one white boy and two fucking Cubans. Claiming that you're *loco* / but you ain't Mexican. . . ." (Westside Connection, "King of the Hill," in *Bow Down* [CD; 1996]). In a response song, B-Real not only affirmed his Cuban identity but carefully placed it in the context of Cuban gangster themes: "Doughboy, you're fuckin' around wit' the real Cuban. I'm no fictional Scarface movie land bullshit" (Cypress Hill featuring Shag, "Ice Cube Killa" [12"; 1996]).

21. I reiterate that I use "black" with hesitation here. See note 9 above on using the term "black" in reference to Latinos.

22. Quoted in Mandalit Del Barco, "Rap's Latino Sabor," in *Droppin' Science: Critical Essays on Rap Music and Hip-Hop Culture,* ed. William Eric Perkins (Philadelphia: Temple University Press, 1996), 81.

23. See South Park Mexican featuring Low-G and Marilyn Rylander, "Who's Over There," in *3rd Wish to Rock the World* (CD; Dope House Records, 1999).

24. Rodriguez-Morazzani, "Beyond the Rainbow," 153. There is a paucity of scholarship on the relationships between African Americans and Puerto Ricans. There is, however, a growing body of work on race and Puerto Ricans. Much of this scholarship confronts the Puerto Rican myth of racial egalitarianism. In fact, this "rainbow people" myth, as Rodriguez-Morazzani notes, is increasingly attacked. Jorge Duany explains how Afro–Puerto Ricans are typically considered "subaltern outsiders" and a marginal group in Puerto Rico where the Spanish farmer *jibaro* is the figurative iconic Puerto Rican. In a similar vein, Miriam Jimenez Roman states that disparaging opinions about people of visible African ancestry are not aberrant among Puerto Ricans. That some of this sentiment was transferred toward African Americans is certain. See Jorge Duany, "Nation on the Move: The Construction of Cultural Identities in Puerto Rico and the Diaspora," *American Ethnologist* 27, no. 1 (2000): 14; and Miriam Jimenez Roman, "Un hombre (negro) del pueblo: Jose Celso Barbosa and the Puerto Rican 'Race' toward Whiteness," *Centro*, 8, nos. 1 and 2 (1996): 10.

25. Wyclef Jean, *Carnival* (CD; 1997).

26. This is not entirely unique in hip-hop. Rappers often employ idiomatic language that is unique to their city or region. Ice Cube, for example, exclaims that "211 is my favorite number" in his song about robbing from the rich and giving to the poor. The number is the California penal code for robbery. This esoteric reference suggests audience exclusivity, but in many ways this is a reflection of the art's tendency to create and extend the dynamic youth idioms pervasive in vernacular English.

27. Del Barco, 86. Here "black" is mutually exclusive with being Latino for Juju, who, with brown skin and frizzy hair is much "blacker" looking than many other black MCs. "African American" is perhaps a more accurate expression of his sentiment.

28. "Latin Lingo," *XXL Magazine*, May 2005, 48.

29. Big Pun, "Dream Shatterer," in *Capital Punishment* (CD; 2000).

30. Judy Tseng, "Asian American Rap: Expression through Alternate Forms," *Model Minority: A Guide to Asian American Empowerment,* http://www.modelminority.com/article128.html; Todd Angkasuwan, "Asian American Hip-Hop: A Commentary," *Model Minority: A Guide to Asian American Empowerment,* November 2004, http://modelminority.com/article924.html; Oliver Wang, "Asian Americans and Hip-Hop," *Asian Week*, November 12–18, 1998.

31. Wang, "Asian Americans and Hip-Hop."

32. See "Top of the Hip-Hop Crop," *Shanghai Daily News,* November 17, 2004, http://english.eastday.com/eastday/englishedition/features/userobject1ai656215.html.

33. In May 2005 Jin announced his retirement from hip-hop and formed Youth Organization for Asian Minorities, whose mission was to foster "unity, positivity and self-awareness"; see http://www.whatsthe411.ca/index.asp?pageID=41.

34. Greg Tate, ed., *Everything but the Burden: What White People Are Taking from Black Culture* (New York: Broadway Books, 2003); Stephan Talty, *Mulatto America: At the Crossroads of Black and White Culture* (New York: HarperCollins, 2003); Burton W. Peretti, *The Creation of Jazz: Music, Race, and Culture in Urban America* (Urbana and Chicago: University of Illinois Press, 1994); Martha Jane Nadell, *Enter the New Negroes: Images of Race in American Culture* (Cambridge, Mass.: Harvard University Press, 2004).

35. Tate, *Everything but the Burden*, 4–6.

36. Bakari Kitwana, *Why White Kids Love Hip-Hop: Wanksta, Wiggers, Wannabes, and the New Reality of Race in America* (New York: Basic Books, 2005), 2.

37. Attention must be directed at white hip-hop artists behind the scenes, where white producers like Arthur Baker, Rick Rubin, DJ Muggs, and the Dust Brothers have all played pivotal roles in the development of new hip-hop sounds.

38. There is a long-circulating rumor among African Americans that Elvis Presley stated in an interview that the only thing that a "nigger" can do for him is buy his records and shine his shoes. Though the rumor has survived since the 1950s, there is no record of the alleged interview in print. No scholarly source can place the name of the publication. *Jet Magazine* in the 1950s attempted to track down the story; it got denials from Presley's camp and found no evidence of the comment. It appears to be a resilient urban legend. See Barbara and David P. Mikkelson, "Shine My Shoes," at *Snopes.com: Urban Legends Reference Pages,* http://www.snopes.com/music/artists/presley1.asp, for further discussion.

39. It is noteworthy that MC Hammer experienced a similar metamorphosis when he reincarnated himself as an "OG"—original gangster—that same year.

40. The video features the group in all-white settings, drinking, smoking, and wearing baggy pants and flannel shirts, similar to Los Angeles–area gangsters. The video is also set against scenes from a Saint Patrick's Day parade with fighting and rowdy behavior. Before lead rapper Everlast enjoyed notoriety as a member of House of Pain, he pursued a career as a solo artist. In 2001 Rhino announced that it planned to reissue *Forever Everlasting,* his 1990 debut solo album recorded for Warner Bros., as Everlast was coming up through Ice-T's Los Angeles–based Rhyme Syndicate Cartel. The album was executive produced by Ice-T and industry legend Benny Medina.

41. Janique Burke, "White Lines," *Source,* July 2003, 50.

42. Anthony Bozza, "Eminem Blows Up," *Rolling Stone,* April 29, 1999, 42.

43. Eminem, "I Remember," in *I Remember* (white label 12"; 2001).

44. Eminem, "Quitter," in *Quitter* (white label 12"; 2001).

45. Toure, "D-12," *Rolling Stone,* February 15, 2000, 70.

46. Quoted in Anthony Bozza, *Whatever You Say I Am: The Life and Times of Eminem* (New York: Crown Publishers, 2003), 194.

47. Kitwana, 139–142.

48. U.S. Census Bureau, Current Population Survey, 2005 Annual Social and Economic Supplement, Washington, D.C.

49. See David Roediger, *Wages of Whiteness: Race and the Making of the American Working Class* (New York: Verso, 1999); Lizabeth Cohen, *Making a New Deal: Industrial Workers in Chicago, 1919–1939* (Cambridge: Cambridge University Press, 1991); Rod Bush, *We Are Not What We Seem: Black Nationalism and Class Struggle in the American Century* (New York: New York University Press, 1999).

50. S. Craig Watkins, *Hip Hop Matters: Politics, Pop Culture, and the Struggle for the Soul of a Movement* (New York: Beacon Press, 2005), 92.

51. "Clap Back," *Source,* February 2004, 80–81.

52. "Chuck D Speaks on Hip Hop, Eminem and Black Death," *Davey D's Hip Hop Political Palace,* December 25, 2003, http://p076.ezboard.com/fpoliticalpalacefrm28.show Message?topicID=226.topic.

53. Zadie Smith, "The Zen of Eminem," *Vibe*, January 2005, http://www.vibe.com/news/magazine_features/2005/01/cover_story_zen_eminem.

54. 504 Boyz featuring Ghetto Commission and Krazy, "We Bust," in *Goodfellas* (CD; Priority, 2000).

55. Mickey Hess, "Don't Quote Me, Boy": Dynamite Hack Covers NWA's "Boyz-N-The-Hood" *Popular Music and Society* 28, no. 2 (May 2005): 179–191.

56. Paul Mooney, a comedian who has used the word professionally and personally for decades, noted that the Michael Richards racist tirade was so offensive that he was moved to abandon the n-word and encouraged hip-hoppers to do the same. DelRay Davis, who appears on Kanye West's first two albums, similarly expressed outrage at Richard's rant, though he, too, uses the word. "SOHH Exclusive: Black Comics Weigh in on Racist Kramer Outburst," *Sohh.com*, November 21, 2006, http://www.sohh.com/articles/article.php/10292; "Daily Hip-Hop News: Update: Comedian Paul Mooney Gives up the 'N Word,' Encourages Fans to Follow," November 28, 2006, http://www.sohh.com/articles/article.php/10336.

57. Many former slaves are on record as referring to black people as "niggas." During audio recordings of ex-slaves in the 1930s made by the Works Progress Administration, elderly black people are documented as referring to enslaved black people in this manner.

58. I have yet to encounter any song or article of protest (or any recognition) on Latinos using "nigga" in rap. KAM, a Los Angeles–based rapper who is African American, refers to Latinos as "kin to me" in a song inveighing against Latino-black violence in California prisons. Several songs have heralded blacks uniting with the "*eses*" in Los Angeles against white supremacy. There was controversy, however, when Puerto Rican superstar Jennifer Lopez uttered the word on her remix for "I'm Real" in August 2001. New York's Hot 97 radio shock jock Buc Wild attacked the singer for using the word, accusing her of "trying to get her ghetto pass back." Buc Wild invited protesters to throw rice and beans at Lopez at her upcoming performance for NBC's *Today Show*. There were no such demonstrations at the show. Lopez explained that she did not mean to offend and that the lyrics were actually written by Irv Gotti and rapper Ja Rule, who are both African American. Her song eventually made it to the number 1 spot on cable channel BET's video countdown, suggesting that little hostility was evoked from the mass of African American fans.

59. The term "Bama" is often used as a term with some degree of stigma to describe southern people who are considered uncouth, ignorant, and rowdy. Used primarily in the South among African Americans, the term can also refer to the variant of AAVE employed by "Bamas." The earliest use that I find for the term in popular film or song is in the Atlanta-set Spike Lee film *School Daze* (1988), where a militant college student (played by Lawrence Fishburne) refers to a local hood (played by Samuel L. Jackson) as a "Bama." The Atlanta-based group Goodie Mob included a translation of this dialect in their *World Party* LP liner notes. Their fellow label mates, the Youngbloodz, similarly translated a conversation from Bama into Standard English for their video "85 South." In a humorous scene in the 2006 movie *ATL,* a conversation is translated from Bama into Standard English. Though not given the scholarly attention that AAVE in general, or another variant, Gullah, has had, this manner of speech deserves more inquiry than it has heretofore received. In fact, beyond these popular culture references, I am unaware of any others beyond anecdotal personal experiences.

60. "Eminem vs. Cage," at *Merry Christmas Eminem and a Happy New Year: Unofficial Fansite*, http://www.eminem.net/enemies/cage/.

61. "Bakari Kitwana on Don Imus and Hip-Hop," editorial, Newsday.com, April 13, 2007, posted at *NewBlackMan* blog, http://newblackman.blogspot.com/2007/04/bakari-kitwana-on-don-imus-and-hip-hop.html.

62. Shaheem Reid, "Hip-Hop on the Defensive after Imus Incident," "MTV News," April 13, 2007, http://www.mtv.com/news/articles/1557094/20070413/index.jhtml.

63. Andre Weston, "Oprah, Imus & Al," *Hip Hop Weekly*, 2, no. 9 (2007): 46.

64. "NAACP to Hold Funeral for 'N' Word," *USA Today*, April 30, 2007, http://www.usatoday.com/news/nation/2007–04–30-n-word-funeral_N.htm.

65. For a discussion on self-criticism in the hip-hop community, see Jeffrey O. G. Ogbar, "Slouching toward Bork: The Culture Wars and Self-Criticism in Hip-Hop," *Journal of Black Studies*, vol. 30, no 2 (November 1999).

66. Jurassic 5, "L.A.U.S.D.," in *Quality Control* (CD; Los Angeles, 2000).

Chapter 3. Between God and Earth: Feminism, Machismo, and Gender in Hip-Hop Music

1. Imani Perry, *Prophets of the Hood: Politics and Poetics in Hip Hop* (Durham, N.C.: Duke University Press, 2004), 58.

2. The popular press—the *Source, Rolling Stone, XXL, Rappages,* and the like—has devoted considerable attention to misogyny in hip-hop. Some of the more nuanced scholarly examinations include Tricia Rose, *Black Noise: Rap Music and Black Culture in Contemporary America* (Hanover, N.H.: Wesleyan University Press, 1994), chap. 5; Eithne Quinn, *Nuthin' but a "g" thang: The Culture and Commerce of Gangsta Rap* (New York: Columbia University Press, 2005), 100–104; Robin D. G. Kelley, *Race Rebels: Culture, Politics, and the Black Working Class* (New York: Free Press, 1994), 185–189; and Kimberle Crenshaw, "Beyond Racism and Misogyny: Black Feminism and 2 Live Crew," *Boston Review* 16, no. 6 (December 1991): 6, 33.

3. This chapter builds upon several examinations of women in hip-hop. Without restating much general information, I attempt to provide a general overview with new attention to the voices of the artists as well as a unique look at male feminist expression. For discussion of the development of women's voices, see Robin Roberts, "Ladies First: Queen Latifah's Afrocentric Feminist Music Video," *African American Review* 28, no. 2 (1994): 245; Rana Emerson, "Where My Girls At?" *Gender and Society* 16, no. 1 (2002): 115–135; Jason Haugen, "Unladylike Divas: Language, Gender, and Female Gangsta Rappers," *Popular Music and Society* 26, no. 4 (2003): 429; Cheryl Keyes, "Empowering Self, Making Choices, Creating Spaces," *Journal of American Folklore* 113, no. 449 (2000): 255–269; J. R. Reynolds, "Women Rap for Dignity: Defiant Voices Fight Misogyny," *Billboard* 106, no. 13 (March 1994): 1; and Nataki Goodall, "Depend on Myself: T.L.C. and the Evolution of Black Female Rap," *Journal of Negro History* 79, no. 1 (1994): 85.

4. Nancy Cott, *The Grounding of Modern Feminism* (New Haven, Conn.: Yale University Press, 1987), 4–5.

5. Judith Grant, *Fundamental Feminism: Contesting the Core Concepts of Feminist Theory* (New York: Routledge, 1993), 1.

6. Ibid., 2–3.

7. Patricia Hill Collins, "Feminism in the United States," *Microsoft Encarta Africana 2000* (CD-ROM; Seattle, Wash.: Microsoft Corp., 1999).

8. Patricia Hill Collins, *Black Feminist Thought: Knowledge, Consciousness and the Politics of Empowerment* (New York: Routledge, 2000), 4–6.

9. For a thorough examination of these ideas, see Patricia Hill Collins, *Black Sexual Politics: African Americans, Gender and the New Racism* (New York: Routledge), 2004.

10. Perry, *Prophets of the Hood*, 58–59.

11. For a very good treatment of black masculinity and its intersection with sports and popular culture, see Todd Boyd, *Young, Black, Rich and Famous: The Rise of the NBA, the Hip Hop Invasion and the Transformation of American Culture* (New York: Doubleday, 2003), and *Am I Black Enough for You: Popular Culture from the 'Hood and Beyond* (Bloomington: Indiana University Press), 1997.

12. Robin D. G. Kelley, *Race Rebels: Culture, Politics, and the Black Working Class* (New York: Free Press, 1994), 214–215. See also Richard Majors and Janet Mancini Billson, eds., *Cool Pose: The Dilemma of Black Manhood in America* (New York: Touchtone, 1993).

13. Kelley, *Race Rebels*, 187.

14. "Gang's Still Here: Sugar Hill Gang Whose 'Rapper's Delight' Was First Hip-Hop Record, Enjoy a Resurgence in Popularity," *New York Newsday*, October 10, 2004.

15. Jon F. Rice, *Up on Madison Down on 75th: A History of the Illinois Black Panther Party* (Evanston, Ill.: The Committee, 1983), 28. Though this book was finally published in 1983, four years after the release of "Rapper's Delight," the writing and research of the book was completed several years earlier. Its focus is on the development of the Black Panther Party in Chicago and the local chapter's attempt to establish constructive alliances with local street gangs. There is, of course, the possibility that street-level raps, such as this one, had been influenced by the rise of hip-hip, and, though attributed to the 1960s, this rap may have borrowed from the commercial release.

16. Sugar Hill Gang, "Rapper's Delight," in *The Sugar Hill Gang* (album; Sugar Hill Records, 1979).

17. Angela Y. Davis, "Billie Holiday's 'Strange Fruit': Music and Social Consciousness," in *Speech and Power*, vol. 2, ed. Gerald Early (Hopewell, N.J.: Ecco Press, 1993), 34.

18. This hip-hop character, alternately known as "nihilism," "gangsta," "misogynist," and "hardcore," has been explored extensively by several scholars. For some of the better examinations, see Kelley, *Race Rebels*; Rose, *Black Noise*; Murray Forman, *The 'Hood Comes First: Race, Space, and Place in Rap and Hip-Hop* (Middletown, Conn.: Wesleyan University Press, 2002); Cheryl L. Keyes, *Rap Music and Street Consciousness* (Urbana: University of Illinois Press, 2002); Quinn, *Nuthin' but a "g" Thang*.

19. Nancy Guevara, "Women Writin' Rappin' Breakin'," in *Droppin' Science: Critical Essays on Rap Music and Hip Hop Culture*, ed. William Eric Perkins (Philadelphia: Temple University Press, 1996), 54–55.

20. Ibid., 56.

21. Elizabeth Fox-Genovese, *Within the Plantation Household: Black and White Women of the Old South* (Chapel Hill: University of North Carolina Press, 1988); Marli

Frances Weiner, *Mistresses and Slaves: Plantation Women in South Carolina, 1830–80* (Urbana: University of Illinois Press, 1997); Angela Y. Davis, *Women, Race, and Class* (New York: Vintage, 1983); bell hooks, *Ain't I a Woman: Black Women and Feminism* (Boston: South End Press, 1981).

22. Darlene Clark Hine, "Female Slave Resistance: The Economics of Sex," in *Black Women in American History,* vol, 2, ed. Darlene Clark Hine (Brooklyn, N.Y.: Carlson, 1990), 657–666; see also hooks, *Ain't I a Woman,* 33; and Deborah Gray White, *Ar'n't I a Woman? Female Slaves in the Plantation South* (New York: Norton, 1999).

23. Collins, *Black Feminist Thought,* 78.

24. Guevara, "Women Writin' Rappin' Breakin,'" 55–57.

25. Ibid., 56.

26. Ibid., 57.

27. Russell A. Potter, *Spectacular Vernaculars: Hip-Hop and the Politics of Postmodernism* (Albany: State University of New York Press, 1995), 33–35.

28. There are, however, other songs that fall into a category of "hopeful" verse, where rappers fantasize about the type of partner they want—but not necessary have. These celebrate a more loving union, not based simply on domination or crude references to sexual relations. See LL Cool J's historic "I Need Love" (1985), Jay-Z's "Excuse Me Miss" (2002), and 50 Cent's "21 Questions" (2003).

29. For example, many MCs adopted names that reflected intelligence: Professor X the Overseer (of X-Clan), Large Professor, Poor Righteous Teachers, and Intelligent Hoodlum, among others. For a more detailed discussion of this era, see Chap. 5.

30. MC Lyte, "I Am Woman," in *Lyte as a Rock* (CD; 1989). Note also that MC Lyte adopts the song title of Helen Reddy's 1972 feminist anthem, suggesting an artistic continuity of feminist discourse in popular music.

31. For a discussion of the female MC types, see Keyes, *Rap Music,* 186–209.

32. Queen Latifah featuring Mark the 45 King, "A King and Queen Creation," in *All Hail the Queen* (CD; Tommy Boy, 1990).

33. Roberts, "Ladies First," 245–257.

34. N.W.A, "Gangsta Gangsta," in *Straight Outta Compton* (CD; Los Angeles: Ruthless Records, 1988).

35. Widely said by artists; for an example, see Tupac featuring the Outlaws, "M.O.B.," in *Until the End of Time* (CD; Los Angeles: Death Row/Makaveli Records, 2001).

36. Perkins, *Droppin' Science,* 26.

37. Lyndah, quoted in Keyes, *Rap Music,* 200.

38. Jennifer Baumgardner and Amy Richards, *Manifesta: Young Women, Feminism, and the Future* (New York: Farrar, Straus & Giroux, 2000); Stacy Gillis, Gillian Howie, and Rebecca Munford, eds., *Third Wave Feminism: A Critical Exploration* (New York: Palgrave, 2004); Daisy Hernandez and Bushra Rehman, eds., *Colonize This! Young Women of Color and Today's Feminism* (Emeryville, Calif.: Seal, 2002).

39. Perry, *Prophets of the Hood,* 159.

40. Lil' Kim featuring Lil' Ceas and Jay-Z, "Big Momma Thang" and "Queen Bitch," in *Hardcore* (CD; 1996).

41. Foxy Brown featuring Jay-Z, "I'll Be," in *Ill Na Na* (CD; 1996).

42. Missy Misdemeanor Elliot, "Lick Shots," in *Miss E . . . So Addictive* (CD; 2001), "Pussycat," in *Under Construction* (CD; 2002), "Let Me Fix My Weave," in *This Is Not a Test* (CD; 2003).

43. Kim Osorio and Jerry L. Barrow, "Lil' Kim, Record Report," *Source*, April 2003, 143–144.

44. In terms of class, wealth is clearly celebrated in hip-hop; however, only a particular type of wealth is acceptable for the sake of credibility. For example, a rapper could not celebrate his Jack and Jill ski trips, Links-sponsored debutante balls, and family outings to the summer home in Oak Bluffs at Martha's Vineyard. These staples of African American elite social life are decidedly black experiences, but only for exclusively upper-class African American circles; they have little cachet in hip-hop circles. Being raised in the affluent home of a banker, physician, businessman, or other professional, going to private school, and living in suburban comfort are anathema to the hardscrabble life typified in hip-hop as "real."

45. Collins, *Black Sexual Politics*, 127.

46. Kenneth J. Neubeck and Noel A. Cassanave, *Welfare Racism: Playing the Race Card against America's Poor* (New York: Taylor & Francis, 2001).

47. Akissi Britton, "Deconstructing Lil Kim," *Essence*, October 2000, 115.

48. Michael Gonzales, "Mack Divas," *Source*, February 1997, 67.

49. Foxy Brown and mother, quoted in Michelle Buford and Christopher John Farley, "Dignity or Dollars," *Essence*, August 1999, 72–76, 132.

50. Ibid., 133.

51. Heidi Siegmund-Cuda, "Breaking Away," *Source*, November 2002, 152.

52. Lil' Kim featuring Mario "Yellowman" Winans, "Single Black Female" in *The Notorious K.I.M.* (CD; 2000).

53. Joan Morgan, "The Bad Girls of Hip-Hop," *Essence*, March 1997.

54. Haugen, "'Unladylike Divas,'" 429.

55. Audre Lorde, "Audre Lorde," in *Black Women Writers at Work*, ed. Claudia Tate (New York: Continuum, 1983), 100–116; see also Robin Roberts, "Music Videos, Performance and Resistance: Feminist Rappers," *Journal of Popular Culture* 25 (1991): 141–152.

56. Lil' Kim, "Suck My Dick," in *The Notorious K.I.M.* (CD; 2000).

57. Lil' Kim, quoted in "Lil' Kim No Fan of Brittney Spears," at RapDirt, http://rapdirt.com/article1474.html.

58. Joan Smith, quoted in bell hooks, *Outlaw Culture: Resisting Representations* (New York: Routledge, 1994), 121.

59. You Go, Girls: Lauryn Hill Leads the Way in a Female-Fueled Grammys," *In Style* 6, no. 5 (May 1, 1999): 196; "Hill, Lauryn," *Microsoft Encarta Africana 2000* (CD-ROM; Seattle, Wash.: Microsoft Corp., 1999).

60. Bahamadia, "Wordplay," in *Kollage* (CD; 1997).

61. Eve featuring Da Brat and Trina, "Gangsta Bitches," in *Scorpion* (CD; 2001).

62. The list of work on the images of women in hip-hop is much too vast to cite here. See Perry, *Prophets of the Hood;* Gwendolyn D. Pough, Elaine Richardson, Aisha Durham, and Rachel Raimist, eds., *Home Girls Make Some Noise! Hip-Hop Feminism Anthology* (Mira Loma, Calif.: Parker Publishing, 2007).

63. See Jeffrey O. G. Ogbar, *Black Power: Radical Politics and African American Identity* (Baltimore: Johns Hopkins University Press, 2004); Maxine Leeds Craig, *Ain't I a Beauty Queen? Black Women, Beauty, and the Politics of Race* (New York: Oxford University Press, 2002).

64. Sir Mix-a-lot, "Baby Got Back," in *Mack Daddy* (CD; New York: Def American Recordings, 1992).

65. Black women like Halle Berry have been featured in *Maxim*. *King* has featured Coco, the white model and wife of Ice-T, whose butt is so large that she has to explain that she does not have butt implants. She is so popular that when she graced the cover of *Smooth*, it became the highest selling issue of the magazine ever. See Carl Chery, "SOHH Exclusive: Ice-T's Wife Coco Poses for 'Playboy,' Working on Reality Show," SOHH.com, May 4, 2007, http://www.sohh.com/articles/article.php/11543; "60 Seconds with Ice-T and CoCo," SOHH.com, November 8, 2006, http://www.sohh.com/articles/category .php?category_ID=106&startAt=40.

66. Also see Heather Day, "How to Treat a Queen: Hip-Hop Media and the Female Body" (unpublished manuscript, Connecticut College, New London, Spring 2006).

67. Paris, "You Know My Name," in *Sonic Jihad* (CD; 2003).

68. bell hooks, *Feminist Theory: From Margin to Center* (Boston: South End Press, 2000), 82.

69. Ibid., 83.

70. Davis, *Women, Race and Class,* 202.

71. The Goats, "Aaah D Yaaa," in *Tricks of the Shade* (CD; New York: Sony Music Entertainment, 1992).

72. Digable Planets, "La Femme Fetal," in *Reachin' (A New Refutation of Time and Space)* (CD; New York: Pendulum Records), 1992.

73. For a greater discussion of black men on patriarchy, see Rudolph P. Byrd and Beverly Guy-Sheftall, eds., *Traps: African American Men on Gender and Sexuality* (Bloomington: Indiana University Press, 2001).

74. bell hooks, *We Real Cool: Black Men and Masculinity* (New York: Routledge, 2004), 49.

Chapter 4. Rebels with a Cause: Gangstas, Militants, Media, and the Contest for Hip-Hop

1. These styles are rooted in the African American urban badman narratives, as I discussed in greater detail in Chapter 3. See Robin D. G. Kelley, *Race Rebels: Culture, Politics and the Black Working Class* (New York: Free Press, 1994), 214–215.

2. William Eric Perkins, ed., *Droppin' Science: Critical Essays in Rap Music and Hip-Hop Culture* (Philadelphia: Temple University Press, 1996), 35–37.

3. Jeru the Damaja, "Come Clean," in *The Sun Rises in the East* (CD; Full Frequency, 1994).

4. Donald Mitchell, *Cultural Geography: A Critical Introduction* (Malden, Mass.: Blackwell Press, 2000), 4.

5. L. Reibstein, "The Right Takes a Media Giant to Political Task," *Newsweek,* June 12, 1995, 23, 30.

6. Lacayo, "Violent Reaction," *Time,* June 12, 1995, 28.

7. Allison Samuels, "Gangsta Rap Label Gets Dissed," *Newsweek,* October 9, 1995, 30.

8. J. Pareles, "On Rap, Symbolism and Fear," *New York Times,* February 2, 1992, 1, 23.

9. Barry Shank, "Fears of the White Unconscious: Music, Race and Identification in the Censorship of Cop Killer," *Radical History Review* 66 (1996): 124–145, esp. 131.

10. The term "house nigga" is a derisive description of a black person accused of enjoying privilege at the expense of endearing himself to white supremacy. It is rooted in the ahistorical assumption that people enslaved in the homes of whites were loyal to their enslavers and hostile to the more rebellious field slaves who did not enjoy the better clothes or food of those enslaved in the home. The most popular slave insurrections in the Unites States were, however, initiated by house slaves: Nat Turner, Gabriel Prosser, and the freedman Denmark Vesey.

11. Michael Roberts, "Rooting Interest." *Denver Westword,* July 17, 1997, http://www.westword.com/1997–07–17/music/rooting-interest/ .

12. From A Tribe Called Quest, "The Pressure," in *Beats, Rhymes and Life* (album; 1996). "The Pressure," written by Fareed, Muhamma, and Taylor. ©1996. Printed with kind permission from Bridgeport Music, Inc.

13. From De La Soul, "Stakes Is High," in *Stakes Is High* (CD; 1996), written by Bobbitt, Brown, Jamal, Jolicoeur, Mason, Mercer, Wesley, and Yoncey. ©1996. Printed with kind permission from Daisy Age/T-Girl Music LLC (BMI), Dynatona Music/Warner Chappell Music (BMI), Ephey Music/Polygram Music (ASCAP), Warner Tamerlane Music (BMI).

14. Lyric is from "When Will They Shoot," in *The Predator* (CD: Los Angeles: Priority Records, 1992).

15. Kelley, *Race Rebels,* 189–195.

16. C. Larkin, ed., "Ice Cube," *The Guinness Encyclopedia of Popular Music* (Chester, Conn.: New England Publishing Associates, 1995), 2052–2053; "From Boyz to Man" *Players,* February 9 1997, 20–23.

17. Selwyn S. Hinds, "An Open Letter to C. Delores Tucker," *Source,* February 1997, 8.

18. Robert H. Bork, *Slouching towards Gomorrah: Modern Liberalism and American Decline* (New York: HarperCollins, 1996), 130–131.

19. Ibid., 125, 133.

20. Ernest Allen, Jr., "Making the Strong Survive: The Contours and Contradictions of Message Rap," in Perkins, *Droppin' Science.*

21. Gene C. Gerard, "The Politics of SpongeBob," *Free Press,* January 23, 2005," http://www.freepress.org/departments.php/display/20/2005/1114.

22. "Tucker Calls for Restrictions," *Yale Daily News,* November 15, 1995.

23. Ibid., p. 2.

24. Ibid.

25. Michael Tonry, *Malign Neglect: Race, Crime, and Punishment in America* (New York: Oxford University Press, 1995); David Cole, *No Equal Justice* (New York: New Press, 1999); Barry R. McCaffrey, "Race and Drugs: Perception and Reality, New Rules for Crack versus Powder Cocaine," *Washington Times,* October 5, 1997.

26. Scott Pfeiffer, "Stop the Witch Hunts! Establishment Organizations Should Fight Conditions Youth Live in, Not Rap," *R.O.C. (Rock Out Censorship) Magazine,* n.d., http://www.theroc.org/roc-mag/textarch/roc-15/roc15–02.htm.

27. Chuck Philips, "At Time Warner Profits from Rap Music Rejected," *Los Angeles Times*, February 23, 1996, D1, D5.

28. KRS-One featuring Channel Live, "Free Mumia," in *KRS-One* (CD; New York: Jive Records, 1995); Federal Bureau of Investigation, *Uniform Crime Reports: Crime in the United States, 2003* (Washington, D.C.: Government Printing Office, 2004).

29. Eminem, "White America," in *The Eminem Show* (CD; Interscope Records, 2002).

30. Dasun Allah, "The Hiphop Soda Pop Shake-up" *Village Voice*, April 3, 2003, http://www.villagevoice.com/news/0310,allah,42290,1.html.

31. Ibid.

32. Bernard Goldberg, *100 People Who Are Screwing up America (and Al Franken Is #37)* (New York: HarperCollins, 2005).

33. See John H. McWhorter, *Losing the Race: Self-Sabotage in Black America* (New York: Harper Perennial, 2001), *Authentically Black* (New York: Gotham, 2004).

34. Michael W. Lynch and Cathy Young, "Internal Constraints: John McWhorter, Author of the Controversial *Losing the Race*, on What's Really Holding African Americans Back," *ReasonOnline*, October 2001, http://www.reason.com/news/show/28173.html.

35. John H. McWhorter, "How Hip-Hop Holds Blacks Back," *City Journal*, Summer 2003, http://www.city-journal.org/html/13_3_how_hip_hop.html.

36. Ibid.

37. John McWhorter, "White Do-Gooders Did for Black America," *London Sunday Times*, September 11, 2005, http://www.timesonline.co.uk/tol/news/world/article565148.ece.

38. Ibid.

39. The literature on the struggle for black freedom is quite vast, but for starters, see Charles Payne, *I've Got the Light of Freedom: The Organization Tradition and the Mississippi Freedom Struggle* (Berkeley: University of California Press, 1995); Clayborne Carson, *In Struggle: SNCC and the Black Awakening of the 1960s* (Cambridge, Mass.: Harvard University Press, 1995).

40. Bill Cosby, "Pound Cake Speech," delivered May 17, 2004, Constitution Hall, Washington, D.C., NAACP Gala to Commemorate the 50th Anniversary of Brown v. Board of Education, http://www.americanrhetoric.com/speeches/billcosbypoundcakespeech.htm.

41. Clarence Page, "Hip-Hop's Dangerous Values," *Washington Times*, March 28, 2004.

42. Juan Williams, "Banish the Bling, a Culture of Failure Taints Black America," *Washington Post*, August 21, 2006, A15.

43. Bob Herbert, "Blowing the Whistle on Gangsta Culture," op-ed, *New York Times*, December 22, 2005.

44. As shown in the government data below, using rates of poverty; homicide; life expectancy; infant mortality; home ownership; high school, college and professional school graduation; teenage births; and other indices, African Americans at the beginning of the twenty-first century are better off than any generation of African Americans in history. But, as also shown, black people continue to lag behind whites in every index noted here. This gap, however, is not a new one but rooted in a history of legalized white supremacy stretching back centuries.

45. James D. Johnson, Sophie Trawlter, and John F. Dovido, "Converging Interracial Consequences of Exposure to Violent Rap Music on Stereotypical Attributions of Blacks," *Journal of Experimental Social Psychology* 33 (2000): 233–251.

46. John McWhorter, "White Do-Gooders."

47. I use the term "hip-hop generation" in line with the definition prescribed by Bakari Kitwana: African Americans born between 1965 and 1984. I would, however, extend the end date forward, considering that those born after 1984 are probably even more attuned to hip-hop as a group, as they have not known of an era without platinum hip-hop records and the art's mainstream success. In terms of the quality of life, this affluence must also account for the prison industrial complex, which houses more black people than ever. I explore this in Chapter 5.

48. McWhorter, "White Do-Gooders."

49. Drop-out rates from high school are slippery. Some rates include students who transferred out of a school or district. They also typically do not count students who eventually earn high school equivalency degrees. A significant percentage of black dropouts have attained general equivalency degrees, resulting in a narrower percentage gap of black and white high school graduates between eighteen and twenty-four years of age. See U.S. Department of Commerce, Census Bureau, Current Population Survey, October 2001, http://www.census.gov/apsd/techdoc/cps/cpsoct01.pdf; National Center for Educational Statistics, "Drop Out Rates in the United States: 2002 and 2003," http://nces.ed.gov/pubs2006/dropout/tables/table_11.asp. The data on all age groups show that the gap between blacks and whites is larger, since older generations of black people have lower rates of graduation from high school. See "High School Graduation Rates Reach All-Time High; Non-Hispanic White and Black Graduates at Record Levels," U.S. Census Bureau News, Press Release, June 29, 2004, Washington, D.C., http://www.census.gov/Press-Release/www/releases/archives/education/001863.html.

50. "Black-White Higher Education Equity Index, *Journal of Blacks in Higher Education*, Winter 2003–2004, 64; "The Good News that the Thernstroms Neglected to Tell," *Journal of Blacks in Higher Education*, Winter 2003–2004, 81–94; "Black-White Higher Education Equity Index," *Journal of Blacks in Higher Education*, Autumn 2005, 48; "The Solid Progress of African Americans in Degree Attainments," *Journal of Blacks in Higher Education Summer* 2006, 54–59.

51. "Subway Victim's Family May Revisit the Scene," *New York Times*, February 16, 2003; "The Rise and Fall of Murder in New York," *New York Times*, December 29, 2003, Federal Bureau of Investigation, *Uniform Crime Reports for the United States, 2003* (Washington, D.C.: Government Printing Office, 2004).

52. Federal Bureau of Investigation, *Crime in the United States, 2000* (Washington, D. C., Government Printing Office, 2001), *Uniform Crime Reports for the United States, 1996* (Washington, D.C.: Government Printing Office, 1997); Joseph P. Fried, "Subway Victim's Family May Revisit the Scene," *New York Times*, February 16, 2003; "The Rise and Fall of Murder in New York," *New York Times*, December 29, 2003; Federal Bureau of Investigation, *Uniform Crime Reports: Crime in the United States, 2005*, Table 8: New York: Offenses Known to Law Enforcement," http://www.fbi.gov/ucr/05cius/data/table_08_ny.html.

53. The Centers for Disease Control statistics reveal that in 1950 the black homicide rate was 28.3 victims per 100,000. By comparison, 1960 had a black homicide rate of 26.0, and 1970 showed an increase to 44.0. The rate was 36.3 in 1990, still much higher than 1950, before the precipitous decline leading to this historic low of 19.7 black homicides per 100,000 in 2004. See U.S. Department of Justice, Office of Justice Programs,

"Homicide Trends in the United States: Trends by Race, 1976–2004," http://www.ojp
.usdoj.gov/bjs/homicide/tables/vracetab.htm; Centers for Disease Control, National
Center for Health Statistics, "Age-Adjusted Death Rate for Selected Causes, According
to Sex, Race, Hispanic Origin: the United States, Selected Years, 1950–2001," http://
www.cdc.gov/nchs/data/hus/tables/2003/03hus029.pdf.

54. Federal Bureau of Investigation, *Uniform Crime Reports, Crime in the United
States, 2005,* Table 1: Crime in the United States by Volume and Rate per 100,000 Inhabitants, 1986–2005," http://www.fbi.gov/ucr/05cius/data/table_01.html.

55. Susan O'Brian, "Troubling Days at U.S. Schools," *USA Today,* October 21, 2003, 1D.

56. As noted in the text, blacks continue to lag significantly behind whites in positive
indices such as employment, net worth, income, and life expectancy. While some of this
can be explained as the legacy of centuries of entrenched legally sanctioned white supremacy, others reflect incessant, informal methods of discrimination. For example, at the
height of the Great Depression in 1932, the black employment rate of 50 percent was
roughly twice that of whites, when employers openly endorsed racism. In every decade
since, including the post-1990s, the black unemployment rate has remained twice that
of whites. Moreover, when education is controlled for, whites outearn blacks, Asians,
and Latinos on every educational level—from high school dropouts to Ph.D.s. See "The
JBHE Black-White Higher Education Equality Index," *Journal of Blacks in Higher Education,* Summer 2003, 76; "Vital Signs," *Journal of Blacks in Higher Education,* Summer
2003, 77; "Searching for Some Good News on African American College Graduation
Rates," *Journal of Blacks in Higher Education,* Summer 2003, 56–57; "African Americans
Continue to Flock to Graduate and Professional Schools," *Journal of Blacks in Higher Ed-
ucation,* Summer, 2003, 10–11; U.S. Department of Labor, Bureau of Labor Statistics,
"Unemployment Rates for Hispanics and Blacks Have Been Consistently Higher than
the Rate for Whites," Washington, D.C., 2003, http://www.bls.gov/cps/labor2005/chart
4–5.pdf; Kay Oehler, "Another Look at the Black-White Trend in Unemployment Rates,"
American Sociological Review 44, no. 2 (1979): 339–342; Centers for Disease Control,
National Center for Health Statistics, "Table 22: Infant Mortality Rates, Fetal Mortality
Rates, and Perinatal Mortality Rates According to Race, United States, Selected Years,
1950–2001," *National Vital Statistics Reports* 52, no. 10 (December 7, 2003), http://www
.cdc.gov/nchs/data/hus/tables/2003/03hus022.pdf, and Tables 1–4, http://www.cdc.gov/
nchs/data/hestat/prelimbirth04_tables.pdf. Also see Marian F. MacDorman, Diane L.
Rowley, Solomon Iyasu, John L. Kiely, Paula G. Gardner, and Michelle S. Davis, "Infant
Mortality," in "From Data to Action: The CDC's Public Health Surveillance for Women,
Infants and Children" (Atlanta: Centers for Disease Control, 1990), http://www.cdc.gov/
reproductivehealth/Products&Pubs/DatatoAction/pdf/birout6.pdf.

57. Centers for Disease Control, National Center for Health Statistics, "Table 10. Non-
marital Childbearing according to Detailed Race and Hispanic Origin of Mother, and
Maternal Age: United States, Selected Years, 1970–2004" (Washington D.C.: U.S.
Government Printing Office, 2006), ftp://ftp.cdc.gov/pub/Health_Statistics/NCHS/
Publications/Health_US/hus06tables/.

58. Cathy J. Cohen, principal investigator, fact sheets from the Black Youth Project,
Center for the Study of Race, Politics and Culture, University of Chicago, accessed June

2007: "Fact Sheet: Gender Roles and Discrimination," http://blackyouthproject.uchicago
.edu/writings/fact_sheet_gender.pdf; "Fact Sheet; Rap Music and Videos," http://black
youthproject.uchicago.edu/writings/fact_sheet_rap.pdf.

59. Mark Hugo Lopez and Emily Kirby, "Electoral Engagement among Minority
Youth," *Circle: The Center for Information and Research on Civil Learning and Engagement Fact Sheet,* July 2005, 1–3.

60. In the late 1980s there were few songs that valorized killing and misogyny. In 1990
many hip-hop artists produced songs that promoted uplift and peace in black communities with such collectives as the Stop the Violence Movement and the West Coast Rap
All Stars. Between 1998 and 2006 only one adult male rapper went platinum—Kanye
West with *College Dropout* (2004) and *Late Registration* (2005)—without lyrical tales of
killing anyone. See Bureau of Justice Statistics, "Homicide Trends in the United States,"
Supplementary Homicide Reports, 1976–2004, http://www.ojp.usdoj.gov/bjs/homicide/
race.htm.

61. "Crime Rates Drop to 30-Year Low," Associated Press, August 25, 2003; U.S. Department of Labor, Bureau of Labor Statistics, "Experiencing Unemployment in 2003," *MLR
(Monthly Labor Review): Editor's Desk,* December 29, 2004, http://www.bls.gov/opub/
ted/2004/dec/wk4/art03.htm, and "Work Experience of the Population in 2003," news release, December 22, 2004, http://www.bls.gov/news.release/archives/work_12222004.pdf.

62. See Bill O'Reilly, *Who's Looking Out for You?* (New York: Broadway, 2003); Ann
Coulter, *How to Talk to a Liberal (If You Must): The World according to Ann Coulter* (New
York: Crown Forum, 2004); Rush Limbaugh, *The Way Things Ought to Be* (New York:
Pocketbook, 1993).

63. See Don Elligan, "Rap Therapy: A Culturally Sensitive Approach to Psychotherapy
with Young African American Men," *Journal of African American Men* 5, no. 3 (Winter
2000): 27–36, esp. 27.

Chapter 5. Locked Up: Police, the Prison Industrial Complex, Black Youth, and Social Control

1. I use this term "community-based hip-hoppers" in reference to those who are not
commercially active participants in hip-hop, e.g., fans or freelance participants in the
culture. This group would include unsigned and local rappers, b-boys and b-girls, graffiti artists, and DJs.

2. Sentencing Project, "Young Black Men and the Criminal Justice System: A Growing
National Problem" (Washington, D.C.: Sentencing Project, 1990).

3. Jewelle Taylor Gibbs, "Young Black Males in America: Endangered, Embittered, and
Embattled," in her *Young, Black and Male in America: An Endangered Species* (Westport,
Conn.: Auburn House, 1988), 1–36; Ronald L. Taylor, ed., *African American Youth: Their
Social and Economic Status in the United States* (Westport, Conn.: Praeger, 1994).

4. Leon Litwack, *Been in the Storm So Long: The Aftermath of Slavery* (New York: Vintage, 1979); Eric Foner, *Reconstruction: America's Unfinished Revolution, 1863–1877*
(New York: Harper & Row, 1988).

5. Nineteen fifty-two was the first year of no recorded lynching in the United States since the nineteenth century. Even the infamous trial of the white men charged with fourteen-year-old Emmett Till's murder in 1955 resulted in an hour-long deliberation by an all-white male jury (in a county that was over 60 percent black) and acquittals. Aware that they could not be retried, the killers later proudly detailed how they murdered the boy for flirting with a white woman. See Stephen J. Whitfield, *A Death in the Delta: The Story of Emmett Till* (Baltimore: Johns Hopkins University Press, 1991); Stewart Emory Tolnay and E. M. Beck, *A Festival of Violence: An Analysis of the Lynching of African-Americans in the American South, 1882–1930* (Urbana: University of Illinois Press, 1995); Ralph Ginzburg, *100 Years of Lynchings* (Baltimore: Black Classics Press, 1997).

6. Vijay Prashad, *Keeping up with the Dow Jones: Debt, Prison, Workfare* (Cambridge, Mass.: South End Press, 2003), 14–15.

7. Federal Bureau of Investigation, *Uniform Crime Reports for the United States, 1996* (Washington, D.C.: Government Printing Office, 1997), http://www.fbi.gov/ucr/cius _04/documents/CIUS2004.pdf; "Subway Victim's Family May Revisit the Scene," *New York Times,* February 16, 2003; Federal Bureau of Investigation, *Supplementary Homicide Reports, 1976–2004* (Washington, D.C.: Government Printing Office, 2005), http:// www.ojp.usdoj.gov/bjs/homicide/tables/ovracetab.htm.

8. Gibbs, *Young, Black and Male.*

9. Robin D. G. Kelley, *Freedom Dreams* (New York: New Press, 2001).

10. X-Clan, "Heed the Word of the Brother," in *To The East Blackwards* (CD; 1990).

11. Quoted in David Marsh and Phyllis Pollack, "Wanted for Attitude," *Village Voice,* October 10, 1989.

12. Ice Cube released two more solo albums, *War and Peace Vol. 1* (CD; 1998) and *War and Peace Vol. 2* (CD; 2000), both of which were decidedly less polemical than his previous work. The first installment of this volume went platinum, making Ice Cube the first rap soloist to go platinum with his first five LPs. LL Cool J would eventually go platinum with five LPs as well. In 2003 DMX joined Ice Cube and LL Cool J with this exceptional record of commercial success with the release of *Grand Champ.* Ice Cube's black nationalist politics were absent as he relied more on the typical content that characterized commercial hits of the late 1990s.

13. Ice Cube, "Steady Mobbin,'" in *Death Certificate* (CD; Priority Records, 1991).

14. Chapter 2 provides further exploration of the illusive meaning of "gangsta" in hip-hop.

15. Da Lench Mob, "Capital Punishment in America," in *Guerillas in the Mist* (CD; Los Angeles: Priority Records, 1993); Perry T. Ryan, *The Last Public Execution in America* (1992), text at http://www.geocities.com/lastpublichang/. Also see National Public Radio, "The Last Public Execution in America," http://www.npr.org/programs/morning /features/2001/apr/010430.execution.html.

16. Da Lench Mob, "Lost in the System," in *Guerillas in the Mists.*

17. "New York Study Finds Racial Disparity in Jail Time," *New York Times,* April 23, 1996, posted at http://www.prisonactivist.org/pipermail/prisonact-list/1996-April/000284.html.

18. In homage to Ice-T, Ice Cube later claimed in 1993 that he was yelling "'cop killer' and 'fuck Time Warner!'"; see Ice Cube, "You Don't Wanna Fuck Wit These," in *Bootlegs and B-Sides* (CD; Priority Records, 1994).

19. Eithne Quinn, *Nuthin' but a "g" Thang: The Culture and Commerce of Gangsta Rap* (New York: Columbia University Press, 2005), 111, 175–176.

20. See Ice Cube featuring WC, "My Skin Is My Sin," in *Bootlegs and B-Sides* (CD; Priority Records, 1994). In "Now I Gotta Wet 'Cha" (in *The Predator* [CD; Priority Records, 1992]), Ice Cube takes aim at gang bangers who have terrorized the black community.

21. Nas featuring Lauryn Hill, "If I Ruled the World," in *It Was Written* (CD; Sony, 1996).

22. "Caution" also provides a reference to Leonard Peltier, member of the American Indian Movement in jail on charges of killing two FBI agents in 1975. Like Mumia, Peltier is widely considered a political prisoner convicted on a weak case. See Dilated Peoples, "Proper Propaganda," in *Expansion Team* (CD; 2002)

23. Jurassic 5, "Freedom," in *Power in Numbers* (CD; 2002).

24. Mike Ladd, "Social Policy Derelicts," in *The Unbound Project* (CD; 2000).

25. While there have been collaborative albums on prisons and the police, no single artist or group created such an album before Spearhead. Other examples of skit-driven stories in albums include issues such as abortion rights (The Goats, *Tricks of the Trade* [CD; 1993]) and drug dealing (Prince Paul, *Prince among Thieves* [CD; 1999]).

26. Bernice A. King, "Uprooting the Seeds of Violence," http://findarticles.com/p /articles/mi_hb5041/is_199709/ai_n18329899.

27. Talib Kweli, "The Human Element," in *The Unbound Project* (CD; 2000).

28. "Intended and Unintended Consequences: State Racial *Disparities in Imprisonment*," *The Sentencing Project,* http://www.sentencingproject.org/pdfs/9050summary.pdf.

29. Manning Marable, "Racism, Prisons, and the Future of Black America," http:// www.afsc.org/pwork/1200/122k05.htm, and *The Great Wells of Democracy* (New York: Basic Books, 2003), 153–159.

30. Jeffrey Reiman, *And the Poor Get Prison: Economic Bias in American Criminal Justice* (Needham Heights, Mass.: Allyn & Bacon, 1996); Prashad, *Keeping Up;* Marc Mauer, *Race to Incarcerate* (New York: New Press, 1999); David Cole, *No Equal Justice: Race and Class in the American Criminal Justice System* (New York: New Press, 1999); Steven R. Donziger, ed., *The Real War on Crime: The Report of the National Criminal Justice Commission* (New York: HarperPerennial, 1996).

31. Prashad, *Keeping Up,* 82.

32. "New York Study Finds Racial Disparity in Jail Time," *New York Times,* April 23, 1996; the Sentencing Project, "Young Black Americans in the Criminal Justice System Five Years Later," http://www.sentencingproject.org/pdfs/9070smy.pdf; "Racial Disparity in Sentencing: A Review of the Literature," http://www.soros.org/Staging/initiatives/ justice/articles_publications/publications/racial_disparity_20050128/disparity.pdf; Michael Coyle, "Race and Class Penalties in Crack Cocaine Sentencing" http://www.sentencing project.org/pdfs/5077.pdf (all retrieved from the Sentencing Project).

33. Salim Muwakkil, "Racial Bias Persists," *Los Angeles Times,* September 26, 2003.

34. Paige M. Harrison and Allen J. Beck, "Bureau of Justice Statistics Bulletin: Prisoners in 2001," U.S. Department of Justice, Office of Justice Programs (July 2002), http:// www.ojp.usdoj.gov/bjs/pub/pdf/p01.pdf; also see Prison Policy Initiative, "New York Times Editorial Calls for Census Bureau to Change How It Counts Prisoners," http:// www.prisonpolicy.org.

35. UNICEF, "Convention on the Rights of the Child," http://www.unicef.org/crc/crc.htm.

36. Prashad, *Keeping Up,* 72.

37. "A Matter of Life and Death," *Socialist Review,* no. 177, July/August 1994, http://pubs.socialistreviewindex.org.uk/sr177/ross.htm.

38. Since the late nineteenth century, hundreds of black people have been killed in Florida, Georgia, Texas, and Mississippi as enslaved or free people. The infamous Rosewood massacre of 1921 accounted for upward of 200 murdered black people. No white person has ever been found guilty of the crime. See "Recent Developments in the Death Penalty in Florida: G. Death Votes and Direct Appeal Decisions," paper presented orally at the "Life over Death" capital litigators training conference held by the Florida Public Defender Association in Orlando, Florida, on September 7, 2001 (no author given), Floridians for Alternatives to the Death Penalty, http://www.fadp.org/pad/apage4.html; "The Texas Death Machine," *Counterpunch,* n.d., http://www.counterpunch.org/death-penalty.html; Bob Herbert, "Tainted Justice," *New York Times,* n.d., reprinted at "No Alla Pena di Morte, Compagna Internazionale," Comunità di Sant'Egidio, Rome, http://www.santegidio.org/pdm/news/06_08_01_b.htm.

39. Bryan Stevenson, "Crime, Punishment, and Executions in the Twenty-First Century," *Proceedings of the American Philosophical Society* 147, no. 1 (March 2003): 24–29.

40. Human Rights Watch, "Incarceration and Race," http://www.hrw.org/reports/2000/usa/Rcedrg00–01.htm.

41. Herbert, "Tainted Justice"; "Hounding the Innocent: Police Use of Racial Profiling," *New York Times,* June 13, 1999, 17.

42. Because of "technicalities," the liner notes explain that some verses were not included on the album, but they were included in the liner notes; *Hip Hop for Respect* (CD; Rawkus Records, 2000).

43. Rakaa Iriscience, personal communication, February 12, 2002.

44. William Upski Wismatt, *No More Prisons* (New York: Soft Skull Press, 1999); *No More Prisons* (New York: Raptivism Records, 1999).

45. D. Reyes, "Rappers dead prez Arrested for Being Minorities," *Amsterdam News,* 94, no. 44 (October 30–November 5, 2003), 1.

46. Eric Schlosser, "The Prison-Industrial Complex," *Atlantic Monthly,* December 1998, http://www.theatlantic.com/doc/prem/199812/prisons.

47. L. Cannon, "One Bad Cop," *New York Times Magazine,* October 1, 2000.

Epilogue

1. In 1950 there were 28.3 black homicides per 100,000 people, compared to 19.7 black homicides per 100,000 in 2004; see Bureau of Justice Statistics, "Homicide Trends in the United States," U.S. Department of Justice, Office of Justice Programs, http://www.ojp.usdoj.gov/bjs/homicide/tables/vracetab.htm; "Age-Adjusted Death Rate for Selected Causes, according to Sex, Race, Hispanic Origin: The United States, Selected Years, 1950–2001, http://www.cdc.gov/nchs/data/hus/tables/2003/03hus029.pdf.

2. "Diddy Declared 'Richest in Hip Hop,'" *EURWeb,* August 9, 2006, http://www.eurweb.com/story/eur27931.cfm.

3. An excellent exploration of the commercial drive of hip-hop is Eithne Quinn's *Nuthin' but a "g" Thang: The Culture and Commerce of Gangsta Rap* (New York: Columbia University Press, 2005).

4. Tariq K. Muhammad, "Hip-Hop Moguls: Beyond the Hype," *Black Enterprise,* December 1999, 78–90; Alan Hughes, "Phat Profits," *Black Enterprise,* June 2002, 149–156; Kawan Ari, "New York State of Mind," *Source,* September 2002, 233–241; "The Source Hip-Hop Power 30," *Source,* February 2006; Alan Hughes, "From New York to Nepal, Hip-Hop Has Become America's Leading Culture Export," *Black Enterprise,* May 2002.

5. "Industry Rule #4080" refers to a famous line from A Tribe Called Quest, "Check the Rhime," in *Low End Theory* (CD; Jive Records, 1991).

6. Much like the myth that the Emancipation Proclamation ended slavery in the United States (it was the Thirteenth Amendment to the Constitution that passed nearly three years after the Emancipation Proclamation) there is a widely held belief that rappers Tupac and Biggie were killed because of "East Coast–West Coast rivalry." There is, however, no credible evidence that Biggie, his label Bad Boy Records, or any East Coast rappers were behind the murder of Tupac. The criminal justice system cannot find guilt without charges being made against a suspect. To date no one has been charged with the murders of Tupac Shakur or Christopher "Notorious B.I.G." Wallace.

7. For an elaborate examination of the recent rise of radicalism in hip-hop, see Jeffrey O. G. Ogbar, "Holla Black: The Bush Administration and the Return of Political Hip-Hop," *Radical Society: Review of Culture and Politics* 32, no. 3 (Autumn 2006): 67–74.

8. Jay-Z, "Moment of Clarity," in *The Black Album* (CD; New York, 2003).

9. Personal communication, Santiago de Cuba, July 2002.

BIBLIOGRAPHY

Books and Chapter Articles

Acland, Charles. *Youth, Murder, Spectacle: The Cultural Politics of "Youth in Crisis."* Boulder, Colo.: Westview Press, 1995.

Adler, Bill. *Rap: Portraits and Lyrics of a Generation of Black Rockers.* New York: St. Martin's Press, 1991.

Adorno, Theodore. *Introduction to the Sociology of Music.* New York: Continuum, 1989.

Agnew, John. "Representing Space: Space, Scale and Culture in Social Science." In *Place/ Culture/Representation,* edited by James Duncan and David Ley. London: Routledge, 1993.

Allen, Theodore W. 1994. *The Invention of the White Race, 2 vols.* New York: Verso, 1994.

Anderson, Elijah. *Streetwise: Race, Class, and Change in the Urban Community.* Chicago: University of Chicago Press, 1992.

Baker, Houston A., Jr. *Black Studies, Rap, and the Academy.* Chicago: University of Chicago Press, 1995.

——. "Hybridity, the Rap Race, and Pedagogy for the 1990s." In *Technoculture,* edited by Constance Penley and Andrew Ross, 197–209. Minneapolis: University of Minnesota Press, 1991.

——. *Long Black Song: Essays in Black American Literature and Culture.* Charlottesville: University Press of Virginia, 1990. First published in 1972.

Berry, Venise. "Feminine or Masculine: The Conflicting Nature of Female Images in Rap Music." In *Cecilia Reclaimed: Feminist Perspectives on Gender and Music,* edited by Susan C. Cook and Judy S. Tsou, 183–201. Urbana: University of Illinois Press, 1994.

——. "Redeeming the Rap Music Experience." In *Adolescents and Their Music: If It's Too Loud, You're Too Old,* edited by Jonathon Epstein. New York: Garland, 1994.

Bogdanov, Vladamir. *All Music Guide to Hip Hop: The Definitive Guide to Rap and Hip Hop.* San Francisco: Backbeat Books, 2003.

Bogle, Donald. *Toms, Coons, Mulattoes, Mammies, and Bucks: An Interpretive History of Blacks in American Films.* New York: Continuum, 1994.

Bork, Robert. *Slouching towards Gomorrah: Modern Liberalism and American Decline,* 125–133. New York: ReganBooks, 1996.

Boyd, Todd. *Am I Black Enough for You? Popular Culture from the 'Hood and Beyond.* Bloomington: Indiana University Press, 1997.

Brewster, Bill, and Frank Broughton. *Last Night a DJ Saved My Life: The History of the Disc Jockey.* New York: Grove Press, 1999.

Campbell, Luther, and John R. Miller. *As Nasty as They Wanna Be: The Uncensored Story of Luther Campbell of the 2 Live Crew.* Fort Lee, N.J.: Barricade Books, 1992.

Capitol D. *Fresh Air: Hip Hop Lit and Lyrics.* Chicago: Writer's Bloc, 1998.

Cashmore, Ellis. *The Black Culture Industry.* New York: Routledge, 1997.

Castleman, Craig. *Getting Up: Subway Graffiti in New York.* Cambridge, Mass.: MIT Press, 1982.

Chalfant, Henry, and Martha Cooper. *Subway Art.* New York: Henry Holt, 1984.

Chang, Jeff. *Can't Stop Won't Stop: A History of the Hip-Hop Generation.* New York: St. Martin's, 2005.

Chapple, Steve, and Reebee Garofalo. *Rock 'n' Roll Is Here to Pay: The History and Politics of the Music Industry.* Chicago: Nelson-Hall, 1977.

Chideya, Farai. "Homophobia: Hip-Hop's Black Eye." In *Step into a World: A Global Anthology of the New Black Literature,* edited by Kevin Powell, 95–100. New York: Wiley, 2002.

Chuck D with Yusuf Jah. *Fight the Power.* Forward by Spike Lee. New York: Delacorte, 1997.

Cohen, Stanley. *Folk Devils and Moral Panics: The Creation of the Mods and Rockers.* New York: Basil Blackwell, 1972.

Cole, David. *No Equal Justice: Race and Class in the American Criminal Justice System.* New York: New Press, 1999.

Collins, Patricia Hill. *Black Feminist Thought: Knowledge, Consciousness, and the Politics of Empowerment.* Boston: Unwin Hyman, 1990.

Conyers, James L. *African American Jazz and Rap: Social and Philosophical Examinations of Black Expressive Behavior.* Jefferson, N.C.: Mcfarland, 2001.

Costello, Mark, and David Foster Wallace. *Signifying Rappers: Rap and Race in the Urban Present.* New York: Ecco, 1990.

Cross, Brian. *It's Not about a Salary . . . : Rap, Race, and Resistance in Los Angeles.* New York: Verso, 1993.

Cubitt, Sean. "Rolling and Tumbling: Digital Erotics and the Culture of Narcissism." *In Sexing the Groove: Popular Music and Gender,* edited by Sheila Whiteley. London: Routledge, 1997.

Dance, Daryl C. *Shuckin' and Jivin': Folklore from Contemporary Black Americans.* Bloomington: Indiana University Press, 1978.

Datcher, Michael, and Kwame Alexander, eds. *Tough Love: The Life and Death of Tupac Shakur.* Virginia: Alexander Publishing Group, 1997.

Davis, Angela. *Blues Legacies and Black Feminism: Gertrude "Ma" Rainey, Bessie Smith, and Billie Holiday.* New York: Pantheon, 1998.

———. *Women, Culture, and Politics.* New York: Women's Press, 1990.

———. *Women, Race, and Class.* New York: Random House, 1981.

Davis, Mike. *City of Quartz: Excavating the Future in Los Angeles.* New York: Vantage Books, 1992.

Dawson, Michael C. "'Dis Beat Disrupts': Rap, Ideology, and Black Political Attitudes." In *The Cultural Territories of Race: Black and White Boundaries,* edited by Michele Lamont, 318–342. Chicago: University of Chicago Press, 1999.

Dee, Kool Moe. *There's a God on the Mic: The True 50 Greatest MCs.* New York: Thunder's Mouth Press, 2003.

Denisoff, R. Serge. *Tarnished Gold: The Record Industry Revisited*. New Brunswick, N.J.: Transaction, 1986.

Dennison, Sam. *Scandalize My Name:* Black Imagery in American Popular Music. New York: Garland, 1982.

Devaney, Micaela. *The Poetry of the Streets*. Norton, Mass.: Wheaton College, 2002.

DMX [Smokey Fontaine,]. *E.A.R.L.: The Autobiography of DMX*. New York: Harper Entertainment, 2002.

Donziger, Steven R. *The Real War on Crime: The Report of the National Criminal Justice Commission*. New York: Harper Perennial, 1996.

Dyson, Michael Eric. *Between God and Gangsta Rap*. New York: Oxford University Press, 1996.

———. *Holler If You Hear Me: Searching for Tupac Shakur*. New York: Basic, 2001.

———. *Reflecting Black: African-American Cultural Criticism*. Minneapolis: University of Minnesota Press, 1993.

Eliot, Marc. *Rockonomics: The Money behind the Music*. New York: Franklin Watts, 1989.

Ely, Melvin Patrick. *The Adventures of Amos 'n' Andy:* A Social History of An African American Phenomenon. Charlottesville: University Press of Virginia, 2001.

Eminem [Marshall Mathers]. *Angry Blond*. New York: Regan Books, 2000.

Eure, Joseph D. *Nation Conscious Rap*. New York: PC International Press, 1991.

Fab 5 Freddy. *Fresh Fly Flavor: Words and Phrases of the Hip-Hop Generation*. Stamford, Conn.: Longmeadow Press, 1992.

Farr, Jory. *Moguls and Madmen: The Pursuit of Power in Popular Music*. New York: Simon & Schuster, 1994.

Faulkner, Janette. *Ethnic Notions: Black Images in the White Mind*. Berkeley, Calif.: Berkeley Art Center, 1982.

Fernando, S. H., Jr. *The New Beasts: Exploring the Music, Culture, and Attitudes of Hip-Hop*. New York: Anchor Books/Doubleday, 1994.

Flanders, Julian. *From Rock and Pop to Hip Hop*. London: Brown Partworks, 2001.

Floyd, Samuel A., Jr. *The Power of Black Music: Interpreting Its History from Africa to the United States*. New York: Colombia University Press, 1995.

Flores, Juan. *From Bomba to Hip Hop: Puerto Rican Culture and Latino Identity*. New York: Columbia University Press, 2000.

———. "Puerto Rican and Proud, Boyee! Rap Roots, and Amnesia." In *Microphone Fiends: Youth Music and Youth Culture*, edited by Andrew Ross and Tricia Rose. New York: Routledge, 1994.

Forman, Murray. *The 'Hood Comes First: Race, Space and Place in Rap and Hip-Hop*. Middletown, Conn.: Wesleyan Press, 2002.

Foucault, Michel. *Power/Knowledge: Selected Interviews and Other Writings, 1972–1977*. New York: Pantheon, 1980.

Franklin, John Hope, and Alfred A. Moss, Jr. *From Slavery to Freedom: A History of African Americans*. 7th ed. New York: Knopf, 1994.

Fricke, Jim, and Charlie Ahearn, eds. *Yes Yes Y'all: Oral History of Hip-Hop's First Decade: The Experience Music Project*. New York: Da Capo, 2002.

Frith, Simon. *Sound Effects: Youth, Leisure, and the Politics of Rock 'n' Roll*. New York: Pantheon, 1981.

———. "Towards an Aesthetic of Popular Music." In *Music and Society: The Politics of Composition, Performance and Reception,* edited by Richard Leppert and Susan McClary, 133–149. New York: Cambridge University Press, 1987.

Garofalo, Reebee. 1992. "Popular Music and the Civil Rights Movement." In *Rockin' the Boat: Mass Music and Mass Culture,* edited by Reebee Garofalo. Boston: South End Press.

Gates, Henry Louis, Jr. *The Signifying Monkey: A Theory of African-American Literary Criticism.* New York: Oxford University Press, 1988.

Gay, Geneva. 1987. "Expressive Ethos of Afro-American Culture." In *Expressively Black: The Cultural Basis of Ethnic Identity,* edited by *Geneva Gay and Willie L. Baber.* New York: Praeger, 1987.

Geertz, Clifford. 1973. *The Interpretation of Cultures.* New York: Basic Books.

George, Nelson. *Buppies, B-Boys, BAPs and Bohos: Notes on Post Soul Black Culture.* New York: HarperCollins, 1992.

———. *Death of Rhythm and Blues.* New York: Pantheon Books, 1988.

———. *Hip Hop America.* New York: Viking Press, 2000. First published 1998 by Penguin, New York.

George, Nelson, Sally Banes, Susan Flinker, and Patty Romanowski. *Fresh, Hip Hop Don't Stop.* New York: Random House, 1985.

George, Nelson, and the National Urban League. *Stop the Violence: Overcoming Self Destruction.* New York: Pantheon Books, 1990.

Gilroy, Paul. *The Black Atlantic: Modernity and Double Consciousness.* London: Verso, 1993.

———. *Small Acts: Thoughts on the Politics of Black Cultures.* New York: Basic, 1993.

———. *There Ain't No Black in the Union Jack: The Cultural Politics of Race and Nation.* Chicago: University of Chicago Press, 1987.

Ginzburg, Ralph. *100 Years of Lynchings.* Baltimore: Black Classics Press, 1997.

Glasgow, Douglas. *The Black Underclass: Poverty, Unemployment, and Entrapment of Ghetto Youth.* San Francisco: Jossey-Bass, 1980.

Gramsci, Antonio. *Selections from the Prison Notebooks.* New York: International, 1971.

Grant, William R., IV. *Post-Soul Black Cinema: Discontinuities, Innovations and Breakpoints, 1970–1995.* New York: Routledge, 2004.

Green, Tony. "The Dirty South." In *The Vibe History of Hip-Ho*p, edited by Alan Light. New York: Three Rivers Press, 1999.

Gugliemo, Jennifer, and Salvatore Salerno. *Are Italians White? How Race Is Made in America.* New York, 2003.

Guerrero, Ed. *Framing Blackness: The African American Image in Film.* Philadelphia: Temple University Press, 1993.

Hager, S. *Hip Hop: The Illustrated History of Break Dancing, Rap Music, and Graffiti.* New York: St. Martin's, 1984.

Hall, Stuart. "Culture, the Media, and the 'Ideological Effect.'" *In Mass Communication and Society,* edited by James Curran, Michael Gurevitch, and Janet Woolacott. Beverly Hills, Calif.: Sage, 1977.

———. "What Is This Black in Black Popular Culture?" In *Black Popular Culture,* edited by Gina Dent. Seattle: Bay Press, 1992.

Hall, Stuart, and Charles Critcher, Tony Jefferson, John Clarke, and Brian Robert, eds. *Policing the Crisis: Mugging, the State, and Law and Order.* New York: Holmes & Meier, 1978.

Haskins, Jim. *The Story of Hip Hop.* London: Penguin, 2000.

Heard, Gladys C. *Empowering the Hip Hop Nation: The Arts and Social Justice.* Norfolk, Va.: Norfolk State University, Department of English and Foreign Languages, 2000.

Hebdige, D. *Cut 'n' Mix: Culture, Identity and Caribbean Music.* New York: Routledge, 1979.

Herskovits, Melville. *The Myth of the Negro Past.* Boston: Beacon, 1958. First published 1941.

Hinds, Selwyn Seyfu. *Gunshots in My Cook-Up: Bits and Bites from a Hip Hop Caribbean Life.* New York: Atria Books, 2002.

Ice-T and Heidi Siegmund. *The Ice Opinion: Who Gives a Fuck?* New York: St. Martin's Press, 1994.

Ignatiev, Noel. *How the Irish Became White.* New York, 1996.

Jackson, Peter, and Jan Penrose. *Construction of Race, Place, and Nation.* Minneapolis: University of Minnesota Press, 1993.

Jackson, Robert. *The Last Black Mecca: A Black Cultural Awareness Phenomena and Its Impact on the African American Community.* Chicago: Research Associates, 1994.

Jah, Yusuf, and Sister Shah'Keyah, eds. *Uprising: Crips and Bloods Tell the Story of America's Youth in the Crossfire.* New York: Scribner, 1995.

Jenkins, Sacha, Elliott Wilson, Jeff Mao, Gabe Alvarez, Brent Rollins, Chairman Mao, and Gabriel Alvarez. *Ego Trip's Book of Rap Lists.* New York: St. Martin's Griffin, 1999.

Jewell, K. Sue. *From Mammy to Miss America and Beyond: Cultural Images and the Shaping of U.S. Social Policy.* New York: Routledge, 1993.

Jones, Charles. *The Black Panther Party Reconsidered.* Baltimore, 1998.

Jones, LeRoi. *Blues People: The Negro Experience in White America and the Music That Developed from It.* New York: Morrow, 1963.

Kelley, Norman. *R & B, Rhythm and Business: The Political Economy of Black Music.* New York: Akashic, 2002.

Kelley, Robin D. G. 1994. *Race Rebels: Culture, Politics, and the Black Working Class.* New York: Free Press.

———. *Yo' Mama's Disfunktional! Fighting the Culture Wars in Urban America.* Boston: Beacon Press, 1997.

Keyes, Cheryl L. *Rap Music and Street Consciousness: Rap from Its Earliest Roots to the Present Day.* Urbana: University of Illinois Press, 2004.

Kitwana, Bakari. *The Hip Hop Generation: Young Blacks and the Crisis in African-American Culture.* New York: Basic, 2002.

———. *The Rap on Gangsta Rap: Who Runs It: Gangsta Rap and Visions of Black Violence.* Chicago: Third World Press, 1994.

Krasilovsky, M. William, and Sidney Shemel. *This Business of Music: The Definitive Guide to the Music Industry.* 8th ed. New York: Billboard Books, 2000.

Krims, Adam. *Rap Music and the Poetics of Identity.* New York: Cambridge University Press, 2000.

KRS-One. *The Science of Rap.* N.J.: L. Parker, 1996.

Krulik, Nancy E. *M.C. Hammer & Vanilla Ice: The Hip-Hop Never Stops!* New York: Scholastic, 1991.

Kunjufu, Jawanza. *Hip-Hop vs. MAAT: A Psycho/Social Analysis of Values.* Chicago: African American Images, 1993.

Labov, William. *Language in the Inner City. Philadelphia:* University of Pennsylvania Press, 1972.

Larkin, C. *The Guinness Encyclopedia of Popular Music.* New York: Guinness, 1995.

Levine, Lawrence W. *Black Culture and Black Consciousness.* New York: Oxford University Press, 1977.

Lhamon, W. T. *Raising Cain: Blackface Performance from Jim Crow to Hip Hop.* Cambridge, Mass.: Harvard University Press, 1998.

————, ed. *The Vibe History of Hip Hop.* New York: Vibe Ventures, 1999.

Lipsitz, George. *Dangerous Crossroads: Popular Music, Postmodernism, and the Poetics of Place.* London: Verso, 1994.

————. *Time Passages: Collective Memory and American Popular Culture.* Minneapolis: University of Minnesota Press, 1990.

————. 1994. "We Know What Time It Is: Race, Class, and Culture in the Nineties." *In Microphone Fiends: Youth Music and Youth Culture,* edited by Andrew Ross and Tricia Rose. New York: Routledge, 1994.

Litwack, Leon. *Been in the Storm So Long: The Aftermath of Slavery.* New York: Vintage, 1979.

Lopiano-Misdom, Janine, and Joanne De Luca. *Street Trends: How Today's Alternative Youth Cultures Are Creating Tomorrow's Mainstream Markets.* New York: HarperCollins, 1997.

Lornell, Kip. *The Beat: Go-Go's Fusion of Funk and Hip Hop.* New York: Billboard, 2001.

Lott, Eric. *Love and Theft: Blackface Minstrelsy and the American Working Class.* New York: Continuum, 1995.

Lott, Tommy. *The Invention of Race, Black Culture and the Politics of Representation.* Malden, Mass.: Blackwell, 1999.

————. "Marooned in America: Black Urban Youth Culture and Social Pathology." *In The Underclass Question,* edited by Bill E. Lawson, 71–89. Philadelphia: Temple University Press, 1992.

Loza, Steven. *Barrio Rhythm: Mexican American Music in Los Angeles.* Urbana: University of Illinois Press, 1993.

Mailer, Norman, and Mervin Kurlansky. *Faith of Graffiti.* New York: Henry Holt, 1974.

Malone, Bonz. *Hip Hop Immortals, vol. 1.* New York: Immortal Brands, 2002.

Marable, Manning. *The Great Wells of Democracy.* New York: Basic, 2003.

————. *Racism, Prisons, and the Future of Black America.* New York: Basic, 2003.

Mauer, Marc. *Race to Incarcerate.* New York: New Press, 1999.

Maxwell, Ian. *Phat Beats, Dope Rhymes: Hip Hop Down Under Comin' Upper.* Middletown, Conn.: Wesleyan University Press, 2003.

Mazur, Eric Michael. *God in the Details: American Religion in Popular Culture.* New York: Routledge, 2001.

McCarthy, Cameron. *Sound Identities: Popular Music and the Cultural Politics of Education.* New York: Peter Lang, 1999.

McCoy, Judy. *Rap Music in the 1980s: A Reference Guide.* Metuchen, N.J.: Scarecrow Press, 1992.

Miller, Ivor L. *Aerosol Kingdom: Subway Painters of New York City.* Jackson: University of Mississippi Press, 2002.

Mitchell, Tony. *Global Noise: Rap and Hip Hop Outside the USA.* Middletown, Conn.: Wesleyan University Press, 2001.

Morgan, Joan. *When Chickenheads Come Home to Roost: My Life as a Hip-Hop Feminist.* New York: Simon & Schuster, 1999.

Murray, James, and Karla Murray. *Broken Windows: Graffiti NYC.* Corte Madera, Calif.: Gingko Press, 2002.

Nadell, Martha. 2004. *Enter the New Negroes: Images of Race in American Culture.* Cambridge, Mass.: Harvard University Press.

Neal, Mark Anthony. *Songs in the Key of Black Life: A Rhythm and Blues Nation.* New York: Routledge, 2003.

———. *What the Music Said: Black Popular Music and Black Public Culture.* New York: Routledge, 1999.

Negus, Keith. *Music Genres and Corporate Cultures.* New York: Routledge, 1999.

Nelson, Havelock and Michael Gonzales A. *Bring the Noise: A guide to Rap Music and Hip-Hop Culture.* New York: Harmony, 1991. First published 1988.

Norman, Kelley. *R&B: Rhythm and Business: The Political Economy of Black Music.* New York: Akashic Books, 2002.

Ogbar, Jeffrey O. G. *Black Power: Radical Politics and African American Identity.* Baltimore: Johns Hopkins University Press, 2004.

Ogg, Alex, with David Upshal. *The Hip Hop Years: A History of Rap.* New York: Fromm International, 2001. First published 1999.

Peretti, Burton. *The Creation of Jazz: Music, Race, and Culture in Urban America.* Urbana: University of Illinois Press, 1992.

Perkins, William Eric, ed. *Droppin' Science: Critical Essays in Rap Music and Hip-Hop Culture.* Philadelphia: Temple University Press, 1996.

Perry, Imani. *Prophets of the Hood: Politics and Poetics in Hip Hop.* Durham, N.C.: Duke University Press, 2004.

Pinn, Anthony B. *Noise and Spirit: The Religious and Spiritual Sensibilities of Rap Music.* New York: New York University Press, 2003.

Potter, Russell A. *Spectacular Vernaculars: Hip-Hop and the Politics of Postmodernism.* Albany: State University of New York Press, 1995.

Pough, Gwendolyn. *Check It While I Wreck It: Black Womanhood, Hip-Hop Culture, and the Public Sphere.* Boston: Northeastern University Press, 2004.

Powell, Kevin, ed. *Who Shot Ya? Three Decades of Hip Hop Photography:* Photographs by Ernie Paniccioli. New York: Amistad, 2002.

Powell, Ricky. *Oh Snap: The Photography of Ricky Powell.* New York: St. Martin's Press, 1998.

Prashad, Vijay. *Keeping up with the Dow Joneses: Debt, Prison,* Workfare. Cambridge, Mass.: South End Press, 2003.

Queen Latifah [Dana Owens]. *Ladies First: Revelations of a Strong Black Woman.* New York: William Morris, 1999.

Ranck, John. *Classified Hip Hop, or, I Wanna Blow up Like Marilyn Monroe's Skirt.* Boston: Simmons College, Simmons College Music Librarianship, 1999.

Reid, Mark. *Redefining Black Film.* Berkeley: University of California Press, 1993.

Rhines, Jesse. *Black Film/White Money.* New Brunswick, N.J.: Rutgers University Press, 1996.

Rivera, Raquel Z. *New York Ricans from the Hip Hop Zone.* New York: Palgrave, 2003.

Ro, Ronin. 2001. *Bad Boy: The Influence of Sean "Puffy" Combs on the Music Industry.* Pocket Star.

———. *Gangsta: Merchandising the Rhymes of Violence.* New York: St. Martin's Press, 1996.

———. *Have Gun Will Travel: The Spectacular Rise and Violent Fall of Deathrow Records.* New York: Doubleday, 1999.

Roberts, Don. *Rap to Live By.* Norfolk, Va.: Hampton Roads, 1993.

Roberts, John W. *From Hucklebuck to Hip-Hop: Social Dance in the African-American Community in Philadelphia.* Philadelphia: Odunde, 1995.

Rodierger, David. *The Wages of Whiteness: Race and the Making of the American Working Class.* New York: Verso, 1991.

Rose, Tricia. *Black Noise: Rap Music and Black Culture in Contemporary America.* Hanover, N.H.: Wesleyan University Press, 1994.

———. "Contracting Rap: An Interview with Carmen Ashhurst-Watson." In *Microphone Fiends,* edited by A. Ross and T. Rose, 122–144. New York: Routledge, 1994.

Ross, Andrew. *Microphone Fiends: Youth Music and Youth Culture.* New York: Routledge, 1994.

Sansevere, John R. *Post-bop Hip-Hop: A Tribe Called Quest.* Racine, Wis.: Western Publishing Co., 1993.

Saxton, Alexander, and David Roediger. *The Rise and Fall of the White Republic:* Class, Politics and Mass Culture in Nineteenth Century America. New York: Verso, 1990.

Saylor-Marchan, Linda. *Hammer: 2 Legit 2 Quit.* New York: Dillon Press, 1992.

Sexton, Adam, ed. *Rap on Rap: Straight Talk on Hip-Hop Culture.* New York: Delta, 1995.

Shabazz, Jamel. *Back in the Days.* New York: Powerhouse Books, 2001. Photographic book.

Shabazz, Julian L. D. *The United States of America vs. Hip-Hop.* Hampton,Va.: United Brothers Publishing Co., 1992.

Shakur, Tupac Amaru. *The Rose That Grew from Concrete.* New York: Pocket Books, 1999. Foreword by Nikki Giovanni.

Shapiro, Peter. *The Rough Guide to Hip Hop.* London: Rough Guide, 2001.

Shaw, Arnold. *Black Popular Music in America: From the Spirituals, Minstrels, and Ragtime to Soul, Disco, and Hip-Hop.* New York: Schirmer Books; London: Collier Macmillan, 1986.

Shaw, William. *Westside: The Coast to Coast Explosion in Hip Hop.* New York: Cooper Square Press, 2000.

Shomari, Hashim A. *From the Underground: Hip Hop Culture as an Agent of Social Change.* Fanwood, N.J.: X-Factor Publications, 1995.

Shuker, Roys. *Understanding Popular Music.* New York: Routledge, 1994.

Simmons, Russell. *Life and Def: Sex, Drugs, Money and God.* New York: Crown, 2001.

Sister Souljah. *No Disrespect.* New York: Time Books, 1995.

Smith, Neil, and Cindi Katz. "Grounding Metaphor: Towards a Spatialized Politics." In *Place and the Politics of Identity,* edited by Michael Keith and Steve Pile. New York: Routledge, 1993.

Smitherman, Geneva. *Black Talk.: Words and Phrases from the Hood to the Amen Corner.* New York: Norton, 1994.

———. *Talkin and Testifyin: The Language of Black America.* Detroit: Wayne State University Press, 1986. First published 1977.

Southern, Eileen. *The Music of Black Americans: A History.* 2nd ed. New York: Norton, 1983.

Spencer, Jon Michael. *The Emergency of Black and the Emergence of Rap.* Durham, N.C.: Duke University Press, 1991.

Speregen, Devra. *Hip Hop till You Drop.* New York: Pocket Books, 1994.

Stancell, Steven. *Rap Whoz Who: The World of Rap Music.* New York: Schirmer Books, 1996.

Stavsky, Lois. *A to Z: The Book of Rap and Hip Hop Slang.* New York: Boulevard Books, 1995.

Stuckey, Sterling. *Slave Culture: Nationalist Theory and the Foundation of Black America.* New York: Oxford University Press, 1987.

Tolnay, Emory Stewart, and E. M. Beck. *A Festival of Violence: An Analysis of the Lynching of African-Americans in the American South, 1882–1930.* Urbana: University of Illinois Press, 1995.

Toop, David. *The Rap Attack: American Jive to New York Hip Hop.* London: Pluto, 1984.

———. 1994. *Rap Attack 2: African Rap to Global Hip Hop.* London and New York: Serpent's Tail. First published 1991 by Pluto, London.

Trotter, Joe. *The African American Experience.* vol. 2: *From Reconstruction.* Boston: Houghton Mifflin, 2001.

Turner, Patricia A. *I Heard It through the Grapevine: Rumors in African-American Culture.* Berkeley: University of California Press, 1993.

Van Deburg, William L. *New Day in Babylon: The Black Power Movement and American Culture, 1965–1975,* Chicago: University of Chicago Press, 1992.

Vanilla Ice. *Ice by Ice: The Vanilla Ice Story in His Own Words.* New York: Avon Books, 1991.

Vibe Magazine. Hip Hop Divas. New York: Three Rivers Press, 2001.

———, ed. *Tupac Shakur.* New York: Crown Publishers, 1997.

Wallace, Michele. "When Feminism Faces the Music, and the Music Is Rap." In *Reading Culture: Context for Critical Reading and Writing,* edited by Diana George and John Trimbur, 25–28. New York: HarperCollins, 1992.

Ward, Brian. *Just My Soul Responding: Rhythm and Blues, Black Consciousness, and Race Relations.* Berkeley: University of California Press, 1998.

Watkins, Craig S. *Hip Hop Matters 2005: Politics, Pop Culture, and the Struggle for the Soul of a Movement.* New York: Beacon, 2005.

———. *Representing: Hip Hop Culture and the Production of Black Cinema.* Chicago: University of Chicago Press, 1998.

Watkins, William H. *All You Need to Know about Rappin'! From Grandmaster Blaster.* Chicago: Contemporary Books, 1984.

Webb, Garry. *Dark Alliance: The CIA, the Contras, and the Crack Cocaine Explosion.* New York: Seven Stories Press, 1998.

West, Cornel. "Black Culture and Postmodernism." *In Remaking History: Discussions in Contemporary Culture,* edited by Barbara Kruger and Phil Mariani. Seattle: Bay Press, 1989.

White, Armond. *Rebel for the Hell of It: The Life of Tupac Shakur.* New York: Thunder's Mouth Press, 1997.

Wilson, William Julius. *When Work Disappears: The World of the New Urban Poor.* New York: Vintage, 1996.

Wimsatt, William. *Bomb the Suburbs.* New York: Subway and Elevated Press Company, 1994.

Zook, Kristal Brent. "Reconstructions of Nationalist Thought in Black Music and Culture." *In Rockin the Boat: Mass Music and Mass Culture,* edited by Reebee Garofalo. Boston: South End Press, 1992.

Periodical Articles, Papers, Theses, Reports, and Recordings

Aaron, Charles. "Gettin' Paid: Is Sampling Higher Education or Grand Theft Auto?" *Village Voice Rock 'n' Roll Quarterly,* Fall 1989, pp. 22–23.

Anderson, Elijah. 1994. "The Code of the Streets." *Atlantic Monthly,* May, 80–94.

Baker, Soren. "Magazine Leads Hip-Hop into Mainstream." *Los Angeles Times,* December 22, 1999.

Ballard, Mary E., Alan R. Dodson, and Doris G. Bazzini. "Genre of Music and Lyrical Content: Expectation Effects." *Journal of Genetic Psychology* 160 (1999): 4.

Barol, Bill. "Some Bad Raps for Good Rap." *Newsweek,* September 1, 1986, 85.

Bartlett, Andrew. "Airshafts, Loudspeakers, and the Hip Hop Sample: Contexts and African American Musical Aesthetics." *African American Review* 28 (1994): 4.

Basu, Dipannita. *"Rap Music, Hip-Hop Culture, and the Music Industry in Los Angeles." Center for Afro-American Studies Report* 15, no. 1–2 (1992): 20–24.

Bateman, Jeff. "Sampling: Sin or Musical Godsend?" *Music Scene,* September/October 1988.

Bernard-Donals, Michael. "Jazz, Rock 'n' Roll, Rap and Politics." *Journal of Popular Culture* 28 (1994): 2.

Binder, Amy. "Constructing Racial Rhetoric: Media Depictions of Harm in Heavy Metal and Rap Music." *American Sociological Review* 58 (1993): 6.

Blair, M. Elizabeth. "Commercialization of the Rap Youth Subculture." *Journal of Popular Culture 27,* no. 3 (Winter 1993): 21–33.

Boyd, Todd. "Check Yo Self, before You Wreck Yo Self: Variations on a Political Theme in Rap Music and Popular Culture." *Public Culture* 7, no. 1 (1994): 289–311.

Braxton, Greg, and Jerry Crowe. "Black Leaders Weighing in on Rap Debate." *Los Angeles Times,* June 14, 1995, F1, F8.

Britton, Akissi. "To Kim with Love: Deconstructing Lil' Kim." *Essence,* October 2000, 112–15, 186.

Brodeur, John M. "Dole Indicts Hollywood for Debasing Culture." *Los Angeles Times,* June 1, 1995, A1, A15.

Chambers, Gordon, and Joan Morgan. "Droppin' Knowledge: A Rap Roundtable." *Essence Magazine* 23 (1992): 5.

Cheney, Charise. "Representin' God: Rap, Religion and the Politics of a Culture." *North Star* 3 (1999):1.

Chomsky Noam, "What Makes Mainstream Media Mainstream," *Z Magazine,* October 1997.

Cobb, Jelani. "The Hoodrat Theory," *Creative Ink,* n.d., http://www.jelanicobb.com/portfolio/hoodrat.html.

————. "We Still Wear the Mask," *Playahata,* June 28, 2006, http://playahata.com/hatablog/?p=1654.

Cornish, James W., and Charles P. O'Brien. "Crack Cocaine Abuse: An Epidemic with Many Health Consequences." *Annual Review of Public Heath* 17 (1996): 259–273.

Cornyetz, Nina. "Fetishized Blackness: Hip Hop and Racial Desire in Contemporary Japan." *Social Text* 41 (1994): 113–39.

Crenshaw, Kimberle. "Beyond Racism and Misogyny: Black Feminism and 2 Live Crew." *Boston Review,* December 1991, 6, 30–33.

Dawsey, Kierna Mayo. 1994. "Caught Up in the (Gangsta) Rapture: Dr. C. Delores Tucker's Crusade against 'Gangsta Rap.'" *Source,* June 1994, 58–62.

Decker, Jeffrey Louis. "The State of Rap: Time and Place in Hip Hop Nationalism." *Social Text* 34 (1993): 53.

Decker, Jeffrey Louis. 1993. "The State of Rap: Time and Place in Hip Hop Nationalism." *Social Text,* no. 34 (1993): 53–84.

Deflem, Mathieu. "Rap, Rock and Censorship: Popular Culture and the Technologies of Justice." Paper presented at the annual meeting of the Law and Society Association, Chicago, May 27–30, 1993, transcribed in *Revisions,* March 2001.

Dery, Mark. "Public Enemy: Confrontation." *Keyboard,* September 1990, 81–96.

Dery, Mark. "Tommy Boy X 3: Digital Underground, Coldcut, and De La Soul Jam the Beat with Audio Junkyard Collisions." *Keyboard,* March 1991, 64–78.

Dimitriadis, Greg. "Hip Hop: From Live Performance to Mediated Narrative." *Popular Music* 15, no. 2 (1996): 179–194.

Dowd, Timothy J. "Introduction: Explorations in the Sociology of Music." *Poetics* 30 (2002): 1.

Dowd, Timothy J., and Maureen Blyler. "Charting Race: The Success of Black Performers in the Mainstream Recording Market, 1940 to 1990." *Poetics* 30 (2002): 87.

Evelyn, Jamilah. "To the Academy with Love, from a Hip Hop Fan." *Black Issues in Higher Education* 17, no. 21 (December 2000): 6.

Ferrell, Jeff. "Freight Train Graffiti: Subculture, Crime, Dislocation," *Justice Quarterly* 15, no. 4 (December 1998): 587–608.

Forman, Murray. "'Represent': Race, Space, and Place in Rap Music." *Popular Music* 19, no. 1 (January 2000): 65–90.

Frammolino, Ralph, and Geoff Boucher. 2001. "Rap Was Eminem's Roots and Road out of Poverty." *Los Angeles Times,* February 21, 2001, A1, A18.

Gallivan, Joseph. "Pop/Guns vs. Girls: The Rap Wars." *Independent,* January 13, 1994, 26.

Garofalo, Reebee. "How Autonomous Is Relative: Popular Music, the Social Formation and Cultural Struggle." *Popular Music* 6 (1987): 1.

———. "Culture versus Commerce: The Marketing of Black Popular Music." *Public Culture* 7, no. 1 (Fall 1994): 275–87.

Gause, Charles Phillip. "Performing Identity/Performing Culture: Hip Hop as Text, Pedagogy, and Lived Practice." *Urban Education* 38, no. 1 (January 2003): 134–140.

Gil, John. 1998. "Thyme and Reason: Outkast's Aquemini." *Source,* December 1998, 46, 48.

Gillard, James. "Jazz Is Hip Hop." *Black Renaissance/Renaissance noire* 4, nos. 2–3 (October 2002): 110.

Gladney, Marvin J. "The Black Arts Movement and Hip-Hop." *African American Review* 29, no. 2 (Summer 1995): 291–301.

Gonzales, Michael A. "Mack Divas." *Source,* February 1997, 62–67.

Goodall, Nakati. "Depend on Myself: T.L.C. and the Evolution of Black Female Rap." *Journal of Negro History* 79, no. 1 (1994): 85–93.

Graham, Renee. "Hip-Hop Doesn't Deserve the Rap for Violence." *Boston Globe,* April 5, 2000.

Hamilton, Marybeth. "The Lure of Black Style." Review article. *Journal of Contemporary History* 34, no. 4 (October 1999): 641–651.

Haugen, Jason. "'Unladylike Divas': Language, Gender, and Female Gangsta Rappers." *Popular Music and Society* 26, no. 4 (2003): 429–44.

Henderson, Alex. "Active Indies: Rap's Cutting Edge Seeks Next New Creative Frontiers to Stay Sharp and Successful." *Billboard,* December 24, 1988.

Henderson, Errol A. "Black Nationalism and Rap Music." *Journal of Black Studies* 26 (1996): 308–339.

Henderson, Robin, and Bob Herbert. *"Hounding the Innocent,"* New York Times, June 13, 1999.

Howard-Spink, Sam. "Grey Tuesday, Online Cultural Activism and the Mash-up of Music and Politics." *First Monday* 9, no. 10 (October 2004) http://firstmonday.org/issues/issue9_10/howard/index.html.

Hutchinson, Janis Faye. "The Hip Hop Generation: African American Male-Female Relationships in a Nightclub Setting." *Journal of Black Studies* 30, no. 1 (September 1999): 62–84.

Iwamato, Derek. "Tupac Shakur: Understanding the Identity Formation of Hypermasculinity of a Popular Hip-Hop Artist." *Black Scholar* 33, no. 2 (Summer 2003): 44–49.

James, Darryl. "Rakim: The Five Percent Science." *Rap Sheet,* October 1922.

Jamison, Laura. "A Fiesty Female Rapper Breaks Hip-Hop Taboo." *New York Times,* January 18, 1998, AR 34.

Johnson, Tom. *"African American Males in the Criminal Justice System."* Council on Crime and Justice, Office of Planning and Development. Minneapolis: Institute on Race and Poverty and the Council on Crime and Justice, 2002.

Judy, R. A. T. "On the Question of Nigga Authenticity." *Boundary 2* 21, no. 3 (1994): 211–230.

Kelley, Norman. "Rhythm Nation: The Political Economy of Black Music." *Black Renaissance/Renaissance noire* 2 (1999): 2.

Kemp, Mark. "Issue by Issue: The Death of Sampling." *Option Magazine,* March–April 1992, 20.

Kessing, Hugo A. "The Pop Message: A Trend Analysis of the Psychological Content of Two Decades of Music." Paper presented at the Eastern Psychological Society meetings, Philadelphia, Pennsylvania, April 18–20, 1974.

Keys, Cheryl L. "Spectacular Vernaculars: Hip-Hop and the Politics of Postmodernism." *Ethnomusicology* 43 (1999): 1.

Kun, Josh. "The Sound of Blacknuss: Rapping Master/Counternarratives of the Hip Hop Imagi-Nation." *Repercussions* 3, no. 2 (Fall 1994): 5–49.

Lacayo, Richard. "Violent Reaction," *Time,* June 12, 1995, 28.

Leland, John, Stanley Holmes, Tim Pryor, Mark Miller, and Charles Fleming. "Gangsta Rap and the Culture of Violence." *Newsweek,* November 29, 1993, 60.

Lena, Jennifer C. "Meaning and Membership: Samples in Rap Music, 1979 to 1995." In "Special Issue: Music in Society: The Sociological Agenda," edited by R. A. Peterson and T. Dowd. *Poetics* 32, nos. 3–4 (2004): 297–310.

———. "Psyops, Propaganda and Gangsta Rap: Why Is Saddam Hussein Rapping for the CIA?" *Radical Society* 30, no. 1 (2003): 25–30.

Lott, Eric. "Raising Cain: Blackface Performance from Jim Crow to Hip Hop." *American Literature* 74, no. 1 (March 2002): 146–147.

Lusane, Clarence. "Rap, Race, and Politics." *Race and Class* 35, no. 1 (1993): 41–56.

———. "Rhapsodic Aspirations: Rap, Race and Power Politics." *Black Scholar* 23 (1993): 37.

Mahon, Maureen. "Black Like This: Race, Generation, and Rock in the Post-civil Rights Era." *American Ethnologist* 27 (2000): 2.

Martinez, Theresa A. "Popular Culture as Oppositional Culture: Rap as Resistance," *Sociological Perspectives* 40 (1997): 2.

Maynard, Dori J. "Growing up Hip Hop." *American Prospect* 13 (2002): 9.

Mayo, Kierna. "2 Proud to Quit: Sisterhood in Baggies and Big Hats." *Source,* June 1992, 46–49, 61.

McAdams, Janine, and Deborah Russell. "Rap Breaking through to Adult Market." *Hollywood Reporter,* September 19, 1991, 4.

McCaffrey, Barry R. "Race and Drugs: Perception and Reality, New Rules for Crack versus Powder Cocaine." *Washington Times,* October 5, 1997.

McLeod, Kembrew. "Authenticity within Hip-Hop and Other Cultures Threatened with Assimilation." *Journal of Communication* 49 (1999): 4.

McWhorter, John. "How Hip-Hop Holds Blacks Back," *City Journal,* Summer 2003.

Middleton, Jason. "The Racial Politics of Hybridity and 'Neo-eclecticism' in Contemporary Popular Music." *Popular Music* 21, no. 2 (May 2002): 159.

Morgan, Joan. "Fly-Girls, Bitches, and Hoes: Notes of a Hip Hop Feminist." *Social Text,* no. 45 (Winter 1995): 151–157.

Muhammad, Tariq. "Hip-Hop Moguls: Beyond the Hype." *Black Enterprise,* December 1999, 78–90.

Muwakkil, Salim. "Racial Bias Persists," *Los Angeles Times,* September 26, 2003.

Negus, Keith. "The Music Business and Rap: Between the Street and the Executive Suite." *Cultural Studies* 13, no. 3 (1999): 488–508.

Ogbar, Jeffrey O. G. "Holla Black: The Bush Administration and the Return of Political Hip-Hop." *Radical Society: Review of Culture and Politics* 32, no. 3 (2006): 67–74.

———. "Slouching Toward Bork: The Culture Wars and Self-Criticism in Hip-Hop Music." *Journal of Black Studies* 30 (1999):2.

Olavarria, Margot. "Rap and Revolution: Hip-Hop Comes to Cuba." *NACLA (North American Conference on Latin America) Report on the Americas* 35 (2002): 6.

Osumare, Halifu. "Beat Streets in the Global Hood: Connective Marginalities of the Hip Hop Globe." *Journal of American and Comparative Cultures* 24, nos. 1–2 (2001): 171–181.

Parels, J. "On Rap, Symbolism and Fear," *New York Times,* February 2, 1992, 23.

Parker, Marc T. "An Analysis of Rap Music as the Voice of Today's Black Youth." Unpublished senior thesis, Gannon University, Department of Theatre and Communication Arts, 1999.

Pfeiffer, Scott. "Stop the Witch Hunts! Establishment Organizations Should Fight Conditions Youth Live in, Not Rap," *The R.O.C.* http://www.theroc.org/roc-mag/textarch/roc-15/roc15–02.htm.

Phillips, Charles. "The Uncivil War: The Battle between the Establishment and the Supporters of Rap Open up Old Wounds of Race and Class." *Los Angeles Times,* July 19, 1992.

Phillips, Chuck. "At Time Warner Profits from Rap Music Rejected." *Los Angeles Times,* February 23, 1996.

Pinn, Anthony B. "'How Ya Livin'?' Notes on Rap Music and Social Transformation." *Western Journal of Black Studies* 23 (1999): 1.

Powell, Catherine Tabb. "Rap Music: An Education with a Beat from the Street." *Journal of Negro Education* 60 (1991): 3.

Powell, Kevin. "Live from Death Row." *Vibe,* February 1996, 44–50.

———. "Tupac Shakur." *Vibe,* April 1995, 50–55.

———. "Live from Death Row." *Vibe,* February 1996, 44–50.

Ramsey, Gutherie P., Jr. "Muzing New Hoods, Making New Identities: Film, Hip-Hop Culture, and Jazz Music." *Callaloo* 25, no. 1 (Winter 2002): 309–320.

Reibstein, L. "The Right Takes a Media Giant to Political Task." *Newsweek,* June 12, 1995, 23, 30.

Roberts. Michael, "Rooting Interest." Denver westword.com. http://www.westword.com/1997–07–17/music/rooting-interest.

Roberts, Robin. "Ladies First: Queen Latifah's Afrocentric Feminist Music Video." *African American Review* 28, no. 2 (1994): 245–257.

———. "Music Videos, Performance and Resistance: Feminist Rappers." *Journal of Popular Culture* 25 (1991): 141–152.

Rose, Tricia. "'Fear of a Black Planet': Rap Music and Black Cultural Politics in the 1990s." *Journal of Negro Education* 60 (1991): 3.

———. "Orality and Technology: Rap Music and Afro-American Cultural Resistance." *Popular Music and Society* 12 (1989): 35–44.

Sacks, Howard L. "Turning about Jim Crow." *American Quarterly* 51, no. 1 (March 1999): 187–194.

Salaam, Kalamuya. "It Didn't Jes Grew: The Social and Aesthetic Significance of African American Music." *African American Review* 29 (1995): 2.

Samuels, Allison. "Gangsta Rap Label Gets Dissed." *Newsweek,* October 9, 1995, 30.

Samuels, David. "The Rap on Rap: The Black Music That Isn't Either," *New Republic,* November 11, 1991, 24–29.

Shank, Barry. "Fears of the White Unconscious: Music, Race and Identification in the Censorship of Cop Killer," *Radical History Review* 66 (1996): 124–145.

Shusterman, Richard. "The Fine Art of Rap." *New Literary History* 22 (1991): 613.

Smitherman, Geneva. "'The Chain Remain the Same': Communicative Practices in the Hip Hop Nation." *Journal of Black Studies* 28 (1997): 1.

Sorensen, Janet. "Showroom Sample: The Visual Politics of Hip Hop." *Afterimage* 21, no. 10 (May 1994): 11.

Stevenson, Bryan. *"Crime, Punishment, and Executions in the Twenty-First Century." Proceedings of the American Philosophical Society* 147, no. 1 (March 2003): 24–29.

Stewart, Jacqueline. "Representing." *Film Quarterly* 54, no. 1 (Fall 2000): 57–60.

Strand, Ginger. "Jails, Hospitals, and Hip Hop." *Theatre Journal* 50, no. 4 (December 1998): 523–525.

Tonry, Michael. *Malign Neglect: Race, Crime, and Punishment in America.* New York: Oxford University Press, 1995.

Tullis, Paul. "The Rap on the Source." *Columbia Journalism Review* 33, no. 5 (January 1995): 15–16.

Wahl, Greg. "I Fought the Law (and I Cold Won!): Hip-Hop in the Mainstream." *College Literature* 26 (1999): 1.

Walser, Robert. "Rhythm, Rhyme and Rhetoric in the Music of Public Enemy." *Ethnomusicology* 39 (1995): 193.

Watkins, Craig L. "A Style That Nobody Can Deal with . . . : Notes from the Doo Bop Hip Hop Inn." *International Review of African American Art* 13, no. 1 (1996): 22.

White, Miles. *The High Fidelity Turntable System and the Creation of Hip Hop Music: An Organological Inquiry.* M.A. Thesis, University of Washington, 1996.

Wong, Celine. "Native Tongues: Hip Hop's Global Domination." *Source,* March 2001, 202–209.

Wood, Brent. "Understanding Rap as Rhetorical Folk-Poetry." *Mosaic: A Journal for the Interdisciplinary Study of Literature* (Winnepeg) 32, no. 4 (December 1999): 129–146.

Vibe Magazine. "Who's Zoomin' Whom?" August 1995, 67.

Zaslow, Emilie, and Allison Butler. "'That It Was Made by People Our Age Is Better.'" *Journal of Popular Film and Television* 30 (2002): 1.

INDEX